THE
ALASKA GARDENER'S
HANDBOOK

by Lenore Hedla

High North Press
6440 West Dimond Boulevard
Anchorage, Alaska 99502

Cover photograph: The Anchorage garden of Sharon and Brian Davies.

The Alaska Gardener's Handbook
by Lenore Hedla

Distributed exclusively by
Todd Communications
203 W. 15th Ave. Suite 102
Anchorage, Alaska 99501
(907) 274-8633
Fax (907) 276-6858

Cover design and production – Mary Spalding
Computer consultant – Robert C. Fitzgerald

First Printing: April 1994   Second Printing: March 1995   Third Printing: December 1996
ISBN 1-878100-56-4
Printed in Korea

TABLE OF CONTENTS

Above: This mid-season border blooms from July through August.

Above: Rosa Rugosa, *Alaska's beloved "Sitka" rose blooms from mid-July and produces large, handsome rose hips—seed pods.*

Right: Feverfew 'Yellow Ball' substitutes for button chrysanthemums in late summer.

CHAPTER 1

FLOWERS FOR ALASKA'S GARDENS

Alaska's gardens put on a grand summer show for camera-toting summer visitors who come to see the igloos. They discover the flowers as they step out of airport terminals and start shooting. For settlers, it's a different story. They are, understandably, baffled. What's so different about Alaska? Why isn't gardening in Alaska the way it was back home?

Precipitation in most of the "big part" of Alaska runs around 15 inches a year, the same as Phoenix, but only half of it falls during the growing season. Cool soil and air temperatures keep Alaska from being a desert.

Cool summer days are relished by most plants, but some easy-to-grow ones, like zinnias, shiver at the prospect of a chilly 70-degree summer day.

Day length confuses some plants, as it does some people. Plants produce a simple sugar during daylight hours, and consume it during the hours of darkness. We don't have many hours of summer darkness, and when it does get dark it doesn't get *very* dark, so some flowers get very large or too tall.

Long summer days fail to give some plants the message that winter is coming, and they don't get ready for it in a timely manner, succumbing to temperatures that don't faze their counterparts in the northern midwest.

Fewer kinds of insects and diseases plague Alaska's gardeners than the beleaguered folk in other states, so plants use less energy fighting the spoilers and more of it getting big and beautiful. Over simplified? Sure, but growing big, beautiful flowers and vegetables in Alaska *is* pretty simple.

The range of adaptable ornamental plants is not as wide as in milder climates, but we can choose from more kinds of plants than most

people know about from new discoveries, the rediscovery of heirloom varieties, and breeding advances. So do the kinds of flower gardens that serve the High North best. In Alaska, there is emerging a singularly Alaska style of gardening, better suited to the High North.

MIXED HERBACIOUS BORDERS are the grand legacy we inherited from England and Denmark. These splendid gardens combine annuals, perennials, biennials, bulbs, and shrubs.

ISLAND GARDENS we lifted from Alan Bloom, the great English nurseryman of Bressingham Gardens where big free-form islands of shrubs and flowers are set in lawns that are simply grassy paths between the islands.

Island beds are useful to Alaska gardeners. Carefully skirting shady areas to grab all the sun there is, we can make flowing borders and islands

Les Brake's Coyote Gardens in Hatcher Pass near Willow borrows from the English border columbines, delphiniums, meadow rue, blue Tibetan poppies, and verbascoms, comfortable in his wild, woodland setting.

Photo by Jerry Conrad

on a north-south axis so that the east side gets morning sun, and the west side the afternoon sun.

You will be less apt to walk on a mounded bed, so plant roots will reach out into the warm surface soil and plants will thank you for not compacting the soil over their feeder roots.

Tall plants can be placed in the center of island beds, with mid-talls on either side, and dwarfs nearer the lawn edges. Leave enough lawn for two people to walk together—about 48 inches, which suits the wheelbarrow, garden cart, with room for a lawnmower to make a couple of passes.

ROCK GARDENS and **ROCKERIES** are not the same, but both have a good place in Alaska gardening. **Rockeries** are gardens planted among rocks, which reflect the sun's heat onto plants that appreciate their warmth. Any low-growing plant that looks right fits into a rockery—annuals, perennials, low-growing shrubs, early spring bulbs.

A rock garden is something else again. The American Rock Garden Society defines rock garden plants as wild annuals, biennials, perennials, shrubs or bulbs from mountains, bogs, woodlands, seacoasts, heaths, prairies or arid plains, from any continent. Some purists limit their definition to alpines (plants growing above tree line) and saxatiles (plants growing among rocks).

A perfect site for a rock garden is a natural out-cropping of rocks; with skill and know-how such a site can be emulated by bringing in rocks and deploying them as they would have been in nature. A pile of rocks does not a rock garden make. If you can lift it, the rock is too small; plan on burying a third of it. Even a raised bed can be made into a miniature alpine garden. Most rock garden plants grow best in the lean sand of the mountain scree.

Woodland flowers do best in the humusy, acid soils of the forest. Alaska has vast resources in plants, but how do you know what to look for? For openers, try hitting the books.

Good glove compartment companions are Verna E. Pratt's *Field Guide to Alaskan Wildflowers,* AlaskaKrafts Publishing; *The Alaska-Yukon Wild Flowers Guide,* and Janice J. Schofield's *Discovering Wild Plants,* both from Alaska Northwest Publishing Company, of Anchorage.

The king of the road that rock gardeners travel is H. Lincoln Foster's *Rock Gardening,* Timber Press, Portland, OR.

The dedicated wild plantsman will need Eric Hulten's *Flora of Alaska* for figuring out what you have found.

Leon C. Snyder's *Native Plants for Northern Gardens,* published by the University of Minnesota Libraries, and the Minnesota Landscape Arboretum is tailored to the Alaska measure.

Butchart Gardens near Victoria B.C. is resplendent with sweeping island beds in the English manner.

Photo: Butchart Gardens

Above: Ellen Lekisch designed this rockery of annual flowers at the head of "Andrews's Trail" in Anchorage's Kincaid Park, a memorial to her son. Like many cyclists who come upon the spectacle, Ann Retherford and Gail Irvine paused to rest and explore its paths.

Ortho Books' *Landscaping with Wildflowers & Native Plants* is an excellent text, beautifully illustrated.

Few gardeners who open this Pandora's box will ever get back to gardening with cell-packs of annuals. Rock gardeners soon crave communication with others of their kind so they join the international rock garden societies, which have annual seed exchanges to which they contribute, and from which they receive seeds of their choice to try in their Alaskan gardens. Addresses are listed in the Addenda.

Susan Condon's entry garden of alpines, designed by Landscaper Suzanne Forster, is artfully composed to utilize both sun and shade to best advantage, and Architect Condon gave it an architectural quality.

Botanical gardens are rarely listed in travel guides or included in package tours; travellers should see some of these great gardens. Vancouver, B.C. and Seattle have several, as does Portland, San Francisco, and the Los Angeles area. Aspen, Colorado's Betty Ford Alpine Gardens are splendid and many plants and cultural methods are transferable to Alaska.

WATER GARDENS. The cool sound of falling water and its flash in the sun may be what you most need when the temperature reaches a hundred or more in the Interior, but the hottest trend in Southcentral is water gardens.

Alaska's first garden pools and fountains were carved in concrete, but today thirty-two mil PVC pool liners take major engineering aspects out of water gardening. Re-circulating pumps are widely available, putting pool and fountain within the grasp of the home gardener. Commercially-manufactured pre-formed pools do not require the design skill that the first free-form pools did. Made from thick fiberglass, some are guaranteed for 50 years and are deep enough to accommodate waterlily tubs.

Pools add charm to a shady garden, but if they are under trees there is a fall leaf-cleaning chore. With a half day of sun they give the gardener an opportunity to grow waterlilies and other aquatic species.

Poolside plants that are not at home in other gardens include the umbrella plant, *Cyperus alternifolius,* and marsh marigold, Alaska cotton and bog rosemary, cattails and sedges, *mimulus,* violets and ferns, the majestic cow parsnip, the red-berried elder, and the native false Solomon's seal, *Smilacina racemosa.*

Installation requires digging a hole and making the bottom level as a billiard table, preferably setting the plastic form on a bed of builder's sand. Directions come with the product. You can fill the pool with a garden hose, letting it stand for 24 hours if it contains chlorine and you plan to add fish, topping it off occasionally as evaporation takes place.

In Anchorage, Water Gardens North designs, sells plants, supplies, waterfalls, fish, and bog, poolside, and some native plants. Call (907) 333-9984 or send a self-addressed stamped business envelope for a free catalogue or an appointment.

Tryck Nursery at 3625 Rabbit Creek Road, 99516 (P.O Box 110104, Anchorage 99511), (907) 345-2507, offers the above and installation service.

COTTAGE GARDENS, informal door yard plantings, are a pleasant, casual mix of annuals, perennials and spring-flowering bulbs that welcome guest and mail carrier.

One of the best guides on cottage gardens is the Brooklyn Botanic Garden bulletin, *American Cottage Gardening*, #123, $6.95, Brooklyn Botanic Garden, 1000 Washington Avenue, Brooklyn, NY 11225-1099.

To avoid a peak bloom explosion, look for early and late bloomers.

The water garden of Linda Teninty of Water Gardens North has columbines, Alchemilla, primulas and irises framing a waterfall and pool of waterlilies.
Photo: Sally Karabelnikof

This Anchorage cottage garden is a mix of Iceland and lettuce poppies, forget-me-nots and sweet alyssum—generous self-seeders.

EARLY BLOOMERS start a garden off with species crocus, which bloom in my garden about April 25th, *Arabis,* an early riser, is the snowy froth that follows on the heels of the real thing. *Bergenia* sends up early pinkish-lavender blooms that resemble hyacinths, which are not hardy here. Pink forget-me-nots make a rosy ground cover and they keep company with the lemon yellow, spring-blooming *Trollius europaea* which follows the Mound of Gold, *Euphorbia polychroma,* which is replaced by the leopard's bane, *Doronicum caucasicum.*

Susan Miller, Municipal Beautification horticulturist in Anchorage must shoot for a city in bloom by June first. She grows thousands of geraniums from seed plus sure-fire annuals, all timed for instant flowering in parks and highway media. Careful deadheading keeps them blooming until first frost.

LATE BLOOMERS don't get the respect they deserve from Alaskans, who want the same plants to bloom early and stay late.

Becky Swanson, grower at the Matanuska Valley Fairgrounds display gardens, knows better than most gardeners what she can count on for spectacular bloom from the last week in August into September, when she is under the gun for timing and must cope with the virtual certainty of rain at Fair time.

"Among the annuals, I can count on *Salvia horminum* 'Bluebird,' 'Pink Sundae' and 'White Swan' to bloom right through the Fair. *Chrysanthemum coronarium* 'Primrose Gem,' *C. segetum* 'Prado,' and *Helianthus* 'Sunspot' are tall and full without staking. *Trachymene,* the blue lace flower, and *Ammi majus*—light and airy—and *Bupleurum* 'Green Gold' are dependable."

It was Becky Swanson who introduced Alaskans to an alternative to hanging basket fuchsias and ivy geraniums with

The William Sherwoods' entry garden is an informal collection of native plants and durable shrubs. It requires minimal maintenance.

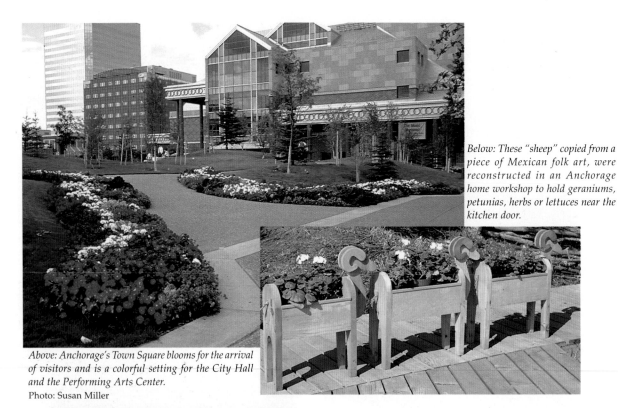

Below: These "sheep" copied from a piece of Mexican folk art, were reconstructed in an Anchorage home workshop to hold geraniums, petunias, herbs or lettuces near the kitchen door.

Above: Anchorage's Town Square blooms for the arrival of visitors and is a colorful setting for the City Hall and the Performing Arts Center.
Photo: Susan Miller

Doronicum, in foreground, and yellow and orange European Trolliuses beyond, like an early wake-up call.

Rhodochiton, "Purple Bells," a vining plant that takes kindly to hanging baskets, now stocked by most garden centers.

'Nutmeg' , a tawny rudbeckia, cries out for a brown bean pot in which to flaunt its autumnal colors, and the bright golden 'Goldilocks' stays with you through thick and thin, and so do the 'Rocket' snapdragons.

With the delphiniums and Maltese-cross gone and the background looking sparse, consider the perennial meadow rue, *Thalictrum aquilegifolium.* The shasta daisy cultivars and their annual kin, *Chrysanthemum paludosum,* are dramatic with red 'Ladybird' poppies or fiery salvias. Foxglove 'Foxy' stoutly resists early frost. The Chinese forget-me-not, *Cynoglossum,* is still with us, as are Tidy Tips and cosmos.

Primula sikkimensis, an orange or yellow exotic beauty, is at its best in late August and September. *Achilleas* 'Ballerina' and the 'Summer Pastels,' are not fazed by summer's end. The mallows consort happily with cleome, godetia, lythrum, the statices, and clary. Feverfew hangs in there, 'Yellow Ball' and 'Santana' the best for now. The geraniums are still good when winter's onset looks ominous.

The Asiatic lilies take up where the delphiniums leave off. 'Sunblaze' roses refused to quit until the first snow had dusted my Zone 4 garden, and two out of three plants came back the next year.

CONTAINER GARDENS were not invented for the high North but they are well suited to the needs of the northern garden. In containers, root runs are warmer. Containers can be moved into the sun, out of the wind, or out back of the garage when they have to be cut back or are not at their best.

Container gardening is the apartment dwellers' alternative to acreage. It is possible to have a salad garden in a half barrel, an herb garden or a garden of mixed annuals in a crate.

Some of the best containers come out of home workshops. Recycled containers are interesting—conveyer buckets from old mines, Blazo boxes, saltery barrels, all reminders of Alaska's past. Some of the most offensive are toy wheelbarrows, infant potties, oil drums.

Hanging baskets get plants up into the warm air and out of the cool, cool ground. Outdoors, the Big Three are fuchsias, tuberous begonias, and geraniums—all gorgeous plants, perfectly suited to Alaska's summer climate. Trailing lobelia, used as a filler with mixed annuals or by itself, is a grace note.

Purchased in March, small plants in three-inch pots are ready to do their stuff by June. Put three fuchsia cuttings in a nine- or 10-inch basket, or one begonia, or one or two geraniums.

A cell-pack of petunias will produce four matching petunia baskets; or a packet of seed will yield a hundred of them for a tenth the cost of a fuchsia basket.

Or, you can have a big ball of bloom from a dozen wax begonias in a 10-inch wire basket. Susan Miller designed spectacular baskets using a mixture of pink and white 'Avalanche' begonias.

Impatiens comes in marvelous new colors, and is the best-seller of the national nursery trade.

Susan Miller designed these lobelia baskets on Anchorage's "Silk Stocking Row." It takes about 30 "plugs" to produce such a basket.

A shade plant farther south, it thrives in the northern sun.

More fun at less cost are several containers of mixed annuals. Good subjects are pansies and violas, lobelias, dwarf nemesias, schizanthus, annual phlox, sweet alyssum, heliotrope, Kenilworth ivy, verbena, and mimulus, often the leftovers from four-packs after planting a neat clump of three in the garden.

The Chinese purple bell vine, Rhodochiton, *R. atrosanguineum,* does well in hanging containers if you are fairly generous with the number of plants, perhaps five to a nine- or 10-inch basket. It germinates erratically and takes four months from seed to flower.

Hanging baskets dry out faster than plants in the ground. The traditional wire baskets lined with sheet moss or sphagnum require vigilant attention to watering. Lining the moss basket with black plastic perforated for drainage, helps. Susan Miller makes the holes big enough to insert her plants by wrapping their roots in a cone-shaped piece of paper.

Plastic pots retain moisture, but they are no great asset to the landscape unless they fit inside more ornamental containers. Hanging containers should be checked daily on sunny days. If this gets to be too much of a nuisance, consider incorporating one of the soil polymers, or hydrogels, in the potting mix. These crystals absorb many times their weight in moisture and release it as needed. The polymers come in fine and coarse grades, and the coarse kind is appropriate for containers. The gels are mixed with water several hours before use, and can be used with established plants as well as in planting mixes.

'Lemon Gem' marigolds are good companions with yellow mimulis, purchased in cell-packs of mixed colors, selected when they show their first bloom.

Rotating hanging baskets to give each side its day in the sun can be tedious. Fishermens' swivels or the swivel-snap devices used on dog leashes can be connected to a basket's support. Wire hangers are not as good as the chain sold at hardware and building supply stores which can be draped over nails in a plywood panel and spray-painted .

PLANTS FOR ALASKA FLOWER GARDENS

ACHILLEA. *Achillea ptarmica,* has been a stalwart in Alaska gardens since the time of the Russians. *A. ptarmica* is still called "Russian daisy" in coastal towns that were once Russian settlements. Mostly it is called "Ladies-in-White," or by its botanical name, pronounced ah-kah-LEE-ah. Not fussy about soil or exposure, it is tolerant of neglect, and accepts the vicissitudes of the north.

The plebeian *A. ptarmica* is usually acquired over the back fence, but it comes easily from seed. It can be a rampant nuisance in a favorable location. You should request the pleasure of its company where not much else will grow. The 'Ballerina' strain is daintier, but still aggressive. 'Summer Pastels,' an AAS award winner, and 'Debutante' are newer and much improved *Achilleas,* worthy additions to the perennial border.

A. filipendula is the good golden-flowered one whose best cultivars are 'Moonlight' and 'Golden Plate'; they must be purchased as plants, vegetatively propagated, given a sunny south wall and a warm summer. The flowers dry well.

AFRICAN DAISY is the common name of two similar species, *Arctotis* and *Dimorphotheca*, both South African natives, both daisies that come in pastel mixtures. Both shut up shop if it looks like rain. Grow them from seed at room temperature. Catalogs list the latter as Star of the Veldt.

AGERATUM, floss flower, is an annual that will edge a bed or fill a container of mixed annuals with pink, white or lavender. Widely available in garden centers, the Thompson & Morgan catalog lists 15 bewildering choices. Seed germinates in 10 to 14 days .

AJUGA, bugleweed, is hardy to Zone 2, but it does not make the great ground cover that it does in milder coastal climates. The plain green is hardier than the variegated or purple kinds, worse luck.

ALLIUMS, onion family members, have some excellent perennials for Alaska flower gardens. Rarely sold in local nurseries, you may get smitten by catalog photography, so bear in mind that they need a 90-day period of moist cold to germinate. Try a jar of seeding mix in the fridge and start checking after two months.

ALYSSUM is now classified as *Aurinia,* a not uncommon happening as taxonomists' studies reveal past errors in nomenclature. You can still call it "Basket of Gold" and be understood. It is not reliably hardy in cool coastal areas, but *A. montana* is, a nice plant for the edge of a flower bed. The annual sweet alyssums make edging and container fillers.

ANEMONES, windflowers, hybrids of *Anemone japonica,* are short-lived in Southcentral, but every now and then somebody pulls it off and the red, white, and blue blooms flare against a south wall. Their tubers are more rot-prone than most and slow to start.

A. richardsonii grows wild over most of Alaska and makes a sprightly ground cover. Its buttercup-like flowers are the first to lift their faces to the tardy spring sun; it does not tolerate commercial fertilizers.

A. narcissiflora, the narcissus-flowered anemone, is also widely distributed in the big part of Alaska, a beauty with creamy flowers above finely cut foliage. *A. altaica baldensis* is yellow. Both are prodigious seed-producers.

A. multifida, the cutleaf anemone, is uncommon except in Southeastern Alaska. All of these native anemones are delightful in the wild garden, but their bloom duration is short and they germinate slowly.

ANTHEMIS, easily grown from seed, is a trustworthy annual. The perennial forms, propagated vegetatively, are shipped in by nurseries and are among our finest summer-blooming daisies. (See MARGUERITES).

ARMERIA, Thrift, has many species but *A. maritima* and its variants are of the most interest for edging and rock gardens. They have grassy foliage and pink, sometimes white, flowers. If it gets too big, a clump can be divided into dozens of plantlets.

ARNICA grows wild throughout Alaska. There are enough native arnicas to keep the plant hunter hunting. Several are worth collecting seeds to grow in town gardens. Some are lanky and weedy, but *A. frigida* and *A. alpina* are short and sweet.

ARTEMESIA, wormwood, is best known for the excellent 'Silver Mound,' a gray perennial foliage plant that makes a good edger and a pleasant mediator of color conflicts. The foliage dries well for winter use. 'Silver Brocade' is a winner, excellent in hanging baskets, or as a spreading mat plant.

Wendy Anderson, horticulturist at the Visitors Information Center in Palmer, introduced Southernwood, *A. arborescens* 'Powis Castle,' a handsome shrubby plant that gets three to four feet tall and densely branched. A real find. *A. schmidtiana* is a beautiful gray, finely cut foliage plant with silky, silver hairs. It may grow to two feet, but probably needs protection in Zone 4. A dwarf form, 'nana' exists.

A. absinthium, the herb that is the flavoring agent in the liqueur absinthe, which reportedly maketh the heart grow fonder, is a perfectly respectable perennial. 'Huntington' and 'Lambrook Silver' are the choice selections, but there are so many interesting Artemesias that keen gardeners should find their own favorites.

ASTER. The perennial cultivars are not hardy, but the annual forms are widely sold in cell-packs. Easy to grow from seed which germinates in 10 to 14 days, asters are a mainstay in many annual gardens.

Siberian aster, *A. sibericus*, is a small lavender wild daisy that is perennial and very much at home in the wild garden or on a sunny bank.

ASTILBE is a shade-loving perennial in milder climates, but requires more sun in most of Alaska, where it is apt to be short-lived. It can be grown from seed in about three weeks at room temperature, but you can save growing-on time by buying plants of this desirable perennial. It accepts pot culture and can be brought into the sunroom.

AVENS have some wild species in Alaska that would enhance any rock garden. Mountain Avens, *Dryas octopetala*, has lovely white flowers above notched small leaves. Yellow Dryas, *Dryas drummondii*, is not as flashy but its silvery seed head mats catch the eye along rocky river banks and gravel pits all over Alaska. *Dryas integrifolia* grows wild over much of the eastern half of Alaska.

BABY-BLUE-EYES, *Nemophila menziesii*, is a neat little true blue trailer that is good in tubs of annuals and in hanging containers. 'Five Spot', *N. maculata*, has white flowers with purple spots.

The Bob Dodds' garden uses 'Silver Mound' to make peace between closely-planted vibrant colors.

'Penny Black' is dark purple with white edges. Our considered opinion: stick with Baby-Blue-Eyes.

BABY'S BREATH, *Gypsophila*, may be the annual *G.elegans* , a lacy little white flower that mixes well in mass arrangements and contrasts prettily with more robust elements in the garden. The perennial baby's breath, *G. paniculata*, is a pink or white froth to trail over a sunny wall in a favored location. It dries well in great billows of tiny flowers for massing in a big container.

BACHELOR BUTTONS, *Centaurea cyanus*, are good mixers and the cornflower blues are effective peace-keepers between combatants in the garden. They germinate from seed sown in place but to be with you all summer give them a four-week head start indoors or use purchased plants. 'Jubilee Gem' is a familiar 12-inch dwarf, and newer kinds like 'Blue Diadem' have more substance. The tall kinds need staking.

There are some perennial *Centaureas* worth growing, mainly *C. macrocephala*, and *C. mochata*, 'The Bride,' oddities that merit more visibility.

BALLOON FLOWER, *Platycodon grandiflorum*, is a good garden perennial for the North, and its dwarf forms are valued in the rock garden. They are easily grown from seed, but the very dwarf forms must be propagated vegetatively. 'Sentimental Blue' has extra large blooms. They germinate in two to four weeks at 70 degrees. 'Mother of Pearl' is a rarely seen pink one.

BEGONIAS. Tuberous-rooted begonias are among the best-adapted flowering plants for the High North. Their spectacular blooms thrive on the misty days similar to those of the famed "begonia belt" of the California coast.

In lower latitudes begonias are shade plants; in Southcentral and Southeastern Alaska they like all the sun there is, but will put up with the unmoving shade of a building, and thrive in dappled shade on the north side of the house.

Tuberous begonias are prime examples of bargain bulbs not being bargains. Buy the biggest, plumpest tubers you can find; small, inexpensive ones produce plants that betray their inferior genes. By March the tubers will be appearing on garden center counters, and those in home basement storage will begin to show small pink buds.

Conventional wisdom has it that you set these tubers in flats of moist sphagnum peatmoss until they have a pair of true leaves before potting them up in individual containers of a humusy, well-drained potting mix. The new 'Non Stops' do as well when set in pots where they are to grow, and they can be stored in the same pots until the following spring when their potting medium is renewed. Non-gardeners may buy them as seedlings and grow them to planting size. The 'Musical' series may be more compact than the 'Non Stops.' They get high marks for 'Illumination Pink,' and 'Pin-up,' a pink picotee.

If you have a seasonal greenhouse that you activate between mid-April and early May, you may need to conserve space by starting your tubers in flats. The round side goes down, the concave side up. To induce a hefty root system, twist the tubers into the mix so that all but the concave basin at the top is covered by the mix.

When the tubers show a pair of well developed leaves, lift them carefully from the mossy rooting medium and set them into pots of a very porous, humus-rich mix.

All the food they need is in their tubers, but by the time you set them out you should begin applications of a soluble fertilizer high in phosphate, the middle number in the fertilizer formula. If you're growing begonias in the ground, bear in mind that blooms tend to face the way the leaves point.

Fibrous-rooted, or wax begonias, *B. semperflorens,* are a far cry from the wax begonias that have long been with us as accommodating houseplants. The hybridizers keep producing more magnificent foliage and larger flowers of melting beauty. These lovely plants are so easy to propagate that you can buy a pair of them for indoors, trim them back when they become too exuberant, root the cuttings, and have enough for patio containers when summer comes.

The Anchorage Municipal Greenhouse liked the 'Encore' series, which is somewhat taller than most, and 'Avalanche.'

BELLS OF IRELAND, *Moluccella laevis,* is a little nothing in the garden but it is big with flower arrangers. The nondescript leaves are snipped out to reveal bell-shaped green calyxes on graceful stems. It dries well for winter bouquets.

BERGENIA crassifolia and *B. cordifolia,* often called Saxifrage, are tough Siberian perennials with leathery evergreen leaves and rosy flower scapes.

They perform well in shade or sun and are useful in woodsy situations. They will make a dense ground cover, or edge a path. They bloom so early that they are good companions for auricula primroses, draba, arabis, spring-flowering bulbs, and forget-me-nots. They are easy to propagate by division or from spring-sown seed. Moose will feed on them, worse luck.

BIDENS is a little known perennial but a star performer. 'Golden Goddess' is 18 inches tall, with ferny foliage and masses of orange daisy-shaped flowers. Its identity is controversial, so you may find it listed in some catalogs under Cosmos, in others as a Coreopsis.

BLEEDING HEART, *Dicentra spectabilis,* **is** hardy to Zone 2. *D. eximia,* the fringed bleeding heart, is a bit less sturdy but its pink, heart-shaped flowers (there is a white form) on shorter plants are a welcome addition to perennial border or rock garden. You can grow Dicentras from seed stratified in moist seeding mix in the fridge for three months.

BRACHYCOME, the Swan River Daisy of West Australia, is a neat little six-inch mound, easy to grow from seed but rarely found in garden centers. Germination is somewhat irregular in 10 to 20 days at room temperature.

BROWN-EYED SUSAN (See RUDBECKIA.)

BULBS, SPRING FLOWERING. Siberian squill and crocuses are hardy to Zone 4, but in the Anchorage area and farther north, as in most places, they are short-lived except in protected locations. Treat them as annuals (which most gardeners in the South 48 have been doing for decades).

A sunny south wall with perfect drainage gives flowers in May, exposed locations in June. Bulbs planted on the north side of the house are later, but they last longer.

The soil should be best under the bulbs, not on top of them, which means digging the bed out and mixing the soil with peatmoss or compost (but not manure) and a slow-release fertilizer or 8-32-16. If you want the tulips to be the same height, make that bed level as a billiard table. Give each bulb, pointed end up, a little twist to make it firmly upright.

Unless this kind of soil preparation has taken place, the tool called a bulb planter does bulbs a disservice. Simply digging holes in the ground and dropping bulbs in is no way to have fine tulips next spring. (Don't throw the bulb planter away, though, because it is a neat tool for picking up volunteer seedlings that you'd rather have someplace else).

If you're serious about tulips, you should have a soil test because they do best in soil that is barely on the acid side of neutral and some Alaskan soils are pretty acid. Planting depth is controversial. You might use as a rule of thumb a depth of three to four times the bulb's height. Or, say, four to six inches deep and two to four inches apart. Bulbs, especially crocuses, look forlorn in rows; they like to huddle in clumps and drifts. Planting bulbs upside down to stagger blooming times is a silly idea. Better to buy different kinds that bloom at different times.

The classic formal beds you see in milder climates are risky in Alaska where there are often some losses. Consider the merits of a mixed bulb planting in the good company of the pasqueflower, yellow draba, arabis, auricula primroses and mound-of-gold.

Plant bulbs on a sunny "Sep-tober" day when golden birch leaves drift down, the geese call a rendezvous for the far flight, and the autumn sun is warm on your head. If it isn't that kind of a day, if it's just a miserable fall day, hang in there. A finger-numbing hour in Sep-tober will pay heart-warming dividends in May, when there's not much else around to warm it. A clutch of little crocuses, braving the breakup by the front step, will do nice things for you. The wild species crocuses have bloomed for us as early as April 25th, and the Kaufmanniana tulips flower on four-inch stems when hardly anything else looks alive.

'Red Riding Hood,' a Greigii, is a good bet and if a hundred of them bloom above a ground cover of big, beautiful blue Altai violets, *Viola altaica,* it will be a bloomin' miracle. Blow the rent money on some Darwins and maybe a dozen lily-flowered tulips that would end the season with style. This is somewhat dependent upon coming into a modest legacy.

The choicest bulbs come from the specialty houses whose catalogs arrive in good time, but whose bulbs may not make it before the ground freezes. The ones that do, come by UPS or Priority Mail, which adds to their cost. Local garden centers advertise the arrival of their bulb stocks, getting first dibs with the wholesalers and taking the risk for you. Sprint over the day the ads appear to get the biggest, firmest ones (before some befuddled nerd has mixed up the colors). Be wary of bargain bulbs in stores that are not in the nursery business. Their bulb bins are a poor place to look for bargains. The best bulbs always cost more than the dogs.

While you're shopping, keep an eye out for the rare species crocuses. The wild botanical tulips do good things for rock gardens. They are short of stem, in rich reds and exotic color combinations, their bulbs no bigger than onion sets.

Their origins are lost in the dawn of history in the high mountain passes of Turkey, Iran, Iraq, Greece, and Afghanistan, which are our principal sources of these treasures, but they also weigh heavily on our horticultural conscience. Dutch growers, who supply most of the minor bulbs, have begun labeling wild-collected bulbs and nursery-grown stock. The Dutch are showing Turkish farmers how to grow species bulbs. The new nursery-grown stock will be superior in quality to the wild-collected and customer insistence on them will halt the depletion of whole genera being dug up in the wild mountain passes of the Middle East. Look for jaw-breaking names like *Tulipa kolpakowskiana*, and *T. dasystemon* (often sold as *T. tarda*, a buttery yellow dipped in cream).

Mulch your bulb bed from a hoard of pea vines or dry leaves mixed with spruce branches. When you shovel the walks, throw a blanket of snow over your grateful bulbs.

Once in a very great while you may buy bulbs whose blossoms "blast" before they bloom. What did you do wrong? Maybe nothing. It occurs when unfavorable weather conditions in their country of origin prevent the development of the flowering bud, and established nurseries replace such bulbs.

When your bulbs have bloomed, cut off the dead flower heads and let the foliage mature. If the summer is a bummer, the foliage may not turn brown. In any case, dig the bulbs around the first of August and let them cure in some cool, dim place. Replant in "Sep-tober." Left in the ground without this step they may multiply, producing fewer and smaller flowers until they check out for good. If you are paying a gardener by the hour, you will be money ahead to treat your bulbs as annuals.

BUTTERCUP, is a common name for the large tribe of *Ranunculus* that grows wild all over Alaska — and for a lot of other wildlings that look like buttercups but aren't. *Ranunculus cooleyae* is a lovely addition to the rock garden. *R. repens*, creeping buttercup, makes a dense ground cover that bears watching; it is useful for weed control in places you'd like to plant and forget. It can become a weed itself.

CALENDULA is easily grown from seed sown six weeks before planting time. The newest kinds are compact, free-blooming plants ranging in

color from cream, to yellow and orange. A fine dwarf in mixed colors, all good, is 'Fiesta Gitana'; 'Coronet' and 'Sonny Boy' are good yellow or orange shorties, but you won't go wrong on any of the new dwarfs. Their single fault is that the blossoms are spoiled by rain and require frequent cutting to keep the plants blooming and neat.

CALLA is a name that can be confusing. *Calla palustris* is the wild calla found in bogs and shallow ponds. The Calla lily is an unrelated species, *Zantedeschia*, and it is no lily. The wild calla, is well suited to a poolside planting. So are the calla cultivars, if treated as seasonal flowers — set out about June first and brought indoors before frost.

CAMPANULA, Bellflowers, thrive in Alaska's cool, moist summer and some are winter hardy. The biennial Canterbury Bell, the "cup and saucer" plant, is worth waiting a second summer for its great show. The out-size pink, lavender, or white bells are stunning, but they require careful attention to grooming for they fade quickly and are easily damaged by rain.

Among the perennial campanulas, *C. persicifolia*, the peach-leafed bellflower, is an excellent garden perennial. *C. glomerata* is a rather coarse old reliable. *C. rapunculoides*, locally called Chimney Bells, has pretty lavender bells on floppy stems that can be invasive. It is rarely sold, but freely traded over the back fence. Don't be shy about inspecting the teeth of this gift horse.

The American Rock Garden Society seed exchange lists 70 species, many hardy to Zone 3. For the rock garden are the much prized *C. rotundifolia*, the Bluebells of Scotland, given to cascading over rock walls, *C. carpatica*, the Carpathian harebell, and *C. lasiocarpa*, a neat little mound covered with pretty mountain bluebells.

CANARY BIRD VINE, *Tropaeolum peregrinum*, close kin to the nasturtium, like other nasturtiums, is finicky about being transplanted, but will accept it if you're cautious. Its deeply lobed, small leaves make a dense screen against a sunny fence and the yellow flowers are sprightly. It will scramble up a trellis against a sunny wall or soften an austere chain link fence. It needs six weeks head start indoors, and will collapse if Jack Frost sneaks even a quick kiss.

CANDYTUFT, *Iberis,* is not hardy in most of Alaska, but the annuals are fine bedding plants. The 'Fairy' mixtures are easy, but the hyacinth-flowered ones are not idiot-proof.

CELOSIA. The annual "plume" and "cockscomb" celosias do better in the Tanana Valley than in cooler locations. Among the plume types, the 'Castle' series has picked up AAS awards for its pink and apricot varieties.

CHRYSANTHEMUMS, are not hardy in mainland Alaska because of our long summer daylight. Days do not get short enough, soon enough, to trigger bud-set.

Some garden centers stock imported plants that had set buds at a lower latitude and they make attractive replacement plants for annuals that have played out, or as bedding plants in sunny locations. Throughout the year potted chrysanthemums make great indoor plants, blooming for six weeks or so. Keeping them over and getting them to bloom again is not easy because of the day length problem. They are attractive to aphids.

Alaska's native Arctic daisy, *Chrysanthemum arcticum,* now classified as *Dendranthemum arcticum,* and the ox-eye daisy, *C. leucanthemum,* now classified as *Leucanthemum vulgare,* (have you got that all straight now?) tend to be sprawlers with sparse foliage, but they have a place in meadow mixes, roadside beautification and informal gardens.

Several annual chrysanthemums are offered by garden centers and seed catalogs. One of the best is *C. paludosum,* a dwarf shasta with one-inch flowers which is generous about self-seeding. *C. multicaule* 'Gold Plate' is a good miniature dwarf. The annual chrysanthemum *C. coronarium* 'Primrose Gem' used to reach for six feet, but Thompson & Morgan now offers one that needs no staking.

CINERARIA, the jewel-toned florists' plants that thrive outdoors in shady West Coast gardens, also appreciate Alaska's cool summers. The long lasting daisy-shaped flowers come in pink, white, purply blues, and bi-colors. They make fine container plants that will bloom in sun or partial shade in Alaska. The bad news is that they must be started from seed in January to bloom six months later, but some garden centers do it for you. Aphids are mad for them. Sown in September they will bloom in a cool sunroom.

Kristen Isacson, a forester by training, showed a landscaper's eye using C. paludosum in a handsome corner planting. A friendly cat volunteered to pose.

CLARKIA, Godetia, a cool weather annual whose pink, lavender and white 24- inch blooms make good hanging basket subjects.

CLARY, a little known member of the salvia tribe is a fine garden plant in soft pink, blue and white which dries well for winter arrangements.

CLEMATIS is a gorgeous flowering vine in milder climates, but the great hybrids are rarely successful in Alaska, perhaps because of soils not sufficiently alkaline (although this is a debatable subject), but also because they are mostly Zone 4 and 5 plants and require more favorable locations than we can provide. The species clematises are a more cheerful subject.

Aline Strutz, an accomplished plantswoman in Anchorage, collected seed of golden clematis, *C. tangutica,* off a fence along the Alaska Highway and passed it around; now it thrives all over Anchorage.

It is a semi-woody subject that blooms on old branches. Its lower foliage is a mess, perhaps best concealed by solitary clematis, *C.integrifolia,* which is not a climber, or by Chinese forget-me-not, *Cynoglossom,* which gets big next to a wall.

Other species clematises that are known to be hardy to Zone 4 include Tube Clematis, *C. heracleifolia,* and Rock Clematis, *C. occidentalis. C. columbiana* is vigorous in Tryck Nursery's garden, producing great silver seed heads. Others available through the rock garden society seed lists are worth trying. Some may decline to crawl a lattice without assistance, and some may suffer die-back, but these are great wild vines.

Ayse Gilbert's Clematis tangutica *reaches for the roof by midsummer.*

CLEOME, a little known annual suited to Alaska's cool summer, has airy, flaring pink flowers and rather coarse foliage, a good three feet tall. Some gardeners find it difficult to germinate. Cold nights are the key to getting cleome to germinate, says John Gale, president and owner of Stokes Seeds. Give the seeds five days in the fridge and sow them in a greenhouse or cold frame between March 5 and April 15. Set them outside at night, even if temps go down to freezing. About four weeks after germination, plants are ready to set out. Travelers to New Zealand in our winter will be agog at their beauty.

COLUMBINE, *Aquilegia,* one of Alaska's most stalwart hybrid perennials, is easily grown from seed or divided crowns. It can be found in talls or shorts, all colors and heights from rock garden dwarfs to three-footers.

Columbines' single fault is their tendency toward promiscuity; natives cross with garden hybrids to the detriment of both, so you may end up with tall, muddy red and yellow plants if you mix a wildling with a hybrid. But sometimes desirable color variants occur and can be propagated by division.

CORAL BELLS, *Heuchera sanguinea,* a pretty white or pink-flowered perennial with tiny bells on upright stems, is maybe hardy to Zone 3. The English plant breeder, Alan Bloom, has been hybridizing heucheras for more than half a century under the distinguished Bressingham hybrid name.

They have beautiful light green foliage. The dramatic 'Palace Purple' was discovered at

London's Kew Gardens among a batch of seedlings labeled *H. Americana*. From this motley crop sprang a great plant with wine-colored leaves and interesting markings. Its seed was re-introduced in the U.S. but, sadly, plants did not come true from seed. You may find seeds but no guarantee that the leaves will be claret-colored and maple-shaped. It is hardy to Zone 4. If they are short-lived, look for a balmier location for they are worth having—and replacing. Some of the 70-odd species native to the western U.S. are found in Alaska and are being used at Blooms of Bressingham to breed winter hardiness into more colorful hybrids.

Alaska's native alpine heuchera, *Heuchera glabra*, is of interest to rock gardeners, and most of the 70-odd species are native to North America.

Alaska's native columbine, A. formosa, *is a short red and yellow, or sometimes just yellow.*

Many are half-hardy to Zone 3; they may not do their best until their third year. They germinate best, but somewhat irregularly, at 70 degrees in daylight.

COREOPSIS. The AAS Gold Metal winner, 'Early Sunrise' was a star performer for Pat Leary at the University of Alaska Anchorage. Started from seed at room temperature, it should show up in two to three weeks.

COSMOS is a great annual for late summer bloom when most others have fizzled out. It is a tall plant that may come in pink, white, or dark maroon daisy shapes. We have tried the much-touted hybrids but keep going back to the 'Sensations,' occasionally found in single colors. True, they require caging and the cages need a tent stake to support all that flower power, but they put on a good show.

DAHLIAS are often thought of as a man's flower because they take a fair amount of muscle. They are so easy to propagate by division of their tubers that dahlia fanciers acquire huge one-of-a-kind collections by trading tubers. These great flowers put on an impressive late summer show but are, truth to tell, more than a little bother.

Dahlias need six weeks' head start indoors before planting. The plants often require caging because their stems are brittle and have to prop up a lot of heavy flowers, and those cages need tent stakes to hold their own against the load. To keep dahlias blooming, they must be kept picked. Once picked, they don't last very long. To produce show-size blooms, they must be disbudded.

The foliage is the most frost-prone in the garden (dahlias are Mexican nationals). When it has blackened it must be cut down and the tubers dug and laid out to dry, then dusted with a fungicide. Cool, frost-free winter storage is not plentiful, and the tubers must be checked in midwinter for shriveling, and lightly sprinkled. If some are moldy they should be discarded and the remaining tubers dusted again with the fungicide.

Dahlias are big eaters and heavy drinkers, asking for deep, amended planting holes and a

Dahlias offer more variety in form and color than any other garden flower, from button to dinner plate size.

handful of 8-32-16 side dressing with more 8-32-16 or 0-20-20 when buds are forming. Large-flowered dahlias need three feet in rows three to four feet apart. Miniatures and pompoms can be planted two feet apart, but they will still need caging because they bloom in the late summer rainy period.

All this fuss brings complaints from dahlia growers, but few drop-outs. Growing dahlias from seed mixtures isn't difficult and if your dahlia budget is modest you may opt to start your collection by saving the tubers of the ones you like and pitching the duds. Barely covered seed will germinate in one to three weeks at 70 degrees.

If you're storing some of the obsolete kinds that don't hold their heads up or are a lurid or insipid color, you should start over. Modern dahlias are fantastic — see them at State Fairs and local garden club flower shows. The Anchorage Municipal Greenhouse likes 'Floodlight,' 'Lavender Perfection' and 'Lula Patti' for show-stoppers. UAA Anchorage liked Park's 'Pompom Mixed' seed.

DAYLILY, *Hemerocallis,* is a sore subject. Several of the species daylilies are hardy in Alaska, but when you say daylilies, it is not these wildlings that put the glint in the gardener's eye. The great modern hybrid daylilies that come in many colors and forms are not hardy enough for most of Alaska. Better ask around among the neighbors before you make a large investment. Among the species that are hardy are the yellow *H. flava,* apricot colored *H. dumortieii,* and the tawny *H. fulva.* The Plant Materials Center at Palmer has tested promising cultivars against a sunny wall next to a heated building with only meager success with orange and yellow varieties.

DELPHINIUMS have a lot going for them: ease of propagation from seed, cuttings, or division; spectacular flowers that tower above six feet at the back of the border; gorgeous colors that include snowy whites, true blues and regal purples, pink and raspberry shades, all hardy to Zone 2.

True, they are a pain in the neck to stake (cages work best, reinforced with a few bamboo canes and maybe a tent stake or two), and they are attractive to the black aphid and the leaf roller. Are you still tagging along?

Garden centers offer seedlings that can be potted up when you get them home and they will bloom by late summer, and some are not so awe-somely tall. You can order seed from many cata-logs and sow them in a cool 60-degree place where they will germinate irregularly in about three weeks.

Grow the seedlings cooler than you would most flowers — say 60 degrees, and set them out in early June. Deep soil preparation pays off with delphiniums. Dig a hole 18 inches or more deep, and mix manure or compost with a generous handful of a balanced fertilizer into the backfill soil. Each plant will need at least two feet of space. Are you still with me?

Seedling plants are so little that they are best grown in a nursery bed for their first summer so they won't have to compete with established clumps for nutrients, water, light and air circula-tion, before being transplanted the following spring to permanent places. New plants will send up a single bloom late in the summer, at about the time your new shasta daisies are doing the same thing, and they make a handsome couple. If you plant them very early, like February, you can treat them as annuals, but do not delude your-self that the blooms will rival the great perfor-mance of established perennial plants.

The Pacific Giants are the majestic tall ones, so heavy-headed in the rain that their brittle canes break unless you are a Master Staker. If you don't thin the shoots to three for a first-year plant and five to seven for mature plants, the canes will be shorter and the flowers smaller, but there will be more of them, in which case you might elect to drive four one-by-one stakes (make the bottom ends pointed!) in a square and circle the clump with a rope to provide support. A better alterna-tive is a six-foot cage reinforced with bamboo canes for individual stems and a tent stake to pre-vent toppling.

Dwarfs in Pacific Giant colors grow only 24 to 30 inches tall, according to the catalogs, but in Alaska's long daylight they get taller. They are easier to stake, but still give the back of the bor-der the skyline it needs. 'Dwarf Blue Butterfly' is an even shorter single, and it gets high marks from the Anchorage Municipal Greenhouse.

DIANTHUS, "pinks," are treasured annuals, bi-ennials, and perennials. The annuals are eight to 15 inches tall and come in bright, fresh colors and bi-colors.

The biennial Sweet William, *D. barbatus*, is a stalwart in the flower garden. Its seeds are started in the spring six weeks before planting out and it spends its first summer growing leaves, so you may want to plant it in a nursery bed, moving the plants that survive the winter to the flower garden the following spring. Carnations are greenhouse plants, but they are so attractive to aphids and red spider that you mix them with tomatoes, cucumbers or peppers at your peril.

The perennials have some delightful species for the rock garden like the tiny Maiden Pink, *D. deltoides*, the Alpine pink, *D. alpinus*, the Sand pink, *D. arenarius*, the Cheddar pink, *D. gratiopolitanus*, and the Grass pink, *D. plumarius*.

The annual pinks and the biennials are sold at garden centers, but you may have to go to cata-logs and the rock garden society seed lists for the species Dianthuses, but they are worth the bother for alpine gardeners.

DORONICUM'S bright yellow daisies come on early above heart-shaped leaves in neat clumps. *D. caucasicum* is offered in catalogs and comes easily, if somewhat irregularly, from seed; starter plants are sold in nurseries.

DRABA is a perennial that self-seeds readily and has numerous species that occur all over Alaska. The white flowered kinds are little nothings but the brilliant yellow-flowered species take the place of the rather unreliable Basket of Gold in the rockery and in wall plantings. It blooms very early, along with Auricula primroses, Bergenia, *Anemone richardsonii* and the Pasque flower, a sight to restore your faith in spring.

DUSTY MILLER is a silver-leafed peacemaker in the garden, good in tubs of mixed annuals, use-ful in bedding plant designs, withstanding frosts with regal poise, and can be dried for winter use. 'Silver Dust' is a finely-cut one; 'Silver Lace' has broader, beautifully carved leaves with a dusting of silver. 'Cirrhus' has white felty leaves, a striking edger for a bed or border. 'Silver Brocade' is an outstanding spreading mat, and makes a distinguished hanging container plant.

EDELWEISS, *Leontopodium alpinum*, is something of a disappointment without Julie Andrews, but its felty white leaves and inconspicuous flowers make a provocative rock garden subject. *L. alpina* is most frequently seen in the market place, but the rock garden society seed lists offer 10 to 20 species. Seed germinates best at 50 degrees on the surface of the seeding medium in 10 days to six weeks. Established plants can be divided to make more. It dries well for wreath-making.

ERIGERON, flea bane, is a wildflower that grows almost everywhere. Some of its numerous species are weedy, some almost as good as Michaelmas daisies which are not hardy here. *E. speciosum* is one of the best and is in its element in a wild garden but, with some encouragement, is good enough for the perennial border.

Seeds, available from the rock garden society seed exchanges, germinate in 15 to 20 days at a chilly 55 degrees, and make lots of daisy-shaped flowers on two-foot bushy perennial plants. The variety 'Profusion' has entered the ranks of cultivars, to the delight of every gardener casting about for a different hanging basket, window box, or garden edging plant.

EUPHORBIA, Mound of Gold, is a heart warming sight in earliest spring with yellow green mounds hard on the heels of breakup. It is lamentably short-lived in the Anchorage area, so if you love it, plant some every year for insurance. It germinates readily in 10 to 14 days at 70 to 80 degrees under a light covering of the seeding medium.

EVERLASTING FLOWERS are getting more space in seed catalogues as the art and craft of drying flowers, grasses and seed pods attract more artisans to create wreaths, swags, topiaries and dried arrangements. The statice seekers among us look for *Limonium* species. The familiar *L. sinuatum* which once came in purple and white is now packaged in separate colors and in mixes like 'Pastel Shades,' 'Sunset Shades,' and the lovely 'Azure.'

The florists' *S. tatarica* is hardy in Zone 4 gardens, providing great bouquets from a single plant and many twigs for wreath-making. Pink Pokers is *S. suworowii*, which has long spikes curved in bizarre ways, good for arrangements (improved by a pass from the hard-to-hold hair spray can).

New varieties tempt craftspeople. Consider the merits of gomphrena, tansy, sea holly, and dwarf strawflowers like the Bikini series. If you have a south-facing hot spot, it might be worth lavishing it on a half dozen plants of the perennial baby's breath, *Gypsophila paniculatum* which will yield enough big sprays for a large basket or an umbrella urn. The pink kind is prettier, but we have overcome our reluctance to spray plants by running a pale golden tint from a spray can past ours in a room of mostly gold and browns.

Flowers that you never suspected would dry include florists' roses, clary, larkspur, "golden ageratum" which is really *Lonas inodora,* and the seed pods of poppies and shrub roses. Among the wildlings don't overlook the seed pods of the native iris and columbines. The dried leaves of Artemesia make dainty sprays. For a sturdy element the ripe stalks of beach wild rye and dock are worth saving. Suzanne Forster, an artist of the craft, is the source of our knowledge.

FELICIA, sometimes called Blue Marguerite, is a nice little lavender daisy that does equally well in the ground or in containers. It is not hardy in most of Alaska and is shipped in as rooted cuttings by many nurseries. It is somewhat expensive, as annuals go, but worth the price if you don't need too many. The seed-grown felicias are not as impressive, but have a place in a meadow mix or wild garden.

FERNS. Alaska has more than 30 kinds, some of landscape importance. The great "lady ferns," *Athyrium filix-femina,* spread wide fronds in the woods and in the foothills of the southern half of the state. They are sought for landscape use on the shady north side, where they perform with distinction, a native horticultural resource of great value. It is common in woods and lowlands in the southern part of Alaska, transplants readily and is hardy to Zone 3.

Planted with the crown level with the soil surface in humisy acid soil it will multiply by spores or its rhizomes.

Southeastern is blessed with the maidenhair fern, *Adiatium pedatum,* and the Matanuska-Susitna Valley has the tall ostrich fern, *Matteuccia struthiopteris,* as ornamental as it is edible for its tasty "fiddleheads," and everybody south of the Arctic Circle can welcome the little oak fern, *Gymnocarpium dryopteris,* when it crashes a garden party.

The Hardy Fern Foundation, (P.O. Box 60034, Richmond Beach, WA 98160-0034) has a fern spore exchange in cooperation with the American Fern Society. Spores and test plants are available to members. Individual memberships at this writing are $20.

FEVERFEW, *Chrysanthemum parthenium,* now classified as *Tanacetum,* is a neat little annual for Alaska gardens. It looks like a button chrysanthemum, smells like one, and has chrysanthemum leaves, is often listed as Matricaria.

'White Stars,' a 15-incher, is the most popular kind, but don't pass up the diminutive 'Golden Ball,' 'Santana,' or 'Butterball,' all good annual edgers and container plants.

FILIPENDULA, a perennial, is often confused with spirea. *Filipendula rubra,* "Queen-of-the-prairie," has large pink flower umbels, a good subject for the back of the border. *F. Ulmaria,* "Queen-of-the-Meadow," is shorter, has creamy white flowers. Don't give up on this perennial until at least its second year.

FLOWERING CABBAGE or **FLOWERING KALE** are good flowers for formal bedding designs, and are useful as edging and in containers. They form green heads splashed with red or pink or creamy white. Flowering cabbage forms a head, the kale is taller. They last well into the fall when we need late bloomers. Moose like all forms of cabbage.

FORGET-ME-NOT, *Myosotis alpestris,* the Alpine forget-me-not, is Alaska's State flower, an inconspicuous little one with true blue flowers. It has been improved by the hybridizers and plants from purchased seeds are the superior *M. sylvatica,* which also comes in pink and white.

M. palustris, the brook forget-me-not, grows wild in Southeastern Alaska but has made itself at home in Southcentral gardens where it is useful as a ground cover and as a rockery plant. It has lighter blue flowers, will grow in quite poor soil, and can be invasive.

M. australis is an Australian native that has yellow flowers. It is not as reliable for us as the blue-flowered cultivars, but it is worth sowing every year.

Chinese forget-me-not, *Cynoglossom Spp.,* has lighter blue flowers and plants up to two feet tall, a nice annual for the north.

Forget-me-nots germinate readily from spring-sown seed and produce green plants the first summer. Those that live over the winter bloom the second summer and then die, usually after profligate self-seeding. The young volunteers can be transplanted in the spring to make a dramatic edging or tucked in where you want them to spread. If one volunteers between cracks in the patio, give it a well-deserved handout now and then.

FOXGLOVE, *Digitalis,* is a biennial that may not survive the winter of its discontent in Zone 3. Against a south wall, with a winter mulch, it sometimes makes it and puts on a great show. Gardeners on the southern coast have it easy.

Elsewhere, foxglove 'Foxy,' sowed in late February or early March will bloom the first summer. The seed comes in a mixture of pinks and lavenders, and the blooms are lovely spires in the garden. It is amiable about sun or shade and tolerant of the first frosts. Many nurseries offer seedling plants.

Digitalis grandiflora is a species foxglove that performs well enough for the flower border. It gets to be a foot tall and has yellow flowers on stocky stems, a neat perennial for a favored location, like a sunny boulder in a rock garden.

FUCHSIA (FEW-sha, to dictionary authorities, FEWK-si-ah to botanists who revere the name of German botanist Fuchs.)

Fuchsias thrive on cool, moist climates and long summer days, and Alaska is pleased to oblige them. There are more than 2,000 named varieties and hundreds of fuchsia societies where devotees trade cuttings and lore. Some fuchsias are more upright than others and do best in patio containers and can be planted in the ground in mild locations. Some are determined to trail and do best in hanging baskets.

Most fuchsias in town gardens are purchased on the brink of full bloom in late May. They should be exposed gradually to the reality of ultraviolet light, and brought indoors on chilly nights or windy days until they are hardened off.

During the summer fuchsias need to be kept moist (check twice on hot days), and they will require feeding every two weeks, or half-strength weekly. Faded flowers should be removed; if seed pods form, bloom slows to a crawl.

When first frost is giving your garden the eye, you have to come to terms with the fuchsia's mortality: store it at a garden center for a little less than the cost of a new, but smaller, plant next spring; store it at home if you have a cool space where you can give it eight hours of artificial light and can remember to water it occasionally; keep it in a cool sunroom where it may continue to bloom for several weeks, but will gradually slip into dormancy. Or, take cuttings and pitch the "mother" plant.

Potting mixes for fuchsias should be very loose and well-drained. Pinching is the key to lots of bloom. If you want a bountiful trailing fuchsia, nip out the growing tip at every second set of leaves until six weeks before you want it to make a big splash.

If you want to go for a tree-form, or "standard," set a stake beside a straight, strong-stemmed, rooted cutting ('Bell Buoy' is a classic selection) and refrain from pinching the center bud, letting it grow as tall as you want your "tree" to be. Then pinch out the growing tip and every alternate terminal bud until the bushy head suits you.

This takes 15 to 18 months from cutting to final triumph and can be done in a sunroom or under lights in a cool, moist place. You'll need a fuchsia "hat" to support the top-growth. For a small standard, an inverted wire hanging basket will do, but you'll need a real fuchsia hat if you have a plant inching up past a $75 price tag.

You will find the fuchsias amiable about bonsai. The miniatures 'Tom Thumb,' 'Isis' and 'Pumilo' are good bets for bonsai treatment. With careful pruning and a bonsai container's constricted space, you can have a six-incher with miniature blossoms and tiny leaves. Watering requires vigilance.

Americans, unlike the great fuchsia-growing New Zealanders, tend to prefer huge double fuchsia blooms, but you might enjoy one of the full size plants with small, single blooms. If you're hopelessly hung up on fuchsias, consider joining the American Fuchsia Society, which advertises its current address and dues in the gardening magazines. The address of the Alaska Fuchsia Society, as of this writing, is P.O. Box 81449, Fairbanks, AK 99708.

GAILLARDIA, Blanket Flower, an annual, has mostly yellow daisy shapes with red markings. The perennial *G. aristata* is hardy to Zone 2.

GERANIUM. The trouble with geraniums is not so much horticultural as it is nomenclatural. The *cognoscente* among us know perfectly well that the garden geranium is really a pelargonium, but cognizant or not, practically nobody calls it that.

The true geranium, *G. sanguineum,* is a wild species that in no way resembles the garden variety, although some have been hybridized to make splendid garden perennials. Alaska's native cranesbill, *G. erianthum,* is a wildling that with good care in fertile soil self-seeds like mad and you may need to control it.

The garden geranium staked out its claim in Alaska when the century was young, peering cheerily from cabin windows. "Slips" got passed around and sourdough gardeners generally agreed that the death rate to "black leg" was a plague of major dimension. Then came a breakthrough: geraniums you could grow from seed. For the price you once paid for a single plant you could have a troop of hybrid geraniums camping by your doorstep, or marching smartly up a flight of steps. True, they took five months from seed to bloom and they had an annoying tendency toward bloom-shatter.

In the 20-odd years since, germination time has dropped from 160 days to less than 80, and the plant breeders have been making progress on more durable blooms. Today most of the geraniums sold in garden centers are seed-grown. They are one of the most satisfactory annuals or they can be over-wintered in a cool, bright place. They will look forlorn by spring, but cuttings can be taken in March. By all means, use a fungicide to prevent "black leg" when taking cuttings.

Picking her way warily through the wholesale catalogs, Susan Miller looks for varieties that thrive in cool summer weather, pits new introductions against proven kinds in a constant effort to upgrade her big show. She leans toward the zonals with the least zonation. The more pronounced the zones, the more prone the leaves are to redden in cool weather.

She liked these for the municipal plantings: 'Cameo,' a sparkling salmon the color of a sockeye; 'Neon Rose,' which is unabashedly incandescent; 'Orbit Rose,' pretty in pink and 'Orbit White.' 'Red Elite' is a shorty, good for window boxes and pots. 'Picasso' is a flamboyant magenta with orange overtones; 'Tetra Scarlet' is another of numerous great reds. For hanging baskets the 'Breakaway' series and the stocky 'Freckles' and 'Orange Appeal' perform well for the Municipality's great public gardens. The 'Sensation' series is obligingly self-cleaning.

Seeds are sown January 15th, programmed to be in bloom by June first when the city plantings come into instant flower. Home gardeners, not under tourist season pressure, might opt for as late as Valentine's Day ("but no later!" says grower Pat Kegel at Bell's Nurseries), and still get lots of bloom in containers in sunny locations.

Sow the seeds in a sterile potting mix and cover them with a quarter inch of vermiculite. They will germinate in 10 to 14 days at 70 to 75 degrees in light or darkness. Once the seedlings are up, the thermostat must come down to 60 to 65 degrees, with artificial light supplementing winter daylight until the days are 10 hours long, about March first. As the plants' first flower buds appear, they should be pinched to induce branching. (Practice will help you tell the flower buds from leaf buds, and you may have to let a bit of leaf develop until you get the hang of it.)

When danger of frost is past and the spring winds have abated, condition the plants for setting out by taking them outdoors for gradually increasing exposure times for a week or 10 days, a task that is more delight than duty to a gardener who has pulled it off. If you can rig up a floating row cover of spun-bonded polyester in a protected place, you may be able to leave them out. If you have a commodious cold frame, park them there.

The zonals thrive on full sun but accept some shade. Removing faded flowers extends bloom by three to six weeks. Keeping temperatures cool helps prevent petal-shatter.

These bedding geraniums are one of the great horticultural strides of recent years. There is still plenty of room for the splendid plants produced vegetatively and listed in specialty catalogs.

The Ivy leaf geraniums make great hanging basket plants if given a spot out of the wind and the traffic pattern; their brittle stems detest buffeting or banging-into. American hybridizers have specialized in breeding large, double flowers, but with the seed-grown ivy leafs gardeners can now have the cascades of floriferous singles

"German" geraniums are trailers, best suited to hanging containers and window boxes. 'Mini Cascade' is more compact than most, says Pat Kegel of Bells' Nurseries. Susan Miller likes to combine the trailers with lobelias of the 'Fountain' series.

Martha Washington geraniums, or the "Regals," have given the royal nod to Alaska's cool plebeian summer. They do well in the ground in protected locations but find their real majesty in containers, either by themselves or with one of the lobelias. They like full sun, plenty of water and a high-phosphorus soluble fertilizer. The "Marthas," as the trade calls them, come in many colors, all luscious.

GERBERA, a florist plant until the introduction of 'Happipot,' is now a fixture in Alaska sunrooms and in patio containers. Gerberas can be grown from seed sown in March and plants are sold by garden centers. They are usually mixtures of spidery, double, or tufted flowers of red, orange, yellow, pink or cream.

GERMAN CHAMOMILE, *Matricaria recutia*, is an ebullient annual that billows with tiny daisylike flowers and, herbal tea drinkers say, makes a soothing brew. Seeds germinate best in daylight in 10-14 days and plants are 18 to 24 inches tall. Give them full sun. The honeybees will hum their thanks.

GEUM, is a small perennial, mostly red and yellow, that is a minor attraction in Alaska gardens. *G. rossii* is an Alaska native that is a good rock garden subject. *G. triflorum,* 'Prairie Smoke,' came to us from the Canadian tundra, and is a nice addition to the wild garden.

Picasso' is shown here with the Benny Benson memorial sculpture. 'Pinto' is a twin.

GLADIOLUS is a tropical flower that is a fair weather friend in Alaska gardens, requiring winter storage of its corms. Start corms indoors in potting mix, about six weeks before planting time, giving them all the light there is when the leaf

Susan Miller, charged with urban beautification for Anchorage, grows 8,000 to 10,000 geraniums each year from seed for the city's parks and public buildings.

spikes appear and growing them in a cool place. If started too early and grown in a warm room, the plants get too tall to transplant well. The advice in garden literature to start several plantings for a succession of bloom is not valid in Alaska, where it is touch-and-go for the late blooming varieties to make it at all.

Glads are not easy to stake gracefully, so many gardeners grow them in a row in the vegetable or cutting garden, running a cord the length of the row on either side of these lanky plants, so they won't topple. They are excellent cut flowers. If cut when the first floret shows color, buds will open gradually to the very tip. Commercial growers extend the life of the stems they ship to distant markets by five to seven days by making a fresh cut after harvesting, plunging them in water up to their lower buds, and pre-cooling them at 40 degrees.

Gladiolus are subject to infestation by thrips, little hyphen-shaped varmints. If you find white stripes between leaf veins or brown, limp buds, spray with Safer's soap, or malathion or Orthene. When frost is imminent, they should be lifted and brought indoors with the foliage intact. If you have a greenhouse, they can be heeled in, in beds or benches, for welcome fall bloom. When foliage turns brown it is useful in dried arrangements and the corms can be stored in paper bags. Dust the corms in the fall with any bulb dust containing carbaryl (Sevin™) and store as close to 40 degrees as you can without letting them freeze.

GLOBE FLOWER (see **TROLLIUS**).

GOAT'S-BEARD, *Aruncus sylvester*, is one of Alaska's best-kept horticultural secrets. It is a big, rangy herbaceous perennial that looks like a shrub, and grows wild in Southcentral and Southeastern. English gardeners appreciate it for its tall plume-like white flowers on arching stems, its usefulness in the back of a flower border, tolerance of some shade, freedom from most insect and disease problems. Male and female plants are separate and the males make the best ornamentals. To tell the boys from the girls, look for stamens; if the flowers have stamens, they're males.

HELIOTROPE has taken on new ways in hanging baskets and tubs of mixed annuals. Give it six weeks head-start indoors if you grow it from seed. 'Mini-Marine' is a good one.

HOLLYHOCK, *Alcea rosea*, is mostly a biennial that may or may not make it through the first winter, depending on where you garden. Some varieties sown from seed in March or purchased from a garden center will bloom late the first summer — but we need some late bloomers to provide a change of scene. For this treatment you might try: 'Indian Spring,' 'Majorette Mixed,' or 'Pinafore mixed.' Hollyhocks are of the complex *Malvaceae*, mallow family. They germinate in 10 to 21 days at 65 to 70 degrees.

Kathi Moon grew her hop vine from seed, planted three where one would have been enough, she admits.

The Keith McCavits face a sunny sidewalk with ice plant.

HOP VINE, *Humulus lupulus*, is one of few perennial vines for southern Alaska, hardy to Cook Inlet. It is the flavoring agent in beer but it won't produce enough of its cone-like fruits to make a six-pack. It will, however, climb a bare chimney or a sunny trellis with determination and considerable grace. The variety 'Aurea' has yellow leaves. Hops can be grown from seed but they take a month to germinate and you need to maintain a 70 to 75 degree temperature, not easy to do. Better buy your beer.

HOSTA, is enjoying a comeback, due in part to Alaska's prolonged warming trend, and partly to our change of heart, having given it a bad press in previous writings. In reasonably favored locations it is perennial in Zone 3, and seems to thrive even in partial shade. Its leaves make lovely mounds and its flowers are elegant. We take ketchup on our crow. It's tricky to grow from seed, germinating in 30 to 90 days at 50 degrees.

HYDRANGEA is, sadly, in the almost-but-not-quite class for Southcentral Alaska. Some are hardy to -20 degrees, surviving in favored locations, but the day length may do them in and they do not get ready for winter in time to get the protection of dormancy against the winter's cold. They are tempting plants for sunrooms and the well-heeled should go for nursery and florist plants in April when spring is eons away.

ICEPLANT, or Livingstone Daisy, *Mesembryanthemum,* shuts up shop on cloudy days and in shady places. Daisy-shaped flowers three to six inches above frosty foliage are dazzlers, a sparkling ground cover for a limited area. It germinates best in the dark, in two to three weeks at room temperature.

IMPATIENS does not deserve its odious common names, "Busy Lizzie" and "Blooming Idiot." It is an accommodating house plant that needs cutting back occasionally to keep it compact. It makes a splendid hanging basket plant for indoors or outdoors. The Anchorage Municipal greenhouse combines the 'Blitz' series with lobelia in lovely compositions for shady locations. It is less successful in the ground, and not at its best in boxes ——it really wants to hang.

Catalogs offer seeds of new varieties almost every year, but they are not the easiest seeds to germinate. They are very small, and should be mixed with a pinch of sand for sowing. Germination time is irregular and may require three to four weeks at 70 to 75 degrees. Seeds germinate best in the light when sown on the surface of the seeding medium and not covered. Enclose the flat in a plastic sack because high humidity is needed for germination. Late February or early March is time to sow seeds, so order when the catalogs hit the mailbox.

The nursery industry now rates Impatiens as its biggest seller and garden centers sell these plants in the early spring—numerous colors, all luscious, singles and doubles, bi-colors, with plain or variegated foliage, in heights ranging from five to 12 inches. The doubles are especially appealing, like tiny rosebuds.

The New Guinea hybrids have variegated, pointed leaves. Grow at least one in a pot outdoors, to bring inside when frost threatens. Or, take cuttings of your favorites and pot them up for houseplants.

Iris flavissima *produces lovely small flowers that live for only a day, but they keep coming through early* spring.

IRIS. The lovely *Iris setosa* is one of Alaska's choicest wildflowers for growing in town gardens. In rich garden soil it tends to get carried away and produce immense clumps that need dividing every few years, a man-sized job. Its colors range from rich purple to a cool violet and a rare white.

JACOB'S LADDER, *Polemonium spp.,* has three lovely wildflowers and some visiting relatives in Alaska. Tall Jacob's Ladder, *P. acutiflorum,* grows wild over the big part of Alaska. Beautiful Jacob's Ladder, *P. pulcherrimum,* is the dwarf one that you see clinging to the rocky bluffs along Turnagain Arm, on roadsides, in the woods, or living it up in town gardens. It is mostly a southern Alaskan native, blooming in early spring.

P. boreale is an eight-incher that braves the Arctic Coast and the Aleutian Chain, but if it can find a toe-hold, it settles elsewhere. If you're trying to grow other Polemoniums, do it at 75 degrees and see if anything happens in three weeks.

JOHNNY-JUMP-UP, *Viola tricolor,* is a perky little weed that self seeds with abandon. Planted in a window box, it will spawn a dense crop beneath it the following year. It makes a pretty fill-in between plants, and if it gets pushy, it is easy to pull. Any neighbor who has it would gladly offer you a shovelful, but in recent years some good strains have been isolated and are sold in garden centers. Isolating a favorite strain is fun for amateur plant breeders.

Use Johnny-Jump-Up in the wild garden, in containers, and put up with it with pleasure wherever it crops up. We never met a weed we liked better.

KENILWORTH IVY, *Cymbalaria muralis,* is the little charmer you get from some nurseries whether you buy it or not. It is a neat little trailing plant with leaves resembling ivy and little pink or lavender flowers, that likes greenhouses and may hitch-hike in on something you did buy.

It transplants easily to hanging baskets of mixed annuals and it will spend the summer outdoors in a sunny wall, or against a rock somewhere, but will not be with you the next time around—you can disregard warnings that it may be invasive, which it is not in the high north. If you love it, catalogs list it.

LADY'S MANTLE, *Alchemilla spp.,* is a recently discovered charmer, perennial to Zone 3. Its toothed leaves catch and hold dew or raindrops like crystal beads and its chartreuse blooms do good things for bouquets and winter arrangements. Sow it at cool room temps and give it three or four weeks to show up. *A. alpina* is a smaller plant.

LAMB'S EARS, *Stachys byzantina,* is an herb, medicinal in bygone days, but makes ornamental low-growing clumps, peacemakers among colorful subjects. It germinates in two to four weeks, or you can buy divided plants. It is inclined to look doleful in rain country.

LARKSPUR, *Delphinium spp.,* is an annual that does not perform well in some places in Alaska, although the perennial delphiniums do. Two species grow wild in Alaska, tall purple-flowered larkspurs that are toxic to livestock. The foliage closely resembles that of *Aconitum delphinifolium,* which is extremely toxic. Eliminate it if you have farm animals.

LAVATERA. (See **MALLOWS.**)

LAYIA, Tidy Tips, is nice to have in a meadow mix, an informal garden, or a container of mixed annuals. It grows about 18 inches tall, and has yellow daisy-like flowers with white tips. It should not be confused with "Fried Eggs," *Limnanthes douglasii,* a six-incher with similar blooms that is not nearly as good (and has that awful name). It germinates irregularly in one to four weeks at room temperature.

LEWISIAS are native to the mountains of Wash-

ington and Oregon. *L. tweedii* is often listed as one of the 10 best wild flowers of the world. If Mrs. Louis Strutz should be cited for only one of her contributions to horticulture in Alaska, it should be for introducing this beautiful native American plant to Alaska's rock gardeners. It is quite variable, ranging from white to melting pinks and yellow. *L. cotyledon* is almost as desirable with pink or white flowers veined in red. *L. pygmaea* has minute pale pink flowers and spreads obligingly in a site to its liking.

All the Lewisias are fussy about wet feet. They need a fast draining soil mix and a ring of pebbles or crushed rock under their rosettes. They excel in a rock wall where their carrot-like roots can find moisture while the sensitive crowns stay dry.

Sow the freshest seed you can find indoors in the early spring at 50 degrees, or in a cold frame in spring or fall. It helps to store the seed three or four weeks at low temperature to speed germination. It may take a year to germinate and when established may self-seed for you. This is a plant you should not give up on easily. Walter Mayr's greenhouse in Sutton sells plants; some catalogs list seeds.

LIGULARIA is a little-known perennial that is worth its space in a mixed border. Hardy to Zone 4, its slender yellow flower spikes look wimpy the first year but will grow three feet tall if it likes you.

LILIES. Among the cultivated lilies, the Asiatic Hybrids are Alaska's best and most reliable performers.

There are pinks, reds, yellows, whites and lavenders, as well as oranges among the Asiatics, and in reasonably favorable locations they should be with you for years. 'Enchantment,' a vibrant orange, is perhaps the most widely grown lily in the world. 'Ming yellow' is a creamy yellow outward-facing Asiatic. 'Zephyr' is pink with maroon dots. Collections of Asiatics are worth experimenting with, but be wary of unnamed grab bags. Look for Asiatic polyploids, which have an extra set of

Theresa Williams, lawyer and lily collector, has drifts of Asiatic lilies in her garden.

chromosomes which make them very durable. 'Red Velvet' is a knockout and so is 'Sally,' with freckles on pink petals.

The *Hollandicum* lilies have been around so long they are called Russian lilies hereabouts. Clumps get divided and passed around and you may find them at garden club plant sales in late May, sometimes offered as "flame" lilies.

The Siberian coral lily is a fiery red rock garden treasure, hardy into the Interior. It is listed in catalogs as *L. tenufolium* or *L. pumila.*

Lily bulbs appear on the market in the spring in Alaska. In a greenhouse or sunroom they could be started in March or April in containers, and set out in the garden in June. Lily plants started in greenhouses bloom the first summer, increasing in size in subsequent seasons. Tender lilies make good sunroom plants.

Fall catalogs make tempting lily offers. If you go this route you might store the bulbs over winter in a refrigerator, starting them into growth in March or April. If you decide to try fall planting, choose a favorable spot close to the house foundation, where there is good drainage and full sun. Plant cultivars about six inches deep, and species lilies only three or four inches deep. University of Minnesota researchers found that a protective mulch was important for the first winter until the plantings were established, and should be left on until frost danger is past.

LILY-OF-THE-VALLEY, *Convallaria majalis,* is one of Alaska's great early-blooming plants. Once established, it spreads, and makes a beautiful ground cover, even in the shade. It is quite aggressive in sunny locations in Zone 3. The tiny bell-shaped white flowers are fragrant.

Thompson & Morgan offers the seed, but Liliesof-the-Valley are usually grown from neighborly handouts or from "pips" sold at garden centers in the spring.

LINARIA, is a sweet little annual that does not deserve to be called Toadflax. It looks like a miniature snapdragon, comes in mixed colors, and 'Crown Jewels' is not mis-named.

It has a black sheep relation, *Linaria vulgaris,* commonly called Butter-and-Eggs, which has the distinction of having made the State's list of noxious weeds. Its yellow and white flowers above attractive gray-green leaves are tempting, but it should not be brought under cultivation, a widely ignored injunction. You'll be sorry.

LOBELIA comes from a large family of annuals and perennials, but only the annuals are of interest in Alaska. There are edging and trailing kinds, and the two overlap. The edgers will trail over a hanging container, but they won't trail as ebulliently as the over-used 'Sapphire.'

'Cambridge Blue' is a delicate, pale blue; its trailing counterpart is 'Pendula Blue Cascade.' Most of the other blues are on the purple side. 'Crystal Palace' is the classic, but 'Bluestone' is also a nice deep blue one. 'Rosamund' and 'Red Cascade' are dark red with white eyes, but new varieties are better. Look for an Irish cultivar with mulberry-colored flowers and a Chilean species, *L. tupa*, with very large flowers and gray-green leaves.

The lobelias are mostly used as mixers, often complementing Martha Washington geraniums or fuchsias, and baskets of mixed annuals. Those great lobelia baskets displayed on antique lamp posts are created by lining wire baskets with black plastic, filling in with fertilized potting mix. Holes are punctured in the plastic and young lobelia plants, encased in protective cones of paper are inserted, root end first, back-filling with potting mix as you add plants. The Anchorage Municipal Greenhouse often puts a dwarf orange mari-

'Sterling Silver' filters through cosmos foliage, a favorite trick of Matanuska Valley landscaper Jim Fox, this one in the Allan Linns' garden.

gold in the top layer to create the colors of Alaska's flag; summer tourists burn up a lot of film on these spectacular baskets.

Lobelias are slow to germinate, so sow them in early March, or even in February, sprinkling a packet of seed on a flat of vermiculite. When you prick them out into pots or cell packs, remember that they are gregarious—they do best when potted up in clumps of several seedlings.

LOTUS. *Lotus bertelotii* is a lacy, gray foliage plant that may surprise you with scarlet sweet pea-like flowers. It is useful in containers.

LUPINE, *Lupinus nootkatensis* and *L. arcticus*, are Alaska's lovely wild lupines, carpeting meadows, roadside ditches, mountain slopes and gravel bars

'Corsica' is a pinkish lavender, lovely with pastel perennials.

from the Arctic Coast into Southeastern and out to the Westward. Why, then, is it so difficult to get them to settle down in town gardens?

Members of the Pea family, these legumes have tap roots that probe deep into the sub-soil for minerals. Transplanting tap-rooted plants isn't easy, so select the youngest you can find and dig deep for the tap root.

Seeding is a better way to go. Harvest fully ripe seed in the fall and sow it where you want it to grow. Or, store it in the refrigerator over the winter and soak the seeds in tepid water for 15 minutes. Nicking the hard outer coating with a file helps moisture to penetrate.

If you sow the seeds indoors, be prepared to set them out when they have a single true leaf, before that tap root gets long. In a year when the Arctic hare's cycle is at its peak, the bunnies will gorge by night on lupines. Lupine seeds are unpredictable, waiting for moisture, temperature and perhaps day length to coincide. One year we had more than an acre in a thick stand; the next year none. Other years they have grown among our choicest alpines, crowding out rarer plants.

Probably nobody knows more about propagating the genus *lupinus* than the Texas Highway Department. Texas bluebonnets, the lupines that are Texas' state flower, once graced the central hill country where buffalo hooves cracked the seed pods and ground them into the dry soil, and the buffalo did it right. Nowadays bluebonnets grow all over, reaching out in a sea of blue to Texas' far horizons and even along the Interstates, where they are let go to seed, mowed once, and the seed-laden hay moved to barren spots where it acts as a mulch until young plants take hold, a method which has possibilities for propagation of Alaska's beautiful native lupines.

The Russell Hybrid lupines, gorgeous perennials in milder climates, are almost as unpredictable here. You sow seeds one year, get flowers the next—*if* they survive the first winter and if the hares don't eat them. Try buying nursery-grown plants in the spring, if you can find small ones, and protect them with cages and a winter mulch. Or wait for a year when the rabbit cycle is down.

If you grow them from seed, nick the hard seeds with a file or let them swell under a moist paper towel in a plate of water. Soaking them in water is trickier—you can drown the embryo if you leave them too long.

LYCHNIS (see also Maltese Cross). The six-footer, Maltese Cross, is well known to Alaskans who mix it with tall delphiniums in the back of the border, a happy combination of fire engine red with blues or white.

But it is not the only Lychnis of merit. *Lychnis x arkwrightii* (also listed as *Lychnis x hagana*) is an 18-inch dazzler in riotous colors that range through the reds into vermilion, orange and hot pinks. 'Vesuvius' is a named variety whose bronze foliage and intense orange-red flowers are stunners among gray-leafed *artemesias*.

L. flos-jovis, sometimes listed as *L. coronaria* 'Angel Blush' has silvery leaves and white flowers with pink centers.

L. chalcedonica alba is a white flowered two-footer that is undistinguished.

LYSIMACHIA punctata, Alaska's "evening primrose," is a two foot, rather shrubby perennial that bears golden yellow whorls of flowers on long arching stems (not to be confused with the genus *Oenothera*, also commonly called evening primrose (a laggard in most of Alaska).

L. nummularia, Moneywort, is a groundcreeper that roots at the leaf nodes and has little yellow flowers. It is at its best in a pool planting, but has not hung around long for most gardeners.

L. clethroides, Gooseneck Loosestrife, has spikes of small white flowers, a good plant for midsummer bloom.

L. terrestris, Swamp Loosestrife, has yellow flowers and grows best in wet places, a possibility for water gardens.

LYTHRUM, Purple Loosestrife, is a tall perennial with magenta flowers in terminal spikes. It is a menace in the South 48, where it has been outlawed in several states

Maltese Cross, Lychnis chalcedonica, makes a bold statement in the midsummer garden, blooming with such attention-getters as the Asiatic trollius and Lysimachia.

MALLOWS are members of a big confusing family; some annual, some biennial, others perennial —all worth sweating a little blood over. You may find them sold as Lavateras, Mallows, Malvas or hollyhocks, a member of the tribe. Among the annual kinds Susan Miller of the Anchorage Municipality likes 'Mont Rose' and 'Mont Blanc,' both real show-offs. 'Ruby Regis,' is positively regal in front of a Canadian chokecherry tree's dark red leaves, and *L. thuringiaca* 'Rose' which is perennial but short-lived. *Malva sylvestris* 'Zebrina' is a tall, dark purple and lavender double for a hollyhock, and more reliable.

Some nurseries start other hollyhocks early enough to give you flowers in late summer. Most will germinate at 70 degrees in two to three weeks. They will require caging but the plants soon filter through the wire to conceal their means of support.

MARGUERITES, *Anthemis tinctoria*, are perennials which are not hardy here. Nurseries ship in plants of rooted cuttings, which are among our best annuals. They come in tall and short white and yellow daisies and are a great garden asset,

Alaska's "Evening Primrose", Lysimachia, makes a good substitute for forsythia, which is more difficult to grow here.

performing well also as container plants. They bend in the breeze, so they are good choices for windy locations. Pink marguerites are the unrelated *Chrysanthemum frutecens,* two-footers that look like pink daisies. Ken Ray of Northern Lights Nursery in Wasilla, grew a hedge of yellow, white, and pink marguerites in front of his nursery, a traffic stopper. "Blue marguerites" are cultivars of *Felicia, i*mported as rooted cuttings by nurseries.

MARIGOLDS are the most obliging of annuals that thrive in Alaska. They come in all sizes from minute edgings to regally tall kinds that need caging. There is a Marigold Society of America, P.O. Box 112, New Britain, PA 18901, for those who want to get deep into marigolds. Dues are $12 a year and there is a seed exchange.

MEADOW RUE, *Thalictrum,* is a native Alaskan, but the cultivars are more interesting. *T.*

Malva mochata rosea *is a nice pink mallow that germinates easily and blooms for a long time.*

Lythrum is a rangy perennial, blooming from midsummer on.

aquilegifolium has foliage like a columbine and foamy lavender flowers. almost three feet tall. The seeds need a 90-day incarceration in a refrigerated jar of moist seeding mix before they will germinate at room temperature. As with all perennials that require stratification, you can sow the seeds in the fall and leave them out under the snow all winter. Protect them from birch tree seeds, which will net you a birch forest. Bring them indoors in the spring and they should produce the goods.

MONARDA, wild Bergamot, is an escapee widely believed to be a native wildflower. It is of invincible hardiness. Be prepared to cage this flopper.

MONKEY FLOWER, *Mimulus,* is usually bought in cell-packs, but gardeners in remote locations can grow it from seed. 'Calypso' is the favored commercial variety, but there are other kinds offered in the catalogs. The seeds are like dust, and should not be covered. Keep the seeding medium moist, dampened from the bottom. The plants accept shade and may grow exuberantly in a south-facing situation.

ORCHIDS. Alaska has several native orchid species distributed throughout the state. The *Cypripediums* are the most sought by gardeners. Collecting these plants is ill-advised; they rarely survive the move because of their dependence on a mycorrhizal association with certain fungi. Native Plant Societies advise members, and often the general public, when areas to be bulldozed contain these plants, and a rescue mission is in order, although survival rate is poor. Buyers should make certain that plants they purchase have been nursery-grown, rather than collected, and they should be cautious about importing any from foreign countries. (Read IMPORTING OF PLANT MATERIALS before you have to report for fingerprinting.)

Monarda is contained here with an arch of farm fencing to support its stems.

Marigolds are a mainstay in Anchorage municipal plantings, filling greenhouse bays to put the city in bloom on June first.

The Large Yellow Lady's Slipper, Cypripedium calceolus, *is found across the northern portion of the U.S. It is hardy in this protected spot in Zone 4.*

PANSY, *Viola tricolor hortensis,* is an annual in the big part of Alaska, although occasionally plants re-up against the side of building or in the garden after a mild winter. They do best in good soil with abundant organic matter and in full sun, but they will tolerate cool locations and some shade. They need to be pinched early on so they won't grow lanky, and you must keep at it as well as conscientiously deadheading spent blooms to keep them blooming. They germinate best in the dark at room temperature in two to three weeks.

If you like yours without "faces" the Crystal Bowl series is the choice of University of Alaska Anchorage grounds supervisor Pat Leary. The Universal Hybrids are also high performers, some with faces, some without. 'Beaconsfield' is a durable, reliable and prolific pansy for window boxes, containers, and locations where compact growth and exuberant flowering are desired. Anchorage Municipal Beautification Horticulturist Susan Miller gives high marks to 'White Crown' and 'Golden Crown,' and to the orange 'Paparadia,' and her staff evaluations' top choice went to 'Majestic Giant Purple,' a truly great pansy in a series for showcase use.

If you're growing your own pansies from seed, they may benefit from a two-week chill in the refrigerator, then sown with a light covering of your seeding medium. They are said to germinate best in the dark, but ours pop up intermittently in 14 to 21 days. They're slow to get to the pricking out stage, so we plant them in early March and they're trying to bloom at planting time.

Viola tricolor (See Johnny-Jump-Up).

PASQUEFLOWER, *Pulsatilla patens,* is one of Alaska's loveliest wild flowers. The Siberians call it "Dream Flower" for its nodding flower head. It self-seeds freely in the garden, but may decline to germinate in the greenhouse. When it has finished blooming, its silvery seed plumes are grace notes in the garden and, when fully ripe, can be distributed where you'd like it to multiply.

The seeds have fairly brief viability. If you want to store it for spring sowing, try snipping the "tails" off, covering the seeds with a light sprinkle of the seeding medium, and holding the flat in a refrigerator for two or three weeks, then exposing it to 60 to 70 degree temperatures.

PEONIES are tough, but regal, demanding almost full sun and withholding their majestic blooms if

Cypripedium guttatum, *Spotted Lady's Slipper, has multiplied from six plants in as many years. Fencing wire deters moose.*

moved peonies will make a comeback in two or three years.

Peonies are expensive because next year's plants are produced by dividing this year's mature plants. Cost-cutters should choose older varieties, which are truly impressive to all save the botanically jaded. Some golden oldies have floppy stems, so ask around.

Peony's gorgeous blooms are heavy-headed. Caging is the best way to stake them unless you have the special peony stakes of commercial manufacture—wire circles mounted on legs that you push into the ground, outside the plant crown. An established clump in an open garden may need a four-foot cage so that rain-drenched full blooms won't bend down to the ground. When installed early in the spring, and held in place with a wooden tent stake on two sides, the cage is virtually invisible.

they don't get it. They can also be petulant if their crowns are set more than an inch or two below the surface of the ground. They detest being moved, or divided, and should be left in their permanent locations, dividing only about every ten years. If you have to move the driveway or put a foundation under the house, they may never forgive you. Sweet talk helps: most divided or

Pasqueflower's silken, silvery seed pods are as interesting as its blossoms. They self-seed freely in a wild garden, attain magnificence in good soil and a favored location. One of the world's best wildlings.

Peonies sold in containers can be planted at any time the ground can be worked, but we lean toward spring planting so their roots can get well established before winter.

Manures should not be used on peonies and they should be fertilized with a low nitrogen fertilizer. After they have bloomed they deserve a light side-dressing of 10-20-10 or 8-32-16 fertilizer and a light application of compost or potting soil. A sprinkle of ground limestone or sifted wood ashes in the spring will keep the soil pH in the 6.5 to 7.0 range.

Since peonies' bloom coincides with the coming of late July rains, fungus diseases are a problem, and fungicides like Zineb or Maneb may be needed, but for the most part these majestic perennials are trouble free.

PETUNIA. The modern hybrid petunias are among the most gorgeous flowers in the garden. They are sun-worshippers and do not thrive in cool, damp, or shady locations. They are outstanding container plants, upright, compact forms in tubs and trailing kinds for window boxes and hanging baskets.

Types of petunias are confusing because seed companies tend to have their own names for the same variety. In general, there are large flowered **grandiflora hybrids** and smaller flowered, but more prolific and weather tolerant, **multiflora hybrids.** The grandifloras may be single or double, ruffled, or picoteed, which means edged in a contrasting color. The multifloras are copy cats with many of the same luscious colors, veined and bi-colored as the grandifloras are.

The multifloras' 'Madness' series is outstanding, but so are the—'Celebrities,' the 'Carpets' and the 'Pearls.' Garden centers offer dozens of the best kinds and you will probably opt for buying them in cell-packs because their fine seed is slow to germinate, three weeks for large and ruffled kinds.

If you are distant from a source, here's how to grow your own plants from seed. Grandifloras will need a January or February start. Multifloras can be sown three or four weeks later. Fill a sterilized flat with a sterile potting mix, level it, and add a quarter-inch of finely sifted peatmoss or horticultural grade vermiculite.

The seeds will be very fine, and there will not be many of them in a packet of the newer kinds. Place them in a moist paper towel inside a plastic bag for 48 hours, then sow the seeds, covering them, if at all, very lightly. Maintain a minimum soil temperature of 75 degrees for best results. Grower Susan Miller of the Anchorage Municipal Greenhouse, transfers the tiny seeds on the moistened tip of a pencil from a towel to her planting medium for even spacing. She does

Horticulturist Susan Miller grows thousands of multiflora petunias for instant bloom in Anchorage parks and streetside display gardens.

not cover her seeds, which are simply pressed into the mix to make good contact with the medium.

Cover the flat with a sheet of plastic wrap and place it where you can maintain a temperature between 70 and 80 degrees. The seeds germinate better in light than in darkness. If you need to moisten them, set the flat in 70-degree water until the surface is moist, then drain. When they have a set or two of true leaves the seedlings can be pricked out into individual pots or cell-packs.

Keep potting them up to larger pots as the roots fill their containers, a fair amount of trouble which is why town gardeners buy theirs from nurseries. If you grow yours on a sunny windowsill, give the pots a quarter turn each day.

POPPIES are trouble-free annuals, and choice perennials. The "lettuce" poppies are *P. somnifera,* the opium poppy, which is one of the most beautiful of the annual poppies, with single and double blooms in red, pink, lavender and other variations. The gray-green leaves are host to the usual mildews that afflict their perennial kin, but they are impressive plants. Don't plan on collecting enough of the milky juice from their seed pods to brew up a batch of opium. That requires acreage —and the risk of doing extended slammer time.

Among the hardy poppies, *Papaver nudicaule,* the Iceland poppy, is the most familiar. Easy to grow from seed, and sold in nurseries, it self-seeds and hybridizes freely with other species, unwelcome if you want to keep a wild strain true to type.

Oriental poppies are great, flamboyant flowers. The common orange one is easy to grow and will stay with you forever despite your best efforts to give it away. The improved hybrids of magnificent pinks, reds, and whites may not be with you forever, but they are worth replanting.

PULMONARIA, a genus that doesn't deserve to be called Lungwort now that there are more efficacious remedies for lung diseases, is a sturdy Zone 4 plant with beautiful blue- or sometimes pink-splotched leaves. It may bloom for you in a favored location, but it is worth having for its foliage alone. Mine is on the north side of an island

bed as an edging plant, where we are happy with each other. Best bets for Zone 4 gardens are *P. mollis, P. officinalis,* and *P. saccharata.* Others are for warmer climes.

PUSSY TOES, *Antennaria,* are hardy perennials that grow wild in Alaska. Some are possibilities for the rock garden and a few are promising as ground cover, notably pink pussy toes, *A. dioica rosea.* The small gray leaves hug the ground, but the blooms are on six-inch stems. When ripe, the seeds disperse and you may want to mow the flowers before you have pink pussy toes all over the place. They dry well and you can save them for use in winter wreaths or arrangements. If you're starting from seed, count on a month or two for germination at 55 to 60 degrees. If this seems like a long time, reflect on how long it will take to eradicate pink pussy toes when they overwhelm you.

PRIMROSES, *Primula ssp.,* The cultivars need a favored location to succeed, the wildlings somewhat less so, and very desirable perennials they are. The **Cortusa** primroses, *P. cortusoides,* are delightful in unpredictable shades of pink, blooming with the forget-me-nots. The **Drumstick,** *P. denticulata,* and the **Sikkimese** primrose, notable for its intense fragrance and unusual yellow or orange flowers, are lovely—but we haven't met a Primrose that isn't.

The *Auriculas* are perhaps the easiest to grow and their many color combinations and spreading habit endear them to Alaska gardeners. Some have "farina," a mealy substance on their leaves, prized by knowledgeable collectors, but novice primula growers have been known to mistake it for a plant disease and throw the plants out.

The English cowslip, *P. veris,* is at home here, as is the oxlip, *P. vulgaris.* Native to the Rocky Mountains, *P. parryi,* does well in Zone 3 and so does one from New Mexico, *P. ellisae.*

There are probably 500 members of the genus, and there are many more than listed that would be hardy somewhere in Alaska. The ones named have been hardy for me and every year I try new ones.

The primroses germinate somewhat irregularly in three to four weeks at 55° to 60° in one of the peaty seed-sowing mixes.

There is a thriving Primrose Society that has a large seed exchange and an informative bulletin. Send $20 for dues to Jay Lunn, Treasurer, 6620 NW 271st Avenue, Hillsboro, OR 97124.

RHODOCHITON, Purple Bells, is an annual vine suitable for sunny locations with something to crawl on. New on the local market, it received favorable comments at the Matanuska Valley Fair. It takes about three months from seed to planting-out time. Parks Seed and Thompson & Morgan list it and some nurseries offer it.

SHRUB ROSES have been loved by Alaskans since the early 1900's when the USDA experiment station at Sitka distributed specimens of *Rosa rugosa* to homesteaders, fishermen, miners—anybody who would plant and evaluate them. The recipients called them the Sitka roses and the name has stuck. The *Rugosas* are very ancient wild roses from Japan and Korea, so they have hybridized among themselves and produced doubles and singles of colors ranging from dark reds to pinks, whites , and, rarely , yellows. (See SHRUBS in Chapter 5).

The **tender hybrid roses** that are the crown jewels of gardens in milder climates are easy enough to grow in Alaska, but keeping them over takes either considerable savvy, or money .

Storage temperatures need to hover between 29 and 32 degrees, so wine cellars and crawl spaces are too warm, unheated garages and storage sheds too cold. Some enthusiasts bury their roses in trenches next to basement walls, digging them up in May to re-plant, reporting good survival but entailing considerable effort.

In cities, nurseries offer storage space and care, returning the rehabilitated plants to their owners in prime condition at modest cost if you have in mind a pair of matched pots, but daunting if you are thinking in terms of Jacqueline Kennedy's rose garden at the White House.

Alaska nurseries sell the best and newest roses, potted up and blooming by Mothers' Day. Grown in containers, they can be shifted to flank the north-facing front door when company comes, and retired to a sunny spot on the deck or patio for your everyday enjoyment and their therapy.

Hybrid roses are subject to assault by insects and fungi and, infrequently, by disease. Serious rosarians must compromise with their repugnance of broad sprectrum sprays to keep these enemies at bay.

Now there is a new race of roses that shows promise for the north. **English Roses,** are now listed in catalogs and attracting excited comment in the horticultural press. We should watch for them in Alaska nurseries,. They are the achievement of English hybridizer David Austin who has developed a strain unlike any other in commerce.

They are so new that we can't give a firm hardiness rating, but their hybridizer rates them for Zone 4, which means a protected spot next to the house in Southcentral and a good possibility for our southern coastal gardens. One rose grower has successfully over-wintered the variety 'Cressida' in her Zone 3 garden. I have bet the farm on 'Heritage' which Austin himself calls "the most beautiful English rose." Stay tuned.

If the English Roses prove to be reasonably durable in Zone 3, David Austin is indeed onto something big. His roses are huge, many-petaled, and very, very fragrant; the colors are of melting beauty.

RUDBECKIA. The rudbeckias are annuals that may be too late for some gardens; for others they are welcome as a plant that comes on as the others play out. We like the species rudbeckia, listed by Thompson & Morgan as 'Dwarf Rustic Mix,' which produces orange, mahogany and ruddy red daisies in early September when the mood for fall colors comes on strong. The AAS winner 'Goldilocks' is a winner with us and so is 'Nutmeg,' a tawny brown.

SAXIFRAGE is a big genus of plants, most of them prized for rock gardens. Alaska's native *S. caespitosa,* tufted saxifrage, is a generous self-

The late Christine Heller, pioneer Alaska botanist, photographed Purple Mountain Saxifrage, S. oppositifolia, on Nome's Anvil Mountain.

seeder, settling into wood cracks and pavement flaws wherever it can find a few grains of soil. Nurseries sell improved cultivars.

They are a bit tricky to germinate, requiring a cooling-off period of two to three weeks in the refrigerator before sowing, barely covered, at room temperature.

SHASTA DAISIES, hybrid beauties that come in large singles, fluffy doubles and quilled types are not always hardy in Zone 3, unlike our native daisies that are toughies almost everywhere. The cultivars are propagated vegetatively from cuttings; you have to buy plants because seeds don't "come true."

Orange 'Sunblaze rose and the Chinese forget-me-not make a nice pair. Two out of three 'Sunblaze' survived their first winter in my Zone 3 garden.

SILENE, Moss Campion, *S. acaulis,* is a mat-forming perennial with pink flowers, best in the rock garden or rockery.

'Peach Blossom' is a hardy annual re-introduced after being lost to cultivation. It forms 12 to 15 -inch plants that could be used as an annual ground cover. Double pink blooms cover the plant.

With some 200 species in the genus, it is inevitable that some make pests of themselves. *S. vulgaris* is a pretty pest with good foliage and you may be tempted to let it go to seed. You'll be sorry, unless it's in a meadow mix.

The annual Silenes germinate readily at room temperature in two to three weeks; the perennials take longer and like cooler temperatures.

SNAPDRAGONS, *Antirrhinums,* may be six-inchers that bloom early in hanging containers or the 'Rockets,' which are six-footers that bloom late and survive frost. There are mid-talls, doubles and ruffled kinds that are favorites for bedding. Garden centers sell thousands of them in cell-packs.

SNOW-IN-SUMMER, *Cerastium tomentosum,* a gray-leafed perennial ground-hugger with starry white flowers, looks ratty in the spring, but cut back to new growth soon recovers its good looks. Seeds germinate in a week and will grow anywhere that a weed will.

SUNFLOWERS, *Helianthus annuus,* are fun to grow, especially the Russian Giants which grow to great heights and attract chickadees who enjoy harvesting the seeds. The hulls are somewhat toxic and there have been complaints that other plants do not thrive under bird feeders stocked with sunflower seed.

TROLLIUS, globe flower. The bright golden haze in midsummer gardens is an Asiatic trollius. *T. ledebourii,* whose foliage makes mounds of deeply cut dark green leaves with stems rising two and a half feet or so and rich orange globe-shaped blossoms that make fine cut flowers. They may get on your nerves near Maltese cross (in a proverbial "riot of color") or overpower pastel neighbors. They are joyful in the company of other sunny yellows and lovely with clear blues. A packet of seed labelled *T. sibiricus,* seemed to me to yield slightly larger flowers. The lemon yellow *T. europaeous,* European trollius, is the early spring-blooming one. If you grow it, you may want to choose tulips of a color other than yellow because they bloom at the same time and are dead-ringers at a distance. A ground-hugging dwarf is *T. pumilis,* which has leaves like parsley and miniature globe flowers, not quite aggressive enough to make a perennial edging, but nice in a rock garden or as a clump down in front in a border.

UMBRELLA PLANT, *Cyperus alternatifolius,* resembles a clump of palm trees about a foot tall. It is easy to grow from seed, makes a good foliage plant indoors but can go outdoors for the summer. It requires lots of moisture and would like nothing better than to have its feet in the mud beside some little pool or stream.

VERBENA. We have been less then thrilled with the annual verbenas in years past because of the tardiness of their bloom. Newer varieties have changed our minds. We are high on the

Rudbeckia 'Nutmeg,' a late bloomer, begs for a brown pottery container.

SEDUMS form large mats that let precious few weeds muscle into their territory. They are good subjects for rockeries and borders, this one in Sharon Davies' Anchorage garden.

spread of the ground hugging, red 'Showtime.' New pastel introductions are zingers, like the Fleuroselect Gold Medal winner, 'Peaches and Cream,' a new hanging basket subject (try three plants in a 10-inch container) and the pretty 'Amour Light Pink' which resembles pink forget-me-nots without their self-seeding propensity. The verbenas germinate best, if somewhat irregularly, in the dark.

'Miss Muffet' got rave notices in Wendy Anderson's Palmer Visitors' Center garden.

The perennial verbenas that are hardy to Zone 3 are not as good as the annuals and the more attractive kinds require warmer climates.

VERONICA, Speedwell, includes species that range from ground covers to two foot-tall clumps of spires that are usually purple but may be pink or white. They are vigorous perennials in Alaska gardens, with big clumps that need dividing occasionally, or you may find them so rampant that you kick them out. The foliage is attractive. *V. grandiflora* is a delightful Aleutian native that makes a pretty ground cover. It is a choice plant for the rock garden. I use it under rugosa roses.

VIOLAS include pansies, violas, and violets, which flourish in Alaska. The dividing line between pansies and violas is not very clear, but *V. cornuta* is the viola that usually, but not always, is without blotches and has a good range of pastel tints.

WINTERGREEN, *Pyrola spp.,* widely distributed throughout Alaska, is of interest to woodland gardeners who have shade and leaf mold cover to offer.

XERANTHEMUM, Immortelle, is an annual everlasting flower whose daisy shapes come in rose, pink, lavender and white. Thompson & Morgan lists separate colors.

ZIGADENUS, Death-camas, is represented in Alaska by *Z. elegans,* a member of the lily family that grows wild all over Alaska and makes a significant plant for the wildflower or rock garden. It is poisonous enough to bring on a number of unpleasant consequences, including coma.

ZINNIAS, greatly to our sorrow, do well only in the Interior and in very favored Southcentral locations. They need a six- to eight-week head start indoors, where aphids lie in wait.

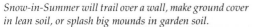

Snow-in-Summer will trail over a wall, make ground cover in lean soil, or splash big mounds in garden soil.

CHAPTER 2

FOOD CROPS FOR ALASKA

To grow food crops successfully in Alaska do these good things:
(1) Grow varieties adapted to Alaska.
(2) Get off to a fast start.
(3) Warm things up.
(4) Clean up your act.

What's in a name? Not much. Some plant varieties are named 'Alaska' because they were introduced the year we became a State (these usually have a sibling named 'Hawaii'), but not because they are especially adapted to cool climates or short growing seasons.

Quite another matter are the vegetables and fruits developed at the Alaska Experiment Stations, like 'Alaska 6467' cabbage, and the potato and strawberry varieties that were bred to order for us.

(1) Alaska-adapted vegetables and other food crops are listed in the free publication of the Cooperative Extension Service, *Vegetables and Fruits for Alaska, Recommended Variety List* (for Southcentral, Southeastern, or Interior Alaska). These are the winners in trials conducted by the State's Plant Materials Center and the University of Alaska Agricultural Experiment Stations, comparing new varieties with the best existing kinds. The list has great merit. Cheechako gardeners should visit any Cooperative Extension Service office to obtain a copy, for a modest fee, of *Sixteen Easy Steps to Gardening in Alaska*, the best vegetable planting guide around. If you're a rookie gardener, tape the back cover to your garden fence to figure out how deep and how far apart to plant.

Assuming that you had your soil tested last fall and applied the prescribed amount of lime, spring is the time to apply fertilizer as specified in the test. If you did not take this prudent step,

Snow melted first on raised beds, warmed up sooner for planting than bare ground on left.

Raised beds are warmer but do not dry out as fast as mounded rows.

spread three pints of 8-32-16 per l00 Square feet and rake it into the top two inches of soil, and hope for the best. But have it tested this fall.

(2). Getting off to a fast start. Most vegetables require a six- to eight-week headstart indoors and a few need more. If you have a greenhouse, or a sunny window sill in a cool room, or a fluorescent light setup in the basement or garage, you're in good shape. If not, you will need to check out the garden centers near you for plants that got their head start there.

You can plant seeds directly in the garden when a fistful of soil crumbles in your hand, which is about May 10th in Anchorage gardens, but it may be earlier or later where you live. You can speed things up by having raised beds or mounded rows, and by pre-warming the soil with a tarp of clear polyethylene plastic.

(3) Warming things up. While the plants are hardening off is a good time to prepare the garden to receive them. Choose a spot in full sun. Run the rows north and south, if you can, so they get morning sun on one side, afternoon sun on the other.

Ideas about spring cultivation have undergone a 180-degree turn since granddad did it. **If you're looking at new ground that has never known a man's plow** and may be rife with alder roots, dead branches, rocks and maybe a Prince Albert can or two, you will probably have to take a heavy duty rotary tiller to it and till in all the organic matter that you can lay a hand on—manure, sod, compost, dead leaves—and spread lime and 8-32-16 granular fertilizer, raking it all smooth.

If a garden has been grown there in past years, the less the ground is disturbed the better, because deep digging turns up dormant weed seeds to plague you and can damage the soil structure. The newer light weight 20-pound tillers are less damaging and easier to operate, but a trowel or a spade may serve you as well if the garden soil is porous and rich in organic matter, and your muscles are up to it.

Mounded rows and raised beds are warmer than level ground. In Southcentral, they are warmer, but they dry out faster during the normally dry early summer, a plus in Southeastern where soggy soil is slow to dry out after a long rainy spell. Both systems prevent soil compaction, and compacted soil is cold and wet, discouraging root development.

Planting-out is hard on the thigh muscles but easy on the spirit. Knock the plants out of their pots or push them out of cell-packs; don't gouge them out. Set the root balls into pre-dug holes, pouring a half cup of starter solution in the hole and filling in with crumbled soil. You can make your own with half-strength soluble fertilizer, or soak a half cup of a granular fertilizer in a three gallon bucket overnight. Or, there are several commercial solutions you can buy.

WARM SEASON CROPS like beans, squash, pumpkins, sweet corn, peppers, and outdoor tomatoes do better when grown through a mulch of clear polyethylene plastic. Most other vegetables do too, but an accelerated harvest is not always desired for all crops. Who wants cabbage, which keeps well in the garden and stores well, when the broccoli is muttering about going to seed? All transplants and seedlings do better when started under **row covers** and they are essential for warm season crops.

Grow-bags have been popular in England, and are catching on in Alaska. Apartment and condominium gardeners can have a little salad garden, a tomato plant or two and an herb garden in plastic bags on a deck or balcony. Heavy plastic bags are filled with a soilless mix to which fertilizer is added. A panel is removed from the top and a stout plastic rope is cinched around the middle. Each end is big enough for a tomato plant. The bags hold heat and moisture well and are free of soil-borne diseases. Drainage holes should be made on the sides of the bags if they are placed on a solid surface.

Looking for Mister Goodspot preoccupies vegetable gardeners, who are also tree-huggers. They would rather throw in their trowel than cut a tree that puts their garden in its shade. Food crops do not do well in the shade. A gentle south slope that gets the all the sun there is, is a gardener's hog heaven. If it is also protected from the prevailing winds of spring and late summer, the times when the seasons' climate patterns change, he will think he has died and gone to heaven.

Alas, such locations do not often come with the lot you fell in love with for its trees and its view of mountains or seascape. The first thing you can do is to choose the sunniest spot you have, which may be the front lawn (see Chapter 3 for

Keith McCavit's mounded rows produced a good crop of leeks, a cool season, but a long season vegetable.

consolation). Next, you can incorporate as much organic material in your soil as you can come by, letting beneficial soil bacteria solve some of your problems.

You can construct **raised beds** and fill them with the best soil you can make—and which you won't be standing on to plant, weed, and harvest. Or you can get on the business end of a rake and push soil into **mounded rows** which are also warmer than level ground. Make them more than 12 inches high because they'll settle a bit, and level off the top of the ridge so that you can plant a single broccoli plants, or maybe a double row of skinny onions or carrots.

You might cover them with clear plastic in the early spring so the sun's warmth can drive the frost out, and perhaps help existing weeds to germinate so that you can eliminate them before you plant seeds or seedlings with which they would compete for moisture and warmth.

Couch potatoes should have gotten off their duffs by the 10th of May in most places and bought their certified potato seed and the seeds of root crops and other cool season vegies. They should hustle their bustles by Memorial Day and set out transplants in X-shaped slits in clear plastic, if they have had the foresight to lay in a supply of #10 galvanized wire or PVC pipe and a roll

of clear plastic to make row covers to protect the tender plants from the wind that ushers in our tardy summer. On sunny days you can roll the covers back to let the bees pollinate your crops.

For warm season crops you may want a WALL O' WATER,™ a commercial plant protector, or a double row cover with a dead air space between layers of plastic stretched over PVC pipe or heavy galvanized wire hoops, or a floating row cover of spun-bonded poly weighted down with rocks or planks. Tuck them in before you say night-night.

There are several "floating" row cover materials on the market. Reemay™ is a spun-bonded fabric resembling the interfacing material long known to seamstresses; Fast Start™ has tiny perforations; both admit sunlight and rainfall or irrigation and keep out the flies and moths that lay insect eggs. Both are useful for hardening off transplants, for speeding early growth, and for holding moisture in and protecting from wind or light frost if you must be away after planting seeds or starter plants.

Why *clear* plastic mulch, gardeners ask testily, under which the weeds, like the transplants, will grow like mad? True. But the weeds push the clear plastic up, creating warm, moist air spaces. And bugs and bees can't get at them to pollinate

Soil was ready to plant earlier when pre-warmed by polyethylene mulch. A "WALL O' WATER" protected an early squash plant.

and make more viable weed seeds.

But gardeners fret about weeds. Black plastic controls weeds admirably, but it does nothing to warm the soil. A more recent development looks better than either. It is 'wavelength selective' plastic that admits infrared rays that warm the soil and blocks the UV rays that encourage weed growth. We tested Gardener's Supply's IRT Mulch™ and found that it did indeed perform as promised. Consult the Addenda for garden supply catalogs.

The CES publication *Plastic Mulch & Row Covers for Vegetable Production in Alaska* is worth the dollar it costs and is a must-have for rookie gardeners.

You can hold the warmth into the chill evening hours by tucking in bottles of water that have been collecting solar heat all day. Liter-size brown beer bottles and 3-liter green wine jugs work best, but both leave a lingering suspicion in neighbors' minds.

Weed 'em and Reap. The worst pests in Alaska food gardens are not insects, but weeds (the Weeder's Digest is in Chapter 7). Weeds rob plants of water and nutrients but, worse, they are hosts to damaging insects.

Harvesting vegetables is the most fun part of gardening. Harvest each in its prime, freezing as you go along, a couple of servings at a time. Some can be left for summer's end: the tender ones that are injured by the first kiss of frost are basil, beans, corn, marjoram, potatoes, summer squash, and tomatoes. Peppers under plastic survive light frosts.

The semi-hardy are good to about 26 degrees. They are beets, carrots, cauliflower, celery, chard, dill, endive, Jerusalem artichokes, lettuce, mustard, parsnips, radishes, and rosemary. Hardy to 20 degrees are broccoli, Brussels sprouts, cabbage, chives, collards, kale, garlic, horseradish, kohlrabi, leeks, onions, peas, rhubarb, rutabagas, sage, scallions, spinach, and turnips.

Whether a vegetable garden pays off in hard cash depends on which year you read the figures.

This asparagus bed backs up to a heated garage and a seasonal greenhouse, producing asparagus from May through June.

The USDA now stands by its estimate that of the $332 billion for 300 million tons of food purchased, more than 70% went for transportation cost, processing and marketing. Almost every state is researching and encouraging local growing of adapted crops, including gourmet, miniature, and ethnic vegetables, for which demand is increasing as people become aware of the nutritional benefits of vegetables which are high in nutrients and fiber and low in calories, sodium, saturated fats and cholesterol.

ARUGULA, Rocket, has been around forever but has only recently been rediscovered by a new generation of gardeners. It is a zesty addition to a bland green salad, slightly hot with a hint of bean or nut flavor. Grow it as you would leaf lettuce, cutting individual leaves as needed.

ASPARAGUS is a perennial vegetable. Once established, it comes up in May when there's not much else to harvest. It has a long list of virtues: almost everybody likes it and it is expensive in the market place. It is relatively free of disease and has few insect enemies. Its faults are few: it takes several years to get settled in and productive, and it demands your most favored microclimate. Winter losses can be heavy.

Give the soil under your asparagus the best humus you have, and have the soil tested so that you can bring the pH up to 6.5 or 7.0. Dig a trench 12 to 18 inches deep, and apply a pound of 8-32-16 per 30 feet of row. Leave three feet between the trenches. Return enough of the topsoil so the trench is six inches deep, and mix the whole works together.

Asparagus can be grown from seeds, transplants, or crowns, but purchased crowns must have been kept moist from harvest to planting time, which is not always easy to pull off so far from their point of origin.

If you're starting from seed, 'Mary Washington' is still listed in seed catalogs and found on seed racks, but asparagas varieties with all-male plants are newer and better because they don't squander their energy producing seeds. Stokes 'Viking' looks good for us, as does Shepherds' 'SYN 4-56,' formerly called 'Jersey Giant,' which produces 60 to 80% male plants and is a promising cold-tolerant hybrid.

Sow the seeds indoors in mid-March, and plant the whole packet; the survivors will be the hardiest.

Set them out 18 inches apart. Do not harvest any stalks during the first three years. In early spring, broadcast one pound of 8-32-16 per 30 feet of row, working it into the top few inches. Six weeks later, give it another quarter pound of high nitrogen fertilizer and keep the bed well watered.

In the fall, mulch the bed with dry leaves and/or pea vines, and don't cut the plants back until the following spring. The prudent will start a few plants each spring to replace the ones that don't re-up.

Harvest eight-inch stalks before they feather out. Harvest begins in mid-May and lasts into June, when you should let the stalks feather out to store food for the next year. With good care an asparagus bed will be with you for several years, but not forever.

BEANS. Bush beans are a marginal crop in Southcentral, and often a lost cause on the Kenai Peninsula. Sourdough gardeners say, "There are bean years and there are lean years." (Gardeners north of the Alaska Range can disregard such talk

Barry Johnson's scarlet runner beans produced an ornamental crop of foot-long beans on the south wall of his garage.

because of long days of high sun and higher temperatures.) Southeasterners, who rarely have enough degree days to make a bean year, may elect to turn the page. About two out of five years turn out to be bean years in Southcentral, but you can make a bean year out of most years if you take these steps:

(1) Pre-warm your raised bed or mounded bean row under a sheet of clear polyethylene plastic for a few days before you plant.

(2) Pre-sprout your beans by soaking them overnight, or wrapping them in a moist towel, or by placing them between moistened paper towels until they sprout in a warm place.

(3) Grow them through a mulch of clear polyethylene plastic, planting when the nights have warmed up.

(4) Place a plastic row cover over the bean row or bed, removing it on sunny days and replacing it at night until the plants get too big.

(5) Avoid handling damp plants.

(6) Stick to the Recommended Variety list unless you have a commodious greenhouse where you can indulge a passion for French horticultural beans or a row of pole beans, which haven't a prayer outdoors.

Runner Beans, and **Fava beans**, are distant relatives, but by no means kissing kin, of other beans. They are of special interest to Alaska gardeners because they are cool season vegetables.

Fava, or broad beans pack an extraordinary payload of protein, and they are rarely seen in stores. They are a popular winter vegetable in Europe and South America and equally at home in Alaska.

The pods are a half-inch wide and six to ten inches long, with big seeds which are the edible part of the bean. Cook them like green limas. Broad beans will germinate at 45 to 50 degrees and their three- to four-foot tall plants will require staking. When the lower trusses of flowers have faded and set pods, pinch out the growing tip of each plant to encourage development of more pods.

Stokes and Thompson & Morgan catalogs list the seeds. Bear in mind that broad beans are an acquired taste. Awfully good for you though.

Their flavor is said to be improved by removing the skins after cooking. Ever tried to skin a bean?

Pole beans. See GREENHOUSE CROPS.

BEET seed is a cluster of seeds and the crop must be thinned as soon as true leaves appear. They do best in soil that is not too acid, with a pH around 6.5, so you may want to save some wood ashes for the beet row. If you have many failures with beets, ask to have your soil tested for boron deficiency, which is easily corrected, but if you overdo it you can't just press the Delete key.

Leaving an inch between plants, you will harvest many pot greens before the main crop is ready for winter storage, so keep thinning young beets for pickling or serving fresh. Cold cooked beets, grated or slivered, are good additions to summer salad plates.

Beets are cool season vegetables that do well in Alaska's cool summer, but the long days tend to make them bolt, or go to seed. To get the kinds less prone to bolting, stick to the Recommended Variety list for your part of Alaska. Beets can be left in the ground until frost has taken the garden; in our climate they do not become woody. The cylindrical types ('Cylindra' and 'Formanova') slice more easily than the whopper round ones, do not sprawl all over the plate, and they taste and yield as well as the big round ones. There are golden and even white beets, of minor interest because a beet should be red as—well, a beet.

Cooked beets can be pureed with red cabbage, potatoes, onions and garlic for hearty Russian borscht, which is complemented by a dollop of sour cream, and Russian rye bread for winter lunches and *apré-ski* feeds. This ruby red puree can be served as is, or thinned to the proper consistency of borscht with beef broth.

BROCCOLI. The Italians introduced us to broccoli, for which we should say a fervent *grazie*, for it is one of Alaska's best-adapted and most nutritious vegetables. Versatile, modern cookbooks are full of new ways to use broccoli. It freezes successfully and microwaves to perfection.

Plants are widely available in garden centers,

but it is easy to grow from seed sown four to six weeks before planting out. Set plants two feet apart to get the most mileage. Broccoli has a tendency to bolt, so harvest the center head at the first sign of a yellow bud. 'Premium Crop' is an early variety that is not bolt-prone, and 'Dandy Early' from Jordan Seeds in Woodbury, MN 55125 was a heavy producer, reports the Alaska State Plant Materials Center. The side sprouts will keep coming if you keep harvesting them.

Such vigor requires ample water and food, so keep it coming until the late summer rains start. Side dress with a high nitrogen fertilizer in early July.

Broccoli and cauliflower are so closely related that broccoli is sometimes called sprouting broccoli to distinguish it from the heading types, of which 'Romanesco' and 'Floccoli' are examples, both yellowish sprouts crammed into a closely formed head. Purple cauliflower, a heading broccoli which turns green when cooked, is one of the most stunning plants in the food garden, and not out of place in the flower border.

BRUSSELS SPROUTS. The Belgians have been licking their chops over this cabbage family member for centuries, but many Americans have not made its acquaintance. Its flavor is robust and cabbagy and it takes about a hundred days to mature, but Brussels sprouts and their preference for a cool summer climate found each other in Alaska.

The plants are sold in cell-packs, but they are easy to grow from seed sown six weeks before planting time. The plants get big and need a good two feet of space. If your fertilizer is too high in nitrogen the sprouts get soft, so 8-32-16 is a better choice. Early in August pinch out the plants' growing tips to encourage development of the upper sprouts, which will be the size of small marbles. Don't start harvesting until after first frost, when the sprouts will be golf ball size.

Brussels sprouts are good served in all the ways you like cabbage, but don't overlook their merits as a chilled vegetable, marinated in a vinaigrette sauce.

CABBAGE presents an embarrassment of riches to Alaska gardeners. Ideally suited to long summer daylight and cool temperatures, these robust plants ask only an abundance of water and two side dressings of a fertilizer moderately high in nitrogen and moderately low in phosphate, like 16-16-16, to do their best, which is sometimes better than a gardener bargains for.

True, cabbage is one of the most nutritious vegetables, and one of the cook's most versatile. Also true, it may blow its cork in response to Alaska's long days, so stick to the Recommended Varieties list.

Cabbage is vulnerable to the root maggot and the cutworm, as it is every place else, but these pests can be controlled (see INSECTS in Chapter 7).

If your definition of Eternity is a cabbage and two people, look for 'Minicole F1,' a wee one that takes up only 10 inches. Try growing open-pollinated varieties which do not mature uniformly, as the hybrids tend to, so you won't get the whole crop at one time. Most commercial varieties are hybrids, which mature uniformly for mechanical harvesting. 'Jersey Wakefield' and 'Golden Acre' are oldies, both open-pollinated, both good, maturing when they get around to it.

Stokes Seeds' 'Castello' and 'Emerald Acre' are listed as 68- and 61-day varieties and Parks' 62-day 'Darkri Hybrid' looked good at the Plant Materials Center trials. 'Bravo' was a great producer in the Interior, but you should plant close together to get heads of manageable kitchen size.

If you hope to make a killing at the State Fair, go for 'O-S Cross,' which attains awesome dimensions (the big money went to Wasilla's Gene Dinkel for a 98-pounder one year). The trick is to keep the monster growing without setback, which means a steady supply of water and nutrients.

Red cabbage is so ornamental in the garden that you may forego eating it at its prime. The Germans were onto something when they braised it with apples in red wine. 'Red Meteor' is the recommended variety. The Japanese named theirs 'Scarlet O'Hara.'

Savoy cabbage is another beautiful, crinkled

kind, maybe too pretty to harvest and spoil the garden's good looks. Most Savoys are late, but the French variety 'Des Vertus' is a 75-day, picture-pretty one. Shepherd's Garden Seeds has it.

Chinese cabbage is ready before you are ready for it, so harvest it early, along with the lettuce crop, seeding directly in the garden. Nichols Garden Nursery lists a tempting choice of oriental cabbages, so try a couple at a time for comparison.

CARROTS do so well in Alaska that it's a shame not to grow them, even though the supermarket product is excellent. Carrots are virtually free of insect or disease predators. In a raised bed or on a double-planted mounded row you can grow enough carrots to have young ones to eat by midsummer and lots to store for winter.

Carrots germinate slowly, like one to three weeks in 68-degree soil, during which you have to hover over them with a watering can and pick the weeds that germinate before the carrots do. The seeds are small and thinning is tedious, so you might buy seed tapes and skip the tedious part. Or, you can broadcast the seed in a raised bed, rake them under an eighth of an inch and tamp them lightly with the hoe, then water with a gentle sprinkler.

However, you can't often buy tapes of the uniformly cylindrical 'Suko,' listed in Thompson & Morgan catalog, or Parks' miniature 'Little Finger' or Burpee's 'Short 'n Sweet,' rarely seen in stores. 'Touchon Deluxe' from Stokes looks good for Alaskans.

Carrots need a deep, friable soil, easy to provide in a mounded row or raised bed. Try a fall planting some year by breaking up the crust of frosty soil and raking in broadcast seed. Cover it with clear polyethylene and a six-inch layer of leaves. Remove the mulch in the spring and, if all goes well, you may have a two- to three-week jump on the season. If it doesn't work, there's still time for a spring planting.

CAULIFLOWER is grown like cabbage, but it needs to be blanched as it heads up. An easy way to do it is to fasten the leaves around the head with a snap clothes-pin or a soft string. Like cabbage, it has a tendency to bolt, or go to curd, so check out the Recommended Variety list.

If such big heads as the excellent 'Snowmound' are too much of a good thing, try one of the mini-cauliflowers like Thompson & Morgan's 'Cargill' six inches àpart. The minis make attractive individual servings, doused with Alfredo sauce.

Keith McCavit's "corn house" once had a roof, which was removed as the corn grew tall.

CELERY thrives in Alaska, but you may decide to pass it up for the produce counter product. It takes 10 to 12 weeks head start, has a massive thirst, and is of considerable interest to maggots. It requires blanching to make it tender-crisp. Half gallon ice cream containers work, or you might make the acquaintance of a rug merchant who will give you a long cardboard tube that can be sawed in celery-lengths. Try 'Utah 52-70' seed or buy nursery-grown plants.

CORN, sweet corn, does better in the Interior than in coastal areas, but in a warm summer Southcentral gardeners get crops they can be proud of. Stick to the Recommended Variety lists ('Earliking,' 'Polar Vee,' 'Super Sweet,' and 'Sundance') and give plants a four-week headstart indoors. Outdoor soil profits by a warm blanket of clear plastic before the plants are set out through X-shaped slits. Cover them with a plastic tunnel. For good pollination, corn should be set out 12 to 14 inches apart in squares rather than in rows. Corn will need lots of water. If this seems like a lot of trouble, consider the rewards of going down in history as the fellow who gave the big corn feed for the guys at work.

CUCUMBERS are a greenhouse crop in Alaska, although some early pickling types can be grown through clear plastic mulch in the Interior and in favored locations elsewhere. See GREENHOUSE CROPS.

ENDIVE, escarole, is grown like lettuce and does well in cool summer climates. It is an Italian favorite, where it is a winter crop, as the variety names indicate: Traviata, Nina, Niuvol. Some upright varieties are naturally blanching, some curlier than others, some with red leaves. Don't write off endive if the only kind you've met was green and bitter.

Belgian endive, **Witloof chicory**, requires special forcing and blanching conditions which appeal to few gardeners. Better hit the produce counter for this one but if you have a bomb shelter or a root cellar dug into the side of a hill, go for it.

GREENS, or pot greens, rarely offered on restaurant menus, are among the most nutrient-packed foods that are grown anywhere. They are especially well-grown in Alaska's cool temperatures and long daylight, packing a heavy pay load of vitamins and minerals, and a new, zippy taste. Jazz them up with bacon bits and a shot of Tabasco.

Swiss Chard is a beautiful plant, especially rhubarb chard which has red stems. The chards are mild-flavored pot greens and mix well with the more pungent turnip greens or kale. They freeze well and are interchangeable with spinach in recipes. Harvest a few leaves at a time and don't bother with a second planting—a spring crop will hold you until frost.

Kale is a non-heading cabbage. All you get is green leaves, but they are attractive enough for flower arrangements. Kale's vitamins A and C are impressive and it packs a heavy pay load of iron. It has an authoritative flavor, reminiscent of the cabbage family, of which it is a member in good standing. Kale has long been known to the Siberians and the Scots, and northern peoples everywhere grow it to prolong their garden's supply of fresh vegetables. You can kick the snow off and harvest good kale well into the winter. It is not surprising that it thrives in Alaska, where it is not impressed by fall frosts, which improve its robust flavor.

'Green Curled Scotch' is a good kind, early and prolific. It can be grown from seed sown where it is to grow, or be given a three-week head start indoors if you crave it before the broccoli and peas come on.

By happy coincidence the first leaves are ready to cut at about the time the beets need thinning, the mild-flavored beet greens and the sharper kale making a good combination. By fall you will have discovered that ham slivers improve it and that it makes a great quiche. Real men eat kale quiche. It also makes the Portuguese *caldo verde*, a hearty green soup, a good choice for winter lunches.

Red Russian kale is ornamental enough for the flower border, its red foliage resembling large oak leaves. Nichols Garden Nursery has it.

Giant Red Mustard came into the country with the Asians who found homes among us, along with other provocative new greens that grow well in our gardens, adding drama to the garden and zip to salads and sandwiches. As the deep reddish-purple textured leaves grow, the flavor gets stouter. Steam or stir-fry it or mix with local greens for color and tang. **Mizuna** is a Japanese mustard that is ornamental in the garden, makes a good salad green, or you can cook the leaves. **Bok Choi** is not unknown to Alaska gardeners, but **Mei ging choi,** a small variety that is harvested when it is about six inches tall produces lime green stems that contrast with the dark green leaves; cooked, the plant has a sweet nutty flavor, not as sharp as other choys. Look for these in oriental grocery stores to check out the ones you like best.

Oriental greens' names may vary from one catalog to another. We found ours in Johnny's Selected Seeds. The Vermont Bean Seed Co., Garden Lane, Bomoseen, Vermont 05732, is a good source and offers a free guide to preparing and cooking oriental greens, but many catalogs now offer selected varieties.

KOHLRABI is a member of the cabbage-turnip clan. It is rarely seen on produce stands, because one bulb to a plant makes it unprofitable to grow commercially. The bulb, unlike that of the turnip, grows above ground, up where the root maggots can't get at it. It is mild tasting, unlike the radish, so that it will double as a water chestnut when cooked tender-crisp and chilled. It can be cooked like a turnip, or served raw, sliced, cubed or grated. It is a versatile vegetable that is a sleeper.

Sow it directly in the garden, or if you can't wait, give it a three-week head start in the greenhouse. 'Gigante' (pronounced hee-GON-tay) took a Grand Championship at an Oregon fair with a 26-pounder in 1992. We were skeptical about such a big kohlrabi lest it be woody and dry; not so. It was big, but it was also juicy and mild and showed no sign of woodiness. Nichols Garden Nursery lists it.

LEEK, *Allium ampeloprasum,* is a member of the onion family which should be more widely grown in Alaska because it supplies a versatile vegetable after the rest of the garden is gone. It stores well into the fall in plastic bags in the refrigerator, and freezes well. Leek is a cool season crop, but it is a long season one, so it needs an early start, 12 weeks before setting out. It germinates best at 70 degrees, and looks like a pathetic little blade of grass when it is ready to be potted up.

Prepare a six inch-deep trench with a couple of inches of manure or compost scratched into the bottom. Set the young plants six inches apart. Every two or three weeks pull a little soil into the trench, taking care to keep the soil line at or just below the point where the leaves begin to part. By fall you will be pulling soil up around the plants, your goal being to get as many inches of blanched white stalk as you can before harvesting, which can last well into the fall with mulch. A little fertilizer applied each time you pull in soil is a timely bribe.

Leeks are not touchy about chilly weather; you can continue to harvest them until snow covers them. Thinly sliced, leek rings make a better addition to a green salad than an onion, and cooked with new potatoes they are the fabled vichysoise soup, chilled with a sprig of dill or a curl of lemon zest for added class. Shepherds' 'Otina,' a French introduction, is a good one for northern gardens.

LETTUCE likes Alaska's cool soils, and long, cool summer days. Alaska gardeners do not exploit these assets enough. Europeans consider the tossed salad an art form and treat it with more respect and imagination. A European garden would have a variety of salad greens—wonderful butterheads, crispheads, cut-and-come-again lettuces and deer-tongues, almost extinct in American catalogs, besides romaine or Cos in a choice of colors and sizes, endives, frilly looseleafs from green-gold to red ones. There would be herbs for chopping fresh or making savory vinegars.

This is no trendy fad; by 800 B.C. the Babylonian kings were into green salads and by the fifth century the Chinese were. By the 17th century, Louis XIV was ordering his lettuce served up with tarragon, sweet basil and a sprinkling of violets. If you are into growing choice lettuces, you are in elite company.

Good catalogs to search for offbeat lettuces are Shepherd's, High Altitude Gardens, Thompson & Morgan, Territorial Seed Company, Cook's Garden, Nichols' Garden Nursery, Epicure Seeds, Le Marché Seeds International, and J.L. Hudson, Seedsman. (See CATALOGS.)

Most gardeners start their lettuce from seed sown directly in the ground in late May. Since it germinates best at 70 degrees, a useful trick is to sow it indoors in three-inch pots of vermiculite every three weeks or so until August, transplanting directly into the garden when the plants have two or three true leaves and are hardened off. You might start indoor seeding about May first for setting out in three weeks under a row cover. You can start earlier in a cold frame, and be serving garden salads by late May. (See FRAMES.)

There are four main types of lettuce, all of which do well in Alaska. They are: **Crisphead** (head lettuce or iceberg), which forms solid heads similar to those you buy at the produce counter, delightfully crisp and icy but a mite skimpy on nutrients and flavor. 'Montello,' introduced by the University of Wisconsin, matures earlier than most. 'Minetto' produces tiny heads suitable for individual servings.

Butterhead forms a soft head with a buttery yellow center, often listed as Boston, Bibb, or limestone lettuce. Superior in flavor and color to crisphead lettuce, it is the choice of chefs. It does not pack or ship as well as head lettuce; to have the best, you must grow your own. In the winter, the greenhouse-grown product is a pallid imitation of the real thing and is relatively expensive. (To do right by it, wash it tenderly, wrap the head in paper towels and store it in a plastic bag in the vegetable drawer. It will not turn brown and will be moist and crisp when you need it to be perfect.)

'Buttercrunch' is a dependable choice. 'Tom Thumb' is a miniature serving-size butterhead. 'Red Perella' is a small, red butterhead of Italian extraction. Burpee's 'Fordhook' is a winner with pulpy outer leaves, one of the best features of the butterheads. From France comes the 'Merveille des Quatre Saisons,' marketed in the U.S. as 'Four Seasons,' a choice red-edged lettuce.

Cos or **Romaine**, forms tall heads with long leaves much like those you see on the produce counter and is the most heat tolerant of the lot. If you make a lot of Caesar salads you'll want to grow it. Cos isn't as attractive when it is cut up as it looks in the garden, but the English 'Little Gem' has leaves small enough to serve whole.

Nichols Garden Nursery catalog lists a romaine with burgundy heads called 'Red Majestic' and Johnny's Selected Seeds has a French butterhead with green leaves and rosy tips named 'Sangria.' 'Rouge d'Hiver' (Winter Red) is a late maturing beauty.

Among the **leaf lettuces**, you may know the popular commercial varieties like 'Grand Rapids' and 'Salad Bowl,' both good, but home gardeners can afford to grow kinds that don't ship and warehouse well. Burpee's 'Green Ice,' 'Oak Leaf,' or 'Ruby,' a pink and red All-America winner, all add zest to the salad bowl. Nichols lists an improved 'Lollo Rossa' called 'Lovina,' a frilly red one. All of these are red or red-tinged, often deeply fringed.

Lettuce does best in a fairly neutral soil that has lots of organic matter. There isn't much you can do to louse up a lettuce crop, but being parsimonious with water will do it, producing stunted, sometimes bitter, leaves. The second route to ruin is over-crowding. If you're sowing the small seeds directly in the garden you are apt to get them so crowded that you must be vigilant about thinning, a character flaw frequently found in gardeners. Transplanting is less tedious than thinning. If you transplant from vermiculite, space the plants four inches apart, and harvest every other plant as needed.

Mesclun is a mixture of tender young salad greens, harvested as baby leaves and the mix sold in open markets in Europe, popular for instant salads. You can buy packets labeled 'Mesclun,' but you do better growing an assortment of lettuces and picking a leaf here and there.

From the sublime let us go to the **Radiccio**s,

red chicories, or endives, known to the Italians before Nero took his first fiddle lesson, but new to Americans, who regard it with the suspicion of a prudent man approaching a mine field. It is an acquired taste, granted, with a bit of a bite, a colorful but slightly sharp addition to a bland tossed salad. For more about radiccios, see—what else—RADICCIO.

ONIONS march to a different drummer in the North. They are a cool season crop, but they are a long season crop, and need frost protection to lengthen the season. "Bulbing" in onions is triggered by day length, and by temperature.

Short-day onions do not form bulbs until the days get short, making them good candidates for scallions, but frustrating if you have in mind enough big onions to dry for winter. Long-day onions will form bulbs when days are long, a bummer when you want arrow-straight scallions, but they are the best bets for storage. For green bunching onions, look for varieties like 'Winter White Bunching,' 'White Portugal,' or 'Evergreen Bunching,' giving the seeds a 10-week head start indoors.

Most gardeners opt for buying their storage onions, freeing up their ground for faster maturing crops. If you enjoy the challenge, or have your eye on a purple rosette for Best of Show at the Fair, you'll have to know your onions. Master Gardener Dick Green of Anchorage does. He took a Grand Championship with 'Kelsae Sweet Giant' which weighed in at 1.9 pounds at the Palmer fair. The balance of the crop stored well under only fair storage conditions. Stokes has it.

Long-day onions like 'Sweet Spanish,' 'Yellow Globe,' 'White Lisbon' or 'Ebenezer' will start bulbing early in the season when days are long. Stokes' Seed, Johnny's Selected Seeds, and Thompson & Morgan catalogs list varieties adapted to northern areas.

Alaskans have long cast covetous eyes on 'Vidalia,' 'Walla Walla Sweet' and 'Maui' onions, all wonderfully sweet for eating raw, but too short-day for us. They are often planted in the fall in their mild winter climates and produce large bulbs the following summer. They are rarely (you learn never to say never in garden writing) hardy in Alaska's colder winters. Texas shippers get them onto produce counters in April. The Vidalias come in mid-May, and the Walla Wallas in July. None will hold in storage more than six weeks. They command a premium price and are worth it if only for one onion sandwich on fresh-baked bread.

Plant breeders are working to produce sweeter onions for northern gardens, but don't hold your breath (no pun intended). Scientists are also working to sweeten the nectar in onion flowers to make them more attractive to honey bees, whose aversion to their odor reduces onion production. The flip side: insects are also turned off by their pungent smell, with the onion maggot one of the few that will pig-out on young onions. Mid-June is the peak egg laying season for maggot flies. (See INSECTS in Chapter Seven.)

Seed-grown onions need to be well established young plants by the time the long days trigger bulbing, so give them a 10-week head start indoors and get them into the ground as early as you can in May, under row covers.

To make the 10 weeks go quickly, reflect upon our Pilgrim Fathers who brought with them from England seeds for their gardens in the New World. The virgin soil produced bountiful crops—except for the onions, which were a dismal failure. They didn't "bulb up" in time to produce onions worth storing.

To make matters worse, the Puritans' Portuguese neighbors, who drank red wine and ate garlic, got fine onion crops from seed they had brought with them from Portugal. The key to the *Portuguesas'* success: Lisbon and Boston are on similar latitudes with similar day lengths; England is farther north, and has longer days.

Seed catalogs and seed packets indicate the bulbing tendencies of their onion varieties. Buying set onions is not as predictable. Suppliers offer garden centers a choice of white, yellow (the trade calls them brown), or red, but they do not specify day length.

Onion seeds germinate best at about 70 degrees. Plant onion sets for scallions two inches apart so they won't be checked when you pull

These garden peas climb netting strung on a slatted fence.

every other one. Plant seedlings out in mid-May and tuck them in under a row cover, which you should keep on until you harvest the onions, to prolong their growing time and protect them from onion maggots. Be mindful that onions require plenty of water to be mild and juicy.

If we don't print it, some seasoned gardener who knows his onions will ask, "What about multiplier onions? And where can I get a start of potato onions?" From Kalmia Farms, that's where. The catalog, available from P.O. Box 3881, Charlottsville, VA 22903, lists such time honored kinds as Egyptian top onions, several shallots almost lost to cultivation, three kinds of garlic plus multiplier and potato onions, all reasonably hardy in most of Alaska.

PARSNIPS. This root vegetable is sown directly in the garden as soon as the ground can be worked. It does best in a deep, well-tilled soil generously amended with organic matter.

It is not harvested until fall and is improved by a kiss from the first frost. 'Hollow Crown' is the standard kind and most years it attains majestic dimensions. Cut into sticks and sauté gently in butter with honey or currant jelly and lemon juice drizzled over it while it candies. This is a delectable vegetable served with ham or roast pork. Trust me.

PEAS thrive on cool summer weather and plenty

Lawrence Clark's ingenious pea fence recycles cot springs. Plastic on both sides increase warmth and moisture retention in normally cool, dry May.

of moisture and are one of Alaska's best-adapted vegetables. They enjoy most favored status as a freezer vegetable. There are three kinds, all dandies, to choose from:

Chinese, or **Snow peas,** edible-podded delicacies that must be harvested almost as soon as they form pods are required for oriental stir-fry dishes, good in chicken soups, and a prime favorite of kid-robbers.

Snap peas, a cross between edible-podded peas and garden peas, combine the best features of both. They can be cooked like snap beans or shelled like garden peas; they are good raw or cooked, although they are better when blanched briefly and chilled. The first 'Sugar Snap' grew too tall for Alaska's long summer daylight; subsequent introductions corrected this and 'Sugar Ann' is shorter, even better eating, and its unifor-

mity makes it a chef's choice.

Garden or **"English"** peas are the kind people think of as peas. The Recommended Variety list has the best kinds. 'Sparkle' is a commercial variety, tending to mature at the same time for mechanical harvesting, but a good choice for home freezing. 'Lincoln' and 'Green Arrow' can be added to the list of good producers of excellent quality. 'Novella,' sometimes sold as 'Bikini' (and, truth to tell, it is virtually leafless) is a good one.

Before planting, pea seeds may be dampened with water and dusted with a legume inoculant, a black powder sold in garden centers, which increases yields on ground where legumes have not been grown before.

The best advice on growing peas is in the Extension Service bulletin, "16 Easy Steps to Gardening in Alaska," which suggests digging a furrow two inches deep, sprinkling into it two pounds of fertilizer per 100 feet of row, partially covering it, and planting the peas an inch apart. When the vines are six inches high they will need another two pints of fertilizer down the side of the 100-foot row, and another in early August to keep the crop coming on until after frost. This works.

In locations where cutworms decimate seeds before they can emerge, you should pre-sprout the seeds. And knock on wood.

PEPPERS were once limited to greenhouse production in Alaska, where they were plagued by red spiders and aphids. The introduction of 'Ace Hybrid' was quickly followed by 'New Ace Hybrid,' which would ripen when grown outdoors where the bugs shunned them.

Grown through clear plastic mulch and under row covers they yielded the ripe, fire engine red peppers that brought premium prices at the market. True, letting peppers ripen cuts down the size of the crop, but that mattered little with ripe peppers several times the cost of the plentiful green peppers.

Now several sweet peppers that will ripen outdoors to red, yellow, or chocolate colors have been introduced.

Each year brings earlier, short season peppers into commerce. We liked Johnny's 62-day 'Gold Crest' and Park's 'Early Thickset'.

Our standards for recommendation are sweetness, earliness and meatiness. We harvested 30 fully ripe peppers from two plants each of 'Gold Crest,' 'Early Thickset,' and 'Italian Sweet,' in a disappointingly cool summer.

Peter Piper may well have picked his fabled peck of peppers for pickling, but he doesn't say if they were ripe and if he did it with eight plants at 60 degrees North Latitude. You should try any that claim to ripen in 60 days or less.

Peppers germinate at between 68 and 86 degrees and require a six to eight-week head start indoors before you can set them outdoors, depending on how warm you can keep your germinating medium and how sunny the spring is. If you introduce into your greenhouse purchased or swapped plants you run the risk of introducing insects. If you start your plants from seed and do not introduce some drooping house plant to the incumbents, you can usually be free of insects and most diseases.

Look for Mister Goodspot, a protected location outdoors that gets all the sun there is. Pave Alaska's cool spring soil with a clear plastic sheet and row covers before setting your plants out. Row covers can be lifted on warm days, lowered at night or kept down on cool or windy days.

Filling wine jugs and brown beer bottles with water and tucking them in around pepper plants helps maintain warm temperatures into the cool evening hours.

Hot peppers are a greenhouse crop, not so subject to aphids and red spiders, which view their fiery flavor with caution.

Freezing peppers is easy because they do not require blanching. A mix of colors, sliced or cut in pieces, is useful for salads and stir-fries, meat loaves and casseroles.

POTATOES. It is important to buy seed potatoes of the recommended varieties from a garden center. Grocery store potatoes are usually treated with chemicals to retard sprouting, and they may be varieties that will not mature in Alaska's short summer. Never plant a potato with a visible sign of disease, nor add potato peelings to the compost heap.

Plant small whole potatoes or large ones cut into pieces with two or more "eyes". Heal cut pieces by placing them in a paper bag at room temperature for several days, until sprouts appear. If the sprouts get broken, discard the potato.

Dig a furrow about eight inches deep and distribute about three pints of fertilizer per 100 feet of row in the bottom, raking back an inch of soil. Plant the potatoes a foot apart, covering with an inch of soil and compacting it.

As the plants grow, rake soil around them. When the plants are a foot high, "hill" them two or three inches higher than the rest of the garden. This is a good way to rid a portion of the garden of weeds.

Irrigated potatoes out-produce non-irrigated crops significantly. New potatoes can be harvested soon after the plants have bloomed. New potatoes may taste sweet to newcomers or people used to store-bought ones. Their natural sugar is converted to starch if they are stored in a warm, dark place, such as under the kitchen sink, for several days. Old Alaska hands don't think new potatoes taste sweet; they think they just taste like potatoes.

The main crop can be harvested when frost takes the vines. Hose the potatoes down or brush the soil from them and store them in a warm place for two weeks, then in a cool but not freezing, well-ventilated place. Handle them like eggs; they bruise easily. In good storage they can be expected to last through March. Store your spuds in the dark because light causes "greening", which impairs flavor.

Several potatoes have been bred for Alaska at the Alaska Experiment Stations. Each has a special characteristic, such as earliness, resistance to scab disease, high dry matter for baking quality, or the waxy quality desired in "plate" potatoes. Amateur potato growers should grow more than one kind for different uses.

Among the top ten producers tested at the Matanuska Experimental Farm were, in this order: Green Mountain, IditaRed, 6-78-139-80, Sable, Rosa, Kennebec, Lemhi Russet, Alaska 114, Superior, and Bake-king.

Harvest your main crop after frost has taken the vines and before the ground freezes. This allows the skins to mature, but you should still handle them like eggs to prevent bruising. "Robbing"—feeling around the roots for edible size new potatoes—is a practice honored out of time. Store your spuds in the dark.

Potato varieties vary in their susceptibility to scab disease, recognizable by corky patches on the skin. It affects appearance, but not quality. The fungus that causes it lives over in the soil, so crop rotation with clean seed is a good practice. Scab can be a problem in alkaline soils, so the addition of lime or wood ashes is not recommended for potato ground, and the use of fresh manure is a dubious practice.

Under test at the Alaska Plant Materials Center the most susceptible to scab were Bake-King, IditaRed, Russet Norkota, Yankee Supreme, and Yellow Finn. If your garden soil is known to be infected, you would be wise to try one of the varieties that is more resistant to the disease, like Avon, Cherokee, Krantz, NorKing, Reddale and Superior. The Cooperative Extension Service issues a bulletin *Potato Growing in Alaska*, that carries a modest price tag, $1.25 at this writing.

PUMPKINS require clear plastic mulch, transplanting indoor-grown plants with great care when they have only one or two true leaves, and protecting them with a row cover. A big cold frame is a good way to go. Don't be too proud to tuck in a few water-filled wine jugs or liter-size brown beer bottles among the vines.

Pumpkins require a growing season slightly longer and warmer than Southcentral can offer. If you have in mind the big money at the State Fair, best you should select a variety known for its tendency toward great girth.

'Cheyenne Bush' has been the recommended variety for years, but the newer 'Atlantic Giant' claims to be two weeks earlier, which may be all that stands between a punkin' eater and a blue ribbon pumpkin grower. Other prize winners are 'Big Moon,' 'Mammoth King,' and 'Prizewinner,' but by the time this book is out of print there will be bigger, earlier ones. Watch the catalogs for introductions that shave a few days off existing varieties, and watch the winners at the Fairs. Bear in mind that giant size is in the genes, not just in cultural methods.

Removing flowers is a good ploy if you're looking for a few good pumpkins instead of several small ones. Leaf pruning is not a good idea. Big pumpkins need the best growing conditions you can provide—full sun, at least eight square feet of good soil at planting time, a pH near neutral, an early start indoors, a clear plastic mulch, row covers at night. The works.

Give them a good soaking during dry spells and refrain from overhead watering, which invites disease. Side dress lightly but frequently, like every two weeks with 8-32-16, or weekly with a high-phosphorus soluble fertilizer. Harris seeds offers 'Munchkin,' a four inch wee one that looks good for a short season crop and a cutie for Halloween.

RADICCIO, a red-leafed chicory, is a northern Italian salad "green." For a heartier fall salad the Italians include slices of ripe olives, artichoke hearts, ripe sweet peppers and croutons fragrant with garlic and olive oil.

In Italy there are many Radiccio varieties on seed racks. There, it is sown in May, matures in fall and produces until a hard frost does it in. One winter we brought back eight kinds of seed and tried them in our Anchorage garden. Some headed up by fall and although the heads were small, their leaves tasted and looked like the real thing.

'Rosso di Verona' did best, perhaps because it is grown in the foothills of the Dolomite Mountains where fall is chilly. It is said to germinate in soils as cool as 40 degrees. Thin it to about 10 inches, or set transplants about 12 inches in the row.

Leaves gradually turn from a bronzy green to red as the weather cools. In the Verona region, it is often dug after the first frost and forced in a cool place, where it reddens.

RADISHES rank with marigolds for ease of culture but no seasoned gardener can forego their

Two good rhubarb plants will keep a family of four in finger-lickin' pleasure for a year.

RHUBARB is happy with cool summers, cold winters, at least a half day of full sun, and quite a chunk of ground.

We have bad-mouthed cow and horse manure, both loaded with pasture weed seeds and salt residues, and we stand by this dour judgment; however, if you have access to either, don't turn down a couple of shovelfuls. Put this good stuff under a rhubarb plant, making sure it is down so far that the weed seeds won't germinate and the salts will leach out far below the plant roots.

The time to look the gift horse in its genes is when you are offered a free rhubarb division ready for planting. If it is an obsolete green kind, back off. Eyeball a nursery's stock and buy a plant or two (no more unless you have a large family of big rhubarb-eaters or plan on going into the rhubarb wine business) of some good kind like 'Apple,' 'Honey Red,' 'Victoria,' or 'Sutton Seedless,' which got top marks from the State of Alaska's Plant Materials Center trials. Older varieties like 'Canada Red' and 'McDonald' are still choice.

Dig a hole two feet deep and a couple of feet wide for each plant and spade in your hoard of manure. If there is no source of animal manure, work in compost and a pint of a complete fertilizer under each plant Set the plant with its crown level with the ground and backfill with good garden soil, settling it with a slow-running hose, not your feet.

Fight off first-year harvesters, and pull only a few stalks the second year; by the third year you can just have at it. In subsequent years, give each plant a half cup of fertilizer in the spring and again in summer. When you start getting more but smaller stalks, it is time to divide the crown and share it with a new neighbor.

Tell him rhubarb isn't like it was in the Old Country. Tell him he can harvest inch-thick stalks

crisp, colorful snap. The seed germinates in about five days and can be harvested a month later. Long cool days and cool soil temperatures grow superior radishes that are not woody or pithy, even when very large. In an unusually warm summer, like the fabled "summer of '93" we had to eat these words—and the biggest, hottest, woodiest radishes anywhere around.

Almost any variety will thrive and seeds can be sown in rows or broadcast in a raised bed. Radish lovers will look far for a radish that will outdo 'Cherry Belle' or 'Cherry Bomb,' 'Burpee White' or 'Champion,' but you'll need 'Jumbo' to fill in between crops and 'Chinese White' for winter stirfries. Running out of radishes is a calamity, so make a planting about every three weeks. As the days grow shorter, radishes do not do as well, so enjoy them at their prime best.

Radish seeds are useful for marking the rows of slower-germinating seeds. They can be used as fillers as other crops are harvested, so you may have some cropping up in several spots in the garden at various stages of development.

Radishes' historic enemy is the despised root maggot. If you can get your first planting in early May you can beat them to the punch, but subsequent plantings require more aggressive measures. (See INSECTS, Chapter 7.)

and they won't be woody when grown under the midnight sun. And he should harvest by *pulling*, not cutting, the stalks. Tell him to tell his wife that rhubarb is not supposed to be a gray, runny sauce. It is supposed to be rosy chunks glazed in their own sweet juice. They get this way by bringing four cups of one-inch chunks of the red part of the stalks to a slow boil with a cup of sugar, simmering gently without stirring until a paring knife barely goes in. If you have a stash of over-age candied dried fruit or strawberry preserves gone to sugar, this is the place for them, cutting back to 3/4 cup of sugar. Let the rhubarb cool in its own juice. Serve with a baron of moose meat.

Freezing rhubarb is easy. It need not be blanched. If you freeze it in four-cup batches, you won't have to measure when you cook it. The sauce, cooled, can be frozen, too.

When rhubarb bolts, or sends up flower stalks, it is a normal part of the plant's life cycle. It doesn't happen every summer, and seems to be triggered by unusually warm weather. You can cut off the flowering stalks, which make dramatic elements in flower arrangements, or leave them on—or chop them off and put them on the compost pile. Horticultural literature reveals divided opinions about rhubarb's flower stalks, so do it your way.

Inexplicably, kids like to munch on raw rhubarb. Remind them that the stems are okay, but the leaves are toxic.

Use water-filled wine jugs or rocks as solar collectors to hold the sun's heat into the evening.

RUTABAGAS. Ever see rutabagas on a restaurant menu? On a dinner party buffet? Maybe it's because cooks haven't discovered 'Altasweet.' Pureed with a little cream and a pass from the nutmeg grinder, 'Altasweet' would give them a new slant on rutabagas. Seeds can be sown in the garden as soon as the soil can be worked, and should be protected by a row cover to keep root maggots

at bay. They can be harvested any time they're big enough to bother with, but can be left in the garden until you harvest the rest of the root crops. They store for months in plastic bags in a refrigerator, or cool, dark place. The puree can be frozen, the goodies added at serving time. Territorial Seed Company has it.

SPINACH is a cool season crop and is sensitive to day length, so it tends to bolt before you've had enough. Planted early in the season, perhaps as early as late April under row covers, it is nothing less than a minor miracle when its sturdy, pulpy leaves present themselves for spring salads before any prudent gardener would plant lettuce in the garden. It germinates best in 60-degree soil.

Start seeds of 'Melody,' 'Marathon,' or 'Bloomsdale' three weeks before you would normally set out plants.

The first spinach is the best, thick and pulpy, for the season's first salad. If you decide this is too much trouble, grow Swiss chard. 'Cold Resistant Savoy' is a new variety to look for.

New Zealand spinach. The Kiwis' "spinach" is no spinach, but it makes another good substitute for its recalcitrant namesake. It is not frost-tolerant, but it's a nice, mild pot green.

SQUASH is a warm season vegetable that requires special selection and handling to make it in Southcentral, but gardeners in the Interior can be more venturesome. The **summer squashes** that do well in most of Alaska are not numerous. The zucchinis are the easiest and most prolific, and there is more variety than most gardeners suspect.

The English call them **'marrows'** and Stokes Seeds, a Canadian company with a U.S. subsidiary, lists a bush-type vegetable marrow with white fruit, and 'Cousa,' a Lebanese marrow of pale greenish white.

The Italians call theirs **zucchini,** and they range in color from gray to a blacky-green. 'Black Jack' gets the nod from the CES Recommended List and deserves it (Denali Seed Company has it). 'Elite,' also a 48-day early bird, is listed by Harris. And don't skip over 'Aristocrat,' which pleased our taste. There are also yellow and golden zucchinis, which taste like any other zucchinis, but you might like the color of 'Gold Rush' in your mostly green vegetable garden, or stir fry.

The French call them **courgettes**, and harvest them when about the size of your middle finger. Any zucchini will make courgettes if you harvest it soon enough—like hovering over it on Friday instead of tooling off to the lake for the weekend.

When they get too big, make zucchini "boats," blanching them briefly and scooping out the seeds. Fill the cavities with ripe pepper and onion bits you've sautéed with the seeds and garlic, topping them with buttered crumbs and parmesan cheese. Brown in the oven. Or, cut an overgrown zucchini in half-inch slices, dip them in a lightly beaten egg, then in parmesan cheese and sprinkle with paprika. Bake until they smell good. Take bows.

Yellow crookneck squash was a lost cause until 'Dixie' was heard from. Grown through a mulch of clear poly, under a rowcap, in a favored location, 'Dixie' was a comely southern belle. But it tolled for her when 'Superset' came on the scene by way of Shepherd's Garden Seeds.

Give it a three-week headstart indoors. All squashes germinate best at soil temperatures between 68 and 86 degrees.

It is possible to transplant indoor-grown squash if you are deft about it. They resent root disturbance and sudden temperature changes, so you may want to start more than one batch to get transplants with one well-developed true leaf. Use clear plastic mulch and a row cover. Peat pots are not satisfactory because they rarely disintegrate soon enough for the expanding root system. Squash enjoys sharing a row cover with water jugs, and solar heat-collecting flat rocks.

Squashes are apt to have blossom-end rot problems in a cool, rainy spell. Best prevention: well drained soil, withhold manure, and water occasionally with a soluble calcium-nitrate fertilizer.

Winter Squashes have problems with Alaska's day length. In early summer our long days delay the onset of female flowers (which makes acorn squash- growers give up), and is true also of cucumbers and watermelons. Study the CES Recommended Variety List for varieties that produce female blossoms earlier, and search the catalogs for the earliest kinds offered.

TOMATOES. New gardeners think first of the delights of tomatoes from their own gardens. The pleasures of vine ripened, home grown tomatoes are real, but getting them can be elusive.

Plant breeders have had some success in developing tomatoes that will set fruit at low temperatures and ripen outdoors in the north. In most of Alaska, getting ripe tomatoes outdoors means using every trick of a wily trade, but gardeners in the Interior, where summer temperatures are higher, can pull it off with greater ease. In the rest of Alaska, here's how:

Choose a kind that is known to set fruit at lower temperatures than most of the outdoor types listed in catalogs aimed at their South 48 clientele.

Under test at Alaska's Plant Materials Center in Palmer in the summer of 1990, the most and earliest ripe fruit was harvested, in this order, from varieties 'Polar Baby' and 'Alpha,' obtained from Fairbanks breeder John Holm, and his 'Polar Gem' was almost as good. Their production far exceeded that of such previous choices as 'Glacier,' the 'Subarctics,' or 'Siberian.'

In this test the Alaska-developed varieties produced the highest yields of ripe fruit; none of the varieties from the Soviet Union produced fruit mature enough to harvest. 'Siberian' produced good quantities of green fruit, but they did not ripen on the vine in this test.

Tomatoes are a warm season crop, not well suited to outdoor culture in the short, cool summer of the High North.

Check the catalog of High Altitude Gardens for new Russian kinds, untested in Alaska at this writing.

Start plants indoors about eight weeks before planting time, or buy them from a local source if you can get young, stocky plants. The seeds germinate in five to seven days at 70 to 86 degrees, and need all the light you can provide.

Outdoors, give them your warmest micro climate. They'll need full sun, and protection from chilling wind. Pre-warm the soil by covering raised beds or mounded rows with clear poly, or plant in large nursery pots. Use the commercial WALL O' WATER or make a cylindrical wire cage and cover it with clear plastic. Row covers or tents are helpful. Cover the plants at night and on cool days.

Water in the morning, preferably with 80-degree water, when plants are cool and less subject to shock.

Outdoor-grown tomatoes may not be as large, sweet, or as red as greenhouse-grown fruit, but in a reasonably warm summer they will make a welcome addition to the garden if you can manage to grow them well.

TURNIPS. In most of Alaska turnips grow to perfection, germinating at cool temperatures and sown as soon as the soil can be worked. 'Purple Top White Globe' is a good producer and 'Tokyo Cross,' which is earlier, is so mild and sweet it can fill in when the radishes have played out. The food processor has made possible the delectable quarter inch sticks drenched in lime juice that are dead ringers for the more costly jicama from Mexico. Serve them as the Mexicans do with a dusting of chili pepper, or with finely chopped dill or mint leaves.

Root maggots also appreciate young turnips and rutabagas. One ploy is to cover the crop with a spun-bonded row cover like Reemay, held firmly in place with planks or rocks so that the flies that make maggots cannot lay their eggs at the base of the young plants. Leave the cover in place until you harvest all of the plants.

It's a good idea to rotate crops so that you don't grow turnips or rutabagas in a bed where one of the brassica family was grown the summer before.

Turnips and rutabagas store well in the refrigerator in plastic bags with holes punched in them. They freeze well also. The greens of both are a welcome fresh vegetable in early summer and they freeze well too.

GARDENING UNDER COVER

Within the recent memory of many gardeners April 15 was a happy day, in spite of the income tax deadline. It was the day they fired up their greenhouses. Like so many lemmings responding to an inaudible call, they trekked across snowy lawns, loaded down with heavy wooden flats filled with garden soil carefully hoarded before the ground froze, and planted their seeds for the customary six weeks' head start.

Today a four-tube fluorescent light fixture strung up in a cool garage or basement provides more plants than there are places for. Full service garden centers offer high quality starter plants, so most greenhouses need not be fired up until May first.

GREENHOUSE CONSTRUCTION

Horticultural literature has much to say about greenhouse construction, but some of it does not meet Alaska's needs. A greenhouse and a sunroom are not the same and they require different orientations.

A free-standing greenhouse ridgepole should run north and south, so that one side of the greenhouse gets the morning sun, the other the afternoon sun. A lean-to greenhouse or sunroom whose long wall faces south may generate too much heat for plants and people if trees or adjacent buildings do not give enough shade to temper solar build-up.

At Alaska's high latitude the glass walls' tilt should be vertical, rather than sloped, for increased solar gain, a plus for a free-standing structure. The greenhouse that is heated from mid-April so that plants can be started there needs the solar heat reflected off the snow.

Tests in cold regions of the Lower 48 have shown that insulating a north wall and roof results in more heat savings than light loss. This is less true at Alaska's high latitude. Reduced light

results in increased leafy growth and decreased fruit production, due to the greater arc the sun travels around the earth and, therefore around the greenhouse, say Alaska agricultural engineers.

In the North where the difference between day and night temperatures can be sharp, the greenhouse ventilation system holds equal rank with its heating system. When the sun goes under a cloud, or drops below the horizon, the vents close to conserve heat. Then the humidity begins to build, inviting fungus diseases in for a feast.

To avert disaster, the thermostat must call for the vents to open and the fans to expel excess humidity, which means a minimum temperature of around 65 degrees at night. Perimeter insulation pays by preventing the greenhouse soil from losing heat to the outside soil.

Should you have beds or benches, or both? If yours is a tomato-cucumber greenhouse you'll find ground beds cheaper to build and they will provide headroom these tall-growing crops require. If your greenhouse is for starting plants in pots, benches are more convenient and attractive. If you want to grow bedding plants early in the season and then set cucumbers and tomatoes into the ground beds, you will most likely want a combination of removable benches for bedding plants, and ground beds for tall-growing vegetables. The removable bench slats are useful for anchoring floating row covers during hardening off. New greenhouse coverings of structured plastic sheets, which are double layers of acrylic or polycarbonate with an air space between, are replacing glass, fiberglass, and polyfilm. They are initially more expensive and transmit somewhat less light, but these modern plastic materials pay for themselves in lower heating costs and their greater resistance to ultraviolet light damage. They are susceptible to scratching, so care must be taken in cleaning.

If you go for glass, go for double glazing if you can afford it. If that isn't practical, consider lining the inside of the greenhouse with polyethylene film, creating a dead air space between it and the glass for a saving of up to 40% in heating cost, but with some light loss.

GREENHOUSE MANAGEMENT. Home greenhouses may have the highest per capita ownership in Alaska, but their management has little in common with home greenhouses in the rest of the country. Alaska greenhouses are used mostly for growing cucumbers and tomatoes, and other warm season crops that do not perform well in our cool summers.

Most Alaska greenhouses are not operated in the winter so they should be given a good cleaning in late April. Check out the heating system while warming up the ground beds. If you do start up in early spring, bear in mind that the sun is 30-odd degrees above the horizon and ricochets off the late snow, roasting seedlings and greenhouse-grown plants. Greenhouse shading compounds and the shading process used on automobile windows in hot climates keep out needed light on cloudy days, and many days have some of both sun and clouds.

Don't be too proud to drape your greenhouse in a funereal black plastic shroud on a bright day, or to tape cardboard where the sun beats in. Most manufacturers of greenhouses sell roller blinds to fit their panels. They are attached to the ridge pole and are raised and lowered by pulleys. They are made of aluminum, bamboo, wood slats or tough plastic fabric. If only the south wall requires shading, the commercial pleated curtain material called Verisol is useful; or, a homemade version of floating rowcover panels may be sufficient.

The best treatment for **insect and disease problems** in the benign atmosphere of the greenhouse is prevention. Relatively easy to keep out, but very difficult to eradicate are fungus diseases, bacterial wilts, and infestations of aphids, red spider and the dreaded white fly.

Growing as many of your plants as you can from seed in a sterile mix is the best insurance. When you bring plants in from a full service garden center they are usually clean, but gardeners are inveterate traders of plants—and bugs and diseases .

You need a quarantine area for such acquisitions to protect your greenhouse from such notably susceptible plants as carnations, chrysanthemums, roses, eggplant, peppers, zinnias, and houseplants that have over-wintered indoors. Often the control, if it is a chemical one, is more devastating than the insects or diseases. (See Chapter 7, FIGHTING BACK.)

Wash your hands with soap and water before handling plants. **Tobacco mosaic** is a virus disease spread by contact with hands and clothing of smokers, not by the smoke itself. There is no cure.

Blossom end rot is not a disease, and many a gardener has emptied a sprayer of fungicide in a vain effort. For many years it has been known that an uneven water supply was a contributing factor, because the soil did not have enough water-holding capacity, or spaces for oxygen. A calcium deficiency is also a factor, so using calcium nitrate as a nitrogen source is a prudent, but somewhat more expensive, move. The use of manure should be avoided. When soil does not drain well the surface can be flooded while the roots are dry. Incorporating lime or wood ashes in the beds or benches the autumn before planting is helpful. The pH should be up around 6.0 to 6.5.

Botrytis, gray mold, appears on greenhouse plants in late summer when the rains come. It can be deterred by adequate ventilation and air circulation, which means keeping those fans going on cool, cloudy days and turning up the thermostat. Condensation on the edges of cucumber leaves and limp, moldy lower leaves of tomato plants comes when condensate streaks down greenhouse walls.

If you or your neighbors use a weed-killer containing 2,4-D on lawns, bear in mind that it takes only one part per million to cripple a greenhouse tomato crop.

Have the soil in greenhouse beds and benches tested every fall, while you still have time to remedy problems related to salt buildup and nutritional deficiencies before the next season.

Ventilation is as important as heat in a greenhouse. You'll need a recording thermometer, a thermostatically-controlled heating and ventilating system, and some method of shading.

Water with warm water, perhaps stored in a plastic barrel with a fitted lid. Plants grown outdoors can stand tap water temperatures that give greenhouse plants a fatal setback. Since condensation is a problem on cloudy days, try to water infrequently but deeply, and do it on sunny days. A long stretch of overcast days will give you fits.

Leaf-pruning of tomatoes and cucumbers reduces the plants' ability to manufacture food, but it's not a bad idea to remove yellow lower leaves to reduce the fungus spores that are flying around.

Soluble fertilizers are less apt to build up toxic salts in the soil than the granular types. If you use garden fertilizers for a few years, the salt buildup could be toxic to plants. It's much cheaper and easier in the long run to use the more expensive, high analysis soluble fertilizers.

Be sure that the soil mix is porous enough to let water run through and leach out any salt buildup. If it isn't practical to replace salt-laden soil you may need to leach it with copious amounts of water between crops.

Weeds attract insects, so it pays to keep the greenhouse weed-free. Refuse should not be kept in an open container in the greenhouse.

Greenhouses limited to tomato and cucumber production in the summer need to be kept about 70 degrees; few blossoms set fruit at less than 65, and cucumbers do better at 75 degrees.

The Cooperative Extension Service issues a helpful bulletin, *Controlling the Greenhouse Environment*, which is free.

BEANS, POLE. Pole beans are a greenhouse crop and it takes a fairly commodious one to give this tall grower the range it requires. But since it's the bean that real bean-eaters crave, it may be worth it to build your greenhouse to its dimensions.

Both Kentucky Wonder and Blue Lake are satisfactory greenhouse varieties, but they have been superseded by newer kinds. Johnny's Selected Seeds (see Catalogs) lists varieties for northern climates. 'Kentucky Blue' is a descendant of both of these fine old kinds, from the breeder of 'Sugar Snap' peas; it was a 1991 All-America winner. 'Northeaster' is earlier and said to perform well under limited light conditions.

CUCUMBERS are a greenhouse crop in Alaska, although some early pickling types can be grown outdoors through clear plastic mulch in the Interior and in favored locations elsewhere.

Monoecious, "standard," cucumbers have both male and female flowers on the same plant, and require pollinating.

The female blossom has a tiny cucumber hiding behind its skirts. If it does not get pollinated it will be aborted. To pollinate, transfer the pollen from the anther of a male blossom to the pistil of a female bloom. This can be done with a small brush, but it's easy to lose track of which blooms have been pollinated.

Most gardeners remove the petals from the male bloom and insert the anther into the center part of a female bloom. (Occasionally you run out of male blooms and have to beg one from another greenhouse gardener who usually lives across town). In the South 48 where cucumbers are grown outdoors, bees and flies take over the pollination chore.

Gynoecious cucumbers are hybrids that have only female flowers, although an occasional male blossom sneaks into the harem and should be evicted. In catalogs these cucumbers may be listed as 'Hybrid Cucumbers,' 'All-female Cucumbers' or 'Gynoecious Hybrid.' They do not produce seeds and are therefore called "burpless."

Parthenocarpic cucumbers do not require pollen from male blossoms to produce fruit, and if they receive it, fruits are misshapen or aborted. They should not be grown in the same greenhouse with other types. These cucumbers are seedless and therefore "burpless." They are usually marketed as European, or greenhouse cucumbers, their long slender fruits encased in plastic to protect tender skin which does not require peeling.

Cucumbers are not easy to transplant from pot to ground bed, but they need a three-week head start and a 75-degree temperature. In cool, cloudy weather cukes tend to abort. Seedless cucumbers are heavy producers, and therefore heavy feeders, and fast growers. Try giving them a cup of soluble fertilizer per plant per week when the plants are small, increasing it to two or three feedings a week as they get larger and start making cucumbers.

Cucumber foliage is attractive to the red spider, so it would be prudent to avoid mixing them with roses, carnations, chrysanthemums, gardenias, or sulking houseplants. The breeder of the parthenocarpic 'Sweet Success' has pulled off a neat trick: he bred the bitterness factor out of the fruit but retained it in the foliage to repel insects.

Cucumbers are also notably susceptible to powdery mildew and various fungus diseases. The best defense is good ventilation, which means keeping the vents open and the fans going, while maintaining optimum temperatures on cloudy summer days. Ouch. It helps if the plants are not so close together that they touch. A square yard per plant is a fair rule of thumb.

Cucumber plants that wilt dramatically may have one of several bacterial wilt diseases, but often the wilting is caused by water stress. On a bright day in a south-facing greenhouse foliage may lose water faster than roots can take it up, and the plant may collapse. Shading the greenhouse and misting the plant helps. Orienting the greenhouse on a north-south axis, planting the cucumbers on the east side and letting the tomatoes take the afternoon heat is a good idea. Water stress should be avoided because even though no disease is present, plant growth and quality are reduced, and such plants may not recover overnight. Salt buildup can also cause a dramatic wilting and the collapse of the plant.

If you're serious about cucumber production, ask the CES for its fact sheet, *Greenhouse Cucumber Production*.

We do not endorse Samuel Johnson's recipe: "Cucumbers should be dressed with salt, pepper, and vinegar, and then thrown out." If yours are bitter, eshew 'Straight Eight' and try a hybrid released sometime in the last twenty-five years, for gosh sakes.

EGGPLANT is usually a greenhouse crop in

Parthenocarpic 'Pandex' is a good home greenhouse variety.

Alaska, but with only indifferent success, and a fatal attraction for aphids reported by gardeners. If grown outdoors it needs to be sowed eight to 10 weeks before planting and requires a 70- to 80-degree temperature for germination. It should be set out under row covers, 18 inches apart. Johnny's Selected Seeds' offers 'Pirouette,' a 50-day F1 hybrid that looks good for Alaska.

TOMATOES are labeled in catalogs as "determinate" or "indeterminate". **Determinate tomatoes** grow to a certain height and quit. Their fruits tend to ripen at about the same time. They may

Steve Robb, Iowa farm boy turned Alaska home gardener, pulled off an eggplant crop with a raised bed covered with clear plastic.

not require staking, acquiring a bush-like shape. 'Patio' is an example, recommended in catalogs for growing in containers on patios and decks. **Indeterminates** keep growing and need staking and tying; they produce ripe fruit over a longer period. For proven varieties, stick with the CES Recommended Variety list unless you get a hot tip from someone who grows tomatoes under conditions similar to yours. Be wary of varieties of unknown adaptability to the high north which have tempting names and unknown characteristics. The current CES list recommends 'Tropic,' 'Vendor,' 'Early Girl' and 'Ultra Girl,' but additions and subtractions occur with updated lists.

The **sweet cherry-size tomatoes** are very different from the large forcing types, and different from commercial cherry tomatoes, which are also little but taste like the big ones.

The little sweeties are 'Sweet 100,' 'Chelsea,' 'Sweetie,' 'Sweet Million' and 'Sugar Lump' (sometimes listed as 'Gardener's Delight'), with more kinds sure to come in seed catalogs. These little fellows are not sold in markets; you have to grow your own from seed or buy starter plants to experience a new taste treat. They are best eaten raw because they lack the tartness needed for cooking.

Do's and Don'ts for Greenhouse Tomato Growers:

(1) Don't start your seeds much more than six weeks before you can set them in greenhouse beds lest they grow so lanky that you may have to pitch the lot and start over. Do space plants so that each has about four square feet of space in ground beds or low benches — they need head and foot room; closer spacing increases disease problems and reduces fruit size. Cringe when somebody says, "You should come see my greenhouse — it's a regular jungle in there!"

(2) Provide support with cages or strong stakes, tying them with soft ropes, cloth ties or re-cycled nylon hosiery. Tomatoes are heavy.

(3) Remove suckers from tall, indeterminate types—the side shoots that develop in the axils of the main stem and the leaves; leaf-pruning is counter productive, except for removing the yellowing lower leaves which are no longer producing chlorophyll, and the terminal bud to encourage ripening as the season draws to a close.

Gardeners report satisfaction with 'Celebrity' and we have great success with 'Super Fantastic,' both listed in the catalog of Tomato Growers Supply Company.

(4) Tomatoes do not set many buds below 65 degrees, so ante up enough heat unless you can be satisfied with a late, sparse crop. Or, grow an outdoor type in an unheated greenhouse. They set fruit at lower temperatures, but determinate types will not climb a pole and keep producing up to the rafters.

(5) Pollinate the blossoms by hand because there are few bees and flies in the greenhouse. It is better to use a commercial pollinating vibrator or an electric toothbrush than to rely on shaking the vines or a commercial blossom-set product which may cause more problems than it solves. When humidity mounts, the pollen may not be dry enough for it to be effective. Keep those fans going, pollinate at noon, or after several hours of sunlight. In an unusually cloudy spring, this can be a problem and fruit-set may be poor.

(6) Ventilation and good air circulation are as important as a reliable heating system. A fan (or two) to keep the air moving prevents cold pockets and condensation on the plants, a cordial invitation to fungus diseases.

Mike Mosesian of Mosesian Farms, Alaska's largest commercial hydroponic producer of greenhouse tomatoes, makes his own growing medium. Here is his formula: mix five pounds of peatmoss with five pounds of horticultural grade coarse perlite. To each cubic yard add five pounds flour lime and five pounds dolomitic lime. He fertilizes with a 10-8-22 soluble fertilizer with trace elements and adds $1/4$ teaspoon epsom salts per gallon of water for the magnesium it lacks. By mid-July he starts removing lower leaves to improve air circulation. His minimum temperature is 60 degrees; he starts exhausting at 78 degrees and never lets the temperature go above 85 degrees.

Sooner or later home tomato growers succumb to the blandishment of hydroponic culture, said to be the Agriculture of the Future, searching for ways to avoid soil disease and drainage problems. Some are successful, but such a system requires an exacting exchange of nutrient solution, automated aeration, plus frequent testing to insure that the nutrient supply is accurate to a gnat's eyebrow. Hydroponic culture lacks the kindly buffering action of soil.

Cornell Universitry has modified an English system that works for us. It involves cutting the bottoms out of five gallon fiber nursery containers, filling them with a commercially manufactured potting mix, and setting them on about five inches of crushed rock (which is a tad smaller than pea gravel) and horticultural grade coarse perlite in deep ground beds.

The tomato plants are watered every other day with Peters Professional 9-45-15 nutrient solution, plus an occasional high nitrogen fertilizer as the plants indicate a need for it. Production exceeds that of previous years' conventionally grown plants, and plants are less prone to blossom end rot because of their even moisture supply and the perfect drainage into their excellent rooting medium.

Most tomato growers in Alaska have green tomatoes at the season's end. They can be sautéed for a tart, different vegetable or they make a trendy quiche. Or, they can be wrapped in paper and will gradually ripen if their storage temperature doesn't drop much below 65 degrees. It is temperature, not light, that causes them to ripen, according to recent Ohio State University research. This works only with tomatoes that are a rich green turning whitish, and are free of bruises, cracks, or blossom end rot, their bulletin states.

BERRIES

BLUEBERRIES, *Vaccinium* Spp. Although wild blueberries grow over most of Alaska, and several cultivars have proved to be hardy, blueberries for the home garden remain in the research arena because of chromosomal differences. If you decide to go for it, buy plants of both sexes and more than one variety. Look for those developed for the northern states. Lotsa luck.

CURRANTS, *Ribes* Spp. Alaska's native currant, *Ribes triste*, the Northern Red Currant, grows all over the big part of Alaska, and the **Northern Black Currant**, *Ribes hudsonianum*, is almost as widespread, and both are edible.

If you want currants for jelly, wine, or pie, you're light years better off with one of the purchased cultivars than with a free wild one. 'Red Lake' is still the standard red one and 'Swedish Black' is still the best of the blacks.

GOOSEBERRIES get a bad press in the Lower 48, where the bushes are host to the infamous white pine blister rust. This is not a problem in pine-poor Alaska and gooseberries enjoy Alaska's invigorating climate. The season is a bit short for them in some places and the berries don't always get ripe enough to eat out of hand, not much of a problem since raw gooseberry devotees are rare birds. The English would think you mad if you

did not harvest your gooseberries to make a batch of tarts or a conserve for scones. 'Pixwell,' which doesn't often get red but does best hereabouts, and 'Champion' are the recommended varieties.

RASPBERRIES. In a country woefully lacking in tree fruits, few Alaskans can forego the goodness of raspberries in season, and later preserved in freezer jams, ruby-toned jellies and a heady liqueur. (The sourdoughs among us make a sweet raspberry-currant dessert wine that warms the cockles.) Raspberries grow wild and some patches produce berries of good size and flavor. However, your best bet is to buy plants of one of the good cultivars which will out-yield the wildlings by a milepost. Good breeding tells, and good weeding, watering, and fertilizing are often wasted on poor plants.

'Trent,' 'Indian Summer,' and 'Chief' are good varieties and garden centers and catalogs offer recent introductions. 'Canby' is excellent in Southcentral, less so in Southeastern where abundant rainfall is not to its liking. If you get your start with raspberries over the back fence, they will most likely be 'Latham,' a berry that has been around for a long time and has earned its kudos.

There are fine Canadian varieties, possibly because the area around Clearbrook, B.C. is called the raspberry capitol of the world, not without reason. The Canadians' 'Boyne' is best in places with cold winters; 'Royalty,' a purple raspberry, 'Haida' (which is susceptible to fruit rot in rainy harvest seasons), and 'Skeena' are all good for us.

Golden raspberries are a cross between the red raspberry and an Asian yellow one. The flavor is sweeter, less tart than the red raspberry. The golden color is lovely, especially when combined with blueberries, but they do not make as colorful or flavorful a jam as the red kinds. Golden raspberries look much like their distant cousin, the cloudberry, but they have more flavor than cloudberries. 'Fallgold' is the one to look for.

Raspberries do not require your most favored site. They have produced well in Alaska's long days if they get at least a half day of sun. They are such enthusiastic growers that they have been known to create bad blood between neighbors. Before you plant a row along the property line, ask the fellow on the other side of the fence if he wants a raspberry patch, because that is what he will get. Raspberries sucker freely and to keep them in rows you have to dig the suckers out and try to find good homes for them.

If you give a sucker an even break, you will have a producing raspberry plant in two years, and it will hit its stride in three. Plant the suckers or the young plants you buy on 30-inch centers in rows seven or eight feet apart—they will look woebegone, but if you cheat on space you will be fighting your way between rows of barbed canes in a couple of years.

If you don't want your raspberries to grow into an impenetrable thicket, stake them in rows or hills. Most people install a double set of stout posts and stretch heavy-gauge wire on two levels, the lower one about two feet high, the upper one four or five feet.

The canes can be interwoven on the wires or tied to them. In areas of strong winter winds, the ties should be snug to prevent chafing. In the Interior exposed canes may die back. A good use for the wire caging you use in the flower border would be to bend the canes over and weigh them down with the uncoupled cages. Snow will offer good insulation and the cages are a somewhat wimpy deterrent to moose pruning. Raspberries are generally self-pollinating, but production may be improved by growing two cultivars next to each other. A hive of bees nearby doesn't hurt.

Spider mites occasionally attack raspberry plants during hot dry spells. Watch for their minute webs at the space between leaf nodes. The raspberry aphid sometimes strikes, but a hard spray from the hose will dispatch these pests, repeated as necessary. Bees, birds and squirrels enjoy raspberries, so if you must resort to malathion or Diazanon, spray in the late evening, when they've retired.

In rainy weather the vines may get powdery mildew, especially if the plants are too close together with poor air circulation. Avoid handling healthy plants. If berries are crumbly, small and dry, it is probably caused by one of the several virus diseases and is apt to reappear, and can spread to neighboring plants. The best cure is to remove the plant and dispose of it, waiting until the next spring to replace it with a new plant.

In the spring, prune weak or malformed canes and reduce the number of strong canes to five or six per plant. If your raspberries get carried away with good care, shorten the canes to about five feet. Weeds will grow at the base of the bushes and hand-pulling may involve some bloodshed. Be cautious with the hoe, lest you damage the shallow roots.

Raspberries are touchy about wet feet. In Southeastern, they do better if planted on mounded rows. In the big part of Alaska they will need deep watering in the normally dry early summer when they are flowering and setting fruit. They are heavy feeders, and three pints of 8-32-16 per 100 feet of row is not too much. We find that a light side dressing when they begin to set fruit increases berry size and quality.

Lime will not be needed unless the soil is very acid. The plants are perennial, but the canes are biennial. The canes that bear fruit this summer will die this fall; the vigorous young canes that had all those green leaves and no berries will be the berry producers next year. The old canes can be removed in either spring or fall, but fall is the better time because some insect eggs and diseased canes are disposed of, and spring is a busier time in the garden.

STRAWBERRIES are grown in every state; good choices for the Alaska garden are kinds that were developed for Alaska or other northern states. (See CATALOGS.) 'Matared,' 'Susitna,' 'Toklat,' 'Squentna' and 'Pioneer' were all developed at the Alaska Agricultural Experiment Stations in Palmer and College, AK. They are marketed through garden centers and commercial greenhouses.

Along with the new berries came the results of research on how to grow strawberries in the North. The best location for a strawberry patch is a slope that faces south, with light soil that has good moisture holding capability. Strawberries need an inch of water per week from bloom time through harvest and, since they bloom in June which is our driest month, their moisture needs should not be neglected.

Strawberries do fine in our moderately acid soils but they benefit from small amounts of lime or wood ashes to provide for their calcium needs. Two and a half pints of 8-32-16 per 100 square feet of row should be worked into the soil for a new strawberry patch. Subsequent fertilizer requirements will be less, one and a half pints plus a light side dressing when fruit-set commences. Every few years a strawberry patch may benefit from an application of 16-16-16 if nitrogen levels have fallen; if the treatment works, be prepared to enlist neighbors to help harvest.

Plant roots must be kept moist, so pour a cup of water into each planting hole as you set the plants. Plant on a cloudy day, if possible, or in the late afternoon.

Conventional wisdom has it that you should pick off all the flowers from new transplants, but this is not recommended for Alaska, unless the transplants are very weak. Set them 30 inches apart in the row and the first runner plants will root between 12 and 18 inches from the mother plant.

Plant in a single hill, a matted row, or a solid planting. Each system has advantages and disadvantages; see CES publications *Strawberries in Alaska*, and *Growing Everbearing Strawberries as Annuals in Alaska* upon which much of this text was based.

There are fewer insects and diseases to plague the strawberry grower than in other places; weeds are the greatest obstacle to a good harvest. Herbicides should be used with the greatest reluctance on food crops, but as a last resort Chloroxon, sold under several trade names, gives good control of annual weeds like chickweed, and Glyphosate ("Round-up") is effective for grasses, but must be kept off the strawberry plants. The bulletins tell how.

Where snow cover does not come early and linger late, a winter mulch may be necessary for plants that are perennial, or that you hope will be. Oat straw is a good mulch, weighted down with spruce boughs, which also help to aerate dried grass and birch leaf mulch, which tend to pack. Treating everbearing strawberries as annuals makes mulching unnecessary, and with winter hardiness not a consideration, you can select for quality.

What's this about "climbing strawberries"? There is a rash of ads every once in a while for them. No strawberry variety will climb, because its runners do not have tendrils, but runners can be tied to supports to make them appear to climb. There is no advantage to this procedure and there are disadvantages in that too many runner plants deplete the strength of the producing plants. *Don't get snookered.*

THE CULINARY HERBS

The best place for a culinary herb garden in Alaska? Hard by the kitchen, which may be in a window box or a container, or a sunny spot snuggled up to the kitchen door. Harried cooks do not sprint out to the vegetable garden for an oregano leaf. And those magazine pictures of little herb pots on kitchen counters are the work of harried photographers, not gardeners.

Culinary herbs, enjoying a brisk revival with interest in ethnic cookery, are easy to grow. They make familiar foods more provocative. When you run out of things to do to a halibut or a head of cabbage, an herb garden offers respite from sameness.

Sources are plentiful. Most garden centers sell the popular herbs. Catalogs list many kinds and nurseries ship perennial plants. In Anchorage, Cathy Sage's Sage Herb Garden sells plants of uncommon kinds.

See good Alaska herb gardens at the Eckert Memorial Garden at the Palmer fairgrounds, where Grower Becky Swanson is on duty daily during the growing season. At the Palmer Visitor's Information Center, Horticulturist Wendy Anderson will talk herbs with collectors.

On the campus of the University of Alaska Anchorage, there is a collection of culinary and ornamental herbs, and Grower Pat Leary is available for consultation. Herb growers would enjoy visiting the two-acre National Herb Garden of the Herb Society of America at the National Arboretum in Washington, DC. Send for the free pamphlet on herbs for flavor and fragrance from Herbs, Dept. FW, Education Office, U.S. National Arboretum, 24th and R. Streets, Washington, D.C. 20002.

This container herb garden is on a deck near the kitchen .

Start seeds of most culinary herbs six weeks before you can plant them outdoors: marjoram, thyme, lemon balm, dill, sage, savory, and sorrel. Parsley, chive and most perennial kinds need an extra three or four weeks.

Basil does best in greenhouses in most of Alaska, in places where tomatoes thrive. It not only has a flavor affinity for tomatoes, but is thought to repel insects that find tomatoes attractive. It does not do well outdoors in Southcentral, but if you are into Italian cooking you will find a warm, protected place for 'Piccolo Verde Fino.' the Italians' pesto basil.

Hap Hollibaugh grows a patch of borage near his vegetable garden to attract bees to pollinate his crops.

Borage is useful primarily for its star shaped, true blue blossoms which can be floated in icy drinks or candied and used as the outrageously expensive candied violets are.

Catnip grows well in the vegetable garden but may attract neighborhood cats. Some cats don't get their jollies from catnip; finiky felines may prefer cat thyme, *Teucrium marum*.

Chive can be grown from seed started from a produce counter pot, or from a wild clump of *Allium schoenoprasum*, the same species. Garlic chive, *Allium tuberosum*, also called Chinese or Oriental garlic, can be found in specialty catalogs and occasionally in garden centers. Nice to know if you live in a rainy place where garlic bulbs tend to rot in the wet ground.

Cilantro is the leaf of the coriander plant. One *Coriandrum sativum* plant of this 18- to 24-inch annual will produce plenty of leaves for culinary use, but the seeds need a warm summer and a long one to mature. The variety 'Santo' is grown especially for its leaves, to be used sparingly in guacamole, chili, ceviche, curries, and Peking duck. It is needed in Latin American, Portuguese, and North African cuisines. Germinate it in a cool, dark place.

Dill you may want to grow in quantity in the vegetable garden if you're into dill pickles or gravlox. A plant or two is nice by the kitchen door, but the tall garden kinds are too lanky for a container garden.

'Bouquet,' 'Petra' and 'Ducat' are not quite so obnoxiously tall , but 'Fernleaf' is the best container subject, a neat little AAS award-winner in 1992. Dill seeds can be stored dry, but dried leaves have a less pleasant flavor as time goes on.

Fennel is useful for flavoring many foods. The plants resemble dill. The strain called Red Leaf Fennel is both ornamental and flavorful.

Garlic is a cool season crop, but it is a long season one. Bulbing and clove formation do not occur until days are short. In milder climates it is planted in the fall, mulched, and harvested in the spring. To be successful with garlic in Alaska, plant as early as you can, using all the tricks of the northern gardener's trade: pre-warming the soil of a raised bed or mounded row with a clear row cover of spun-bonded polyester or clear plastic. Plant the cloves, pointed end up, from the largest bulbs you have (the size of the cloves doesn't matter). A cooling period in the refrigerator for a couple of weeks helps.

Garlic needs plenty of water and regular fertilizing to make leaves—and the more leaves it makes before bulbing, the bigger the bulbs. When bulbing occurs the leaves collapse, so not to worry when that happens. Harvest when the leaves turn yellow, and let the bulbs cure until the wrapper leaves are wrinkled. Store at 50 to 60 degrees.

It takes about 25 feet of row to make a garlic braid. It won't store all winter at kitchen temperature, but no garlic grower wants to hide such a feat in the basement either.

Elephant garlic, *A. scorodoprasum*, is a separate species from true garlic, *A. sativum*. It was introduced to the trade by Nichols Garden Nursery which is still the principal source for it. It has a milder flavor and because of its larger size is easier to use.

The practice of soaking garlic in cooking oil should be avoided because of the possible development of the botulism organism.

Ginger can be started from a produce counter root that has three or four eyes. If you start it in the spring you can harvest the roots in late fall. Store them in the refrigerator where they keep for a long time. Be wary of this herb—it is so pungent that an overdose may ruin the family for everything from gingerbread to gingerale.

Good King Henry is a 10-inch ornamental pot herb, a spinach substitute that sends out billows of white flowers. It is a good under planting for leggy dill beds. It is an introduced weed from Europe and is related to lambs' quarters.

Horseradish is grown from root cuttings sold by garden centers and listed in catalogs. Once you have a start you can save a piece of the root you dig in the fall and replant it the following spring. However, the plant is perennial in most of Alaska. The roots are ground to make fresh horseradish, and teary eyes.

Lemon Balm is best treated as an annual.

Cathy Sage starts her herbs in a cool garage under fluorescent lights.

Offered by garden centers and easily grown from seed, like most mints, it is easy to root from cuttings or divisions. Carol Murkowski gave us this easy recipe for lemon balm butter, a quick fix for fish, which she serves frequently from her Aleutian Island kitchen: chop a handful of lemon balm leaves and blend with four ounces of butter or margarine, season with salt and pepper, store in the fridge.

Mints do well in Alaska and do not require the shade ordained by texts written for lower latitudes. The common field mint, *Mentha arvense*, grows wild, and peppermint or spearmint, including a golden one, are widely sold; a pot of mint beside a patio chair would not be amiss on a hot afternoon when cold drinks are passed.

Corsican mint, *M. requieni*, has tiny leaves on a sweet creeping plant. Curled mint, *M. spicata crispata*, has crinkled leaves. *M. piperita citrara*, combines peppermint with a mild orange fragrance. *M. suaveolens* is apple-scented. Pineapple mint, *M.'varigata'* is variegated green and white. Lemon mint is *Monarda citriodora*. The Italians could not long sustain life without *M. origanum*, a fortuitous combination of Italianate flavors.

Oregano's botanical identity is in dispute;

Dill is not too tall for a mixed flower border where this one volunteered from seed in the vegetable garden.

Greek oregano, *O. vulgare.*, is the standard, *O. heraclium* is the chef's choice.

The plants you buy at one nursery may not be the same that you buy at another. **Marjoram** is the annual one. If you cook in Italian, one of the oreganos is a must-have.

Parsley is a slow germinator (11 to 28 days and not fussy about temperature) and it is a slow grower, but it will mature if planted in March—most nurseries sell it in cell-packs. You might like to try one of the more pungent Italian kinds like 'Catalonon' in addition to the popular 'Extra Dwarf Curled.' Italian parsleys have flat celery-like leaves. The curled kinds make more attractive garnishes and garden edgings. Since parsley freezes well without blanching, you could grow a couple of plants in your container garden for kitchen use, and more in the vegetable garden for freezing. Freeze some with chopped chives and lemon balm.

After a mild winter parsley may re-up the following spring, for it is really a biennial. It is easier and safer to start over each spring. Successive plantings are not necessary.

Rosemary is best propagated by cuttings, or purchased from garden centers. It accepts lower light than most herbs and will continue to produce if you bring your herb garden into a sunroom or cool window for the winter. Rosemary is decorative in a hanging basket and it is a show-stealer when trained to tree form.

Sage is attractive in the herb garden, easy to grow from seed, and a single plant will keep most cooks in enough sage to flavor meats and poultry for a year.

Sorrel, especially French Sorrel, is a two-footer with heart-shaped leaves, used to flavor cream soups, fish, or cabbage. The French would be bereft without it.

Summer Savory is a dandy annual that makes a nice mound of flavorful leaves and then showers of minute lavender blooms. Bring a potted plant indoors some year and when it has bloomed on into the fall, let its leaves drop to reveal bare branches that resemble a small desert tree.

Sweet Woodruff, *Galium odoratum*, is hardy to Zone 4 and is the flavoring agent for the Germans' May wine. It works in non-alcoholic beverages as well.

Tarragon, *Artemesia dracunculus*, is French tarragon, propagated from cuttings and divisions because it does not produce much seed and the seed does not "come true." Plants cost more, but are so useful that you should bite the bullet. Seed-grown tarragon is Russian tarragon, a weed of no value as a condiment. When frost is imminent, harvest the stems and stuff them in bottles of wine vinegar.

Thyme is as ornamental as it is useful, coming in many scents and colors.

Watercress comes easily from seed sown about a month before setting out, and it would grow in a pot of moist soil or in a well-watered garden spot. It thrives in the greenhouse, but is an aphid's fatal attraction.

Drying herbs is easy. For maximum flavor, harvest when blossoms first begin to form. Do it on a sunny day when the leaves are dry. You can safely prune up to two-thirds of most plants. Rinse them if necessary, then air-dry. Ideally herbs should be bunched and hung in a dark place with good air circulation, but a dark paper bag with holes for ventilation will work.

Herbs are dry enough to strip the leaves off when they crumble in your fingers. Dried herbs do not have indefinite shelf life and should be replaced when their fragrance fades.

Herbal vinegars are an easy way to preserve pungent fresh herbs and they make dressing a green salad an easy route to fame.

Cathy Sage gives charming gifts of her **Four Thieves Vinegar**. Here is her recipe: combine several cloves, a few cinnamon sticks, black pepper corns, whole allspice berries, mustard seed, fennel seed, garlic cloves, rue, sage, spearmint, rosemary, tarragon, salad burnet, and salt. Add red wine vinegar to cover. Strain when they have steeped to your liking. Use in marinades for red meats and game, for pickling eggs, in salad dressings. It is a complex, heady brew.

Nancy Groczek's **Dilly Vinegar** is satisfyingly pungent. She saves wine bottles, stuffs them with dill, adds several garlic cloves, backfills with red wine vinegar, and displays them against a window or gives them to deserving friends.

Cooking oils pose a more serious problem.

The practice of putting a small red pepper and fresh garlic cloves in oil for use in cooking has potential danger. The exclusion of air by the oil makes the growth of the botulism bacterium in fresh garlic possible. Refrigerating it would lesson the danger, but if the refrigerator temperature should fluctuate, it could be dangerous.

Herbal Teas enjoy a certain mystique and offer an alternative to coffee. Federal Drug Administration has raised troubling questions about the toxicity of some teas sold in bulk to stores. **Teas made from garden herbs should avoid lobelia, sassafras, comfrey, tonka bean, wormwood, shavegrass, burdock, penny royal and pokeroot.** Most commercially packaged products are safely consumed in moderation, like two or three cups a day. Those concocted by amateur herbalists may be experimental and merit caution.

MELONS

Melons are warm season crops that rarely mature in Alaska's brief growing season. They decline to make female blossoms in the long daylight of our early summer, but certain **muskmelons** will produce the goods with special treatment. They like warm feet and cool heads, appreciating soil temperatures as high as 110 degrees and accepting quite cool air temperatures.

Dave Schroer's garden hobby is growing what doesn't grow easily in Homer, where there aren't enough "degree days" for most warm season crops, but the first time he tried, he harvested over 100 ripe 'Minnesota Midget' muskmelons from eight plants in four hills.

He started his seeds indoors three weeks before he thought he could set the plants out under row covers. He warmed his garden soil with a clear polyethylene mulch, and made himself a giant double plastic row cover. Under it he planted his melons in soil fertilized with 8-32-16, digging the holes 18 inches deep and working in a bucket of compost.

Shroer, a retired teacher, experiments with ways to warm things up in his cool garden. He uses double row covers early in the season when the nights are chilly, one six inches above the other to create a dead air space. He tucks boulders in among the plants to soak up the sun's heat and release it in the cool hours of the evening. He fills jugs with water and uses them as solar collectors. None of this, he says deprecatingly, is very scientific. But a hundred muskmelons from eight plants in *Homer, Alaska*?

The next year Schroer's neighbor installed a hive of bees, which found good sources of pollen and nectar in Schroer's big garden. That year he harvested *two hundred* muskmelons. Some were only tennis ball size, he concedes, but many would have been acceptable on the produce counter.

Are muskmelons cantaloupes by another name? Not quite. Both are botanically *Cucumis melo*; Muskmelons are variety *reticulatus*, native to Persia and Central Asia. They have netted skin, ribs, and the flesh may be green or orange, ripening rapidly, making them poor shippers, but a better bet for the northern gardener. Cantaloupes, variety *Cantaloupsis*, are thicker skinned, ripen more slowly, and ship better.

Most of these melons are 70- to 85-day melons; Farmer Seed & Nursery of Faribault, Minnesota, which specializes in varieties suited to northern climates, lists some that may be early enough for Alaska. Le Marché International lists an early casaba variety called 'Santa Claus,' a so-called winter melon that has been grown as a short-season summer melon.

Why not grow muskmelons in a heated greenhouse? Pollination time is critical, and even the most conscientious gardener armed with a camel's hair watercolor brush may not be around when the female blossom is receptive to the male pollen. Bees and other insects do a better job, staying on duty more faithfully.

How to tell when muskmelons are ripe? Not easy, but the best indicator is when the connection between stem and fruit is dry and scabby, with pale threads between stem and melon. If you wait until the melon is soft, it will be too far gone. Trust me.

Growing melons in Southcentral Alaska is the sort of challenge that tempts an Alaska gardener to take the bait; as more Russians venture across the Bering Strait into Alaska, we hear of muskmelons being grown under plastic in Novosibirsk; of watermelons, a new pink-fleshed Siberian variety called 'Vesenny' and a yellow-fleshed American variety, 'Yellow Doll,' being grown there under plastic cover outdoors.

Lawrence Clark grafted 17 apple varieties onto the Siberian crab rootstock pictured here.

TREE FRUITS

Tree fruits have been frustrating Alaska gardeners for decades. Efforts the Pioneer Fruit Growers Association brought to this prodigious task are paying off.

The fruit growers report that more than 50 kinds of apple and crabapple trees have produced ripe fruit in Alaska.

There are sour cherries, apricots, plums, and a wild Ussurian pear that show promise. The Pioneer Fruit Growers Association has regular meetings for instruction and exchange of scion wood.

In Siberia, gardeners have also grafted large-fruited apples onto the lower part of crabapple trees, and when planted where they will be protected by snow in winter, have been successful. There is little doubt that large-fruited apples will be available to Alaska growers in the near future.

Some Matanuska Valley growers have espaliered apple trees against south-facing house walls successfully. Some south walls may be too hot and east or west walls may be a better choice.

The introduction of the 'Summer-red' apple by the late Dr. Curtis H. Dearborn, research horticulturist at the Alaska Experiment Station in Palmer, was a major breakthrough. Here was an apple of excellent flavor, bright red color, and good storage quality that ripened on the tree in Southcentral Alaska. When it was grafted onto Siberian crabapple rootstock, it was reliably hardy. Many successful varieties of cold-hardy apples have crab apple blood in their heritage.

Not all available genetic material has yet been tried on hardy rootstocks, so it appears likely that there will be more breakthroughs.

Other apples of eating quality that have been grown successfully include 'Yellow Transparent,' 'Norland,' 'Chinese Golden Early,' 'Anoka,' 'Yephorys Chernogous,' 'Lodi,' 'Canada Red,' 'Vista Bella,' 'Mantet' and several apple-crabs and crabapples.

The problems do not lend themselves to quick solution. The foremost one is not cold, but latitude. The metabolic changes that bring about dormancy and hardiness are triggered by day length and declining temperature. Trees acclimated to lower latitudes do not get the message that they should get ready for winter. By March 21st the sun is 29 degrees above the horizon at Anchorage and strikes the thin barked apple tree trunks, unshaded by foliage. Sap that flows during the day and freezes at night, ruptures the capillaries.

Only early and mid-season apples have time to ripen in the brief growing season. Early apples are poor keepers, some maintaining quality under refrigeration for less than a month, but they make good pies for freezing. Gardeners along the southern coast have a small advantage, with somewhat more moderate temperatures and a slight edge on day length. 'Winter Banana' succeeds there.

Apricots have been grown in the Anchorage area. The Manchurian apricot, *Prunus armeniaca*

off, the Pioneer Fruit Growers organization recommends a sunny, east-facing slope for planting, and clear plastic mulch or a soil heating cable to warm the soil. Topsoil fortified with lime, manure and a slow-release fertilizer should go into a planting hole two to three feet wide and at least a foot and a half deep.

Many fruit trees are not self-fertile and require another tree nearby that blooms at the same time. Plant your fruit trees in your warmest micro-climate, in well-drained soil, and give them the best possible care for the first three years while they are becoming acclimated.

Moose are a serious problem for fruit tree

Above: 'Norland' ripened at Eckert Nursery in Palmer by early September. Photo by Jim Fox

Right: Lilian Eckert "cuffed" her six year-old 'Norland' tree to prevent girdling by rodents. Photo by Jim Fox

var. mandshurica, produced fruit suitable for preserving for experienced fruit tree grower Lawrence Clark. Plums are hardy ornamental trees in Zone 3, but have not produced ripe fruit. **Sour Cherries** suitable for pies and preserves have been grown in the Anchorage area.

Fruit trees are beautiful in bloom, and the immense satisfaction of producing an edible crop keeps Alaskans working toward the next big breakthrough. If you'd like to try to pull it

Diana and Clem Tillion of Halibut Cove in Kachemak Bay cover their orchard with a plastic structure.

Onion bags offer some protection against moose browsing, but they must be securely tied, and caged in wire fencing to be really effective.

at Dimond Greenhouses, 1050 Dimond Blvd., Anchorage, AK 99502) is hands-on information by an old hand at planting trees. Municipal Park Departments release lists of plant materials hardy in their areas, often with useful comments on cultural practices.

growers, and many ploys have been tried, but few have worked. (See Chapter 7, FIGHTING BACK)

For more information ask the Extension Service for *Tree Fruits & Small Fruits for Alaska* and *Landscape Plant Materials for Alaska* by Alan C. Epps. *Gardening in Alaska* by Wayne Leiser ($9.95

When a heavy wet snow comes before leaves have fallen, it behooves the gardener to apply his lawn rake, but gently.

CHAPTER 3

A LANDSCAPE FOR ALASKA

The landscape revolution that changed the face of American cities was late coming to Alaska. Alaskans long ago settled for the front lawn and back yard they knew back home and resigned themselves to familiar plants used in time worn ways.

There were good reasons why they were slow to scuttle tradition. Less research was done on what horticulturists call "ornamentals" than on the food and feed crops needed for our self-sufficiency. Garden writing had, and still has, little to say about gardening in the High North.

A quick survey of horticultural literature reveals that the "Far North" is the northern tier of states. Alaska's "High North" has little in common with that Far North. In the High North, latitude calls the tune, with long summer days. Plants don't get the message that winter is coming and do not initiate the physiological changes needed for dormancy. Short winter days and long winters sorely try plants' winter survival. Cold is not so much Southcentral's problem as day length, and plants' response to it.

Conventional ideas about landscaping have yielded to the realities of living in the High North. Time was, a proper landscape included a foundation planting of shrubs to conceal the basement, a front lawn, and a back yard for the clothesline and trash burner. A matched pair of little spruce trees on either side of the front steps was a nice touch, and a round puddle of marigolds centered on the front lawn was a traffic-stopper.

A lawn is mostly ceremonial, says Dr. Marc Cathey, Director of the National Arboretum. It consumes too much water. The nitrogen fertilizer and pesticides it requires drain into the water table. Its weekly mowing is mind-numbing. This heresy is now gaining widespread acceptance.

In Alaska the most favorable micro-climate on the property, usually the south side of the house (of which, lamentably, there is only one), takes first priority—which may be a rose garden, a fenced patio or deck, a vegetable garden, or a flower border. A lawn may be pretty far down on the list of priorities.

The idea of dividing one's property into "rooms" is not new, but it serves Alaskans well. On sloping hillside properties or level city lots, a sunny "room" may get the sun-loving flowers and

Sherman and Peggie Reynolds of Bush Landscaping and Nursery achieved levelment on their sloping property by installing retaining walls. Design by Jeff Dillon, ASLA.

'Hap' Hollibaugh, whose vocation is set design but whose avocation is gardening, concealed sound baffles behind trees to create a private garden for his parents' home.

shrubs, with grassy paths between borders and beds. A room may be a ground-covered expanse with "borrowed scenery," where traffic and high maintenance are not desired, a Japanese concept. Another may be an off-street parking area screened by tall shrubs. Some properties need "rooms" for the less than ornamental functions of composting, storage of machinery and scrap lumber, a woodpile, dog run, or a gaggle of wire plant cages.

Problem growing areas are outdoor rooms of great distinction when a moist shady spot becomes a fernery where mosses, mushrooms and liverworts thrive. A sun-baked rocky bank could be a rock garden where alpine plant roots go deep

David and Sandy Harrington transformed a shade problem into a landscape asset, a snug nook for a small garden.

for moisture and minerals. A hard surfaced patio makes a room for outdoor meals, summer entertaining, or game watching. In winter it transforms into a backyard skating rink, in summer a place for toddlers to toddle, and tool around by tricycle. A landscape is an evolving design. One day the basketball hoop will be gone from the garage, and the backyard skating rink will be converted to a patio.

Most such landscape designs require the services of a landscape architect or landscape designer. These talented people are not often found in small cities and rural areas, but there are a few, and many in larger cities take out-of-town jobs.

Many homeowners have a collection of magazine pictures and article ideas and can design their own landscape with books borrowed from far-flung libraries or landscape software brought up on a computer monitor.

Sharon Davies designed her own fence to screen a vegetable garden and work area from public view.

LANDSCAPE ARCHITECTS are professionals who are qualified by education and supervised experience to plan new communities, parks, freeways, recreation areas, and land use on a regional scale. They also design or consult on home landscape projects, and some are design/build architects who both plan and supervise the installation of their designs.

In Alaska, where factors such as day length, seasonal temperature swings, planting methods, plant hardiness, and structural concerns are critical, you will want to know if the person or firm has practiced in Alaska or where he or she had practiced previously.

How do you find a qualified landscape architect? Call any member of the American Society of Landscape Architects, listed in the Yellow Pages, and ask if his or her firm does home landscape jobs and if not, who does.

Ask what services are offered—consultation, design, installation; ask about the fee schedule. Ask for references from jobs similar to the one you need. If your requirements fit more closely the services of a landscape contractor, ask the same questions of that entrepreneur.

LANDSCAPE CONTRACTORS may also design landscapes, and install walks, walls, plantings, patios, or decks. Some limit their work to topsoil and lawn installation. Some sell and install shrubs and trees, and offer maintenance service.

Some advertise that they are "licensed, bonded, and insured." The license may be simply an Alaska business license. As with any independent contractor, it would be a prudent business procedure to ask to see the supporting documents defining the bond and insurance coverage. Inquire about training and experience under professional supervision in Alaska, or a similar environment. It is perfectly acceptable to ask for references and to see jobs they have done.

LANDSCAPE GARDENERS range from boys who mow lawns (better check laws about age requirements for operating power equipment) to individuals with graduate degrees in horticulture, to persons who have had experience in installation and/or maintenance.

They may charge on an hourly basis or have a flat rate for services. Some provide their own equipment, others use yours, in which case you should inquire of the Internal Revenue Service as to your payroll tax liability.

Weekly lawn service is a blessing to busy homeowners and folks with bad backs. If the contractor has not had some supervised experience and you are not qualified to evaluate his work, better go for one with references; lawn mowing is not as simple as it sounds.

ARBORISTS are shrub and tree specialists who meet the requirements of a professional organization and can give competent advice and service on shrub and tree problems.

To possess a piece of the wild is the dream that brings many people to the High North to live. More than any other urban people northern city

Untended woodlands fall victim to a "killer snow," a heavy, wet, early snowfall that finds deciduous trees with leaves still on them. They often bend down to touch the ground, never to stand tall again, or crack off in mid-trunk.

dwellers often live intimately with trees. Most people in these choice locations yearn to keep them wild, to savor the healing balm of the woodland, and then to pass it on as unspoiled as when

it first came into their trust. Yet bad things happen to spoil the private woodland.

Weeds, especially quack grass, get a toe-hold and crowd out desirable native plants, giving the woods a weedy, abandoned look. If it looks untenanted it is subject to forays by firewood hunters and tree diggers. Trash, junked cars and appliances get left there.

A diseased tree infects its neighbors and a precious windbreak is breached.

Adjacent land clearing takes its toll. The water table recedes, trees compete for moisture and none achieves anything like its destiny. It takes only a few inches of soil from a basement excavation spread over tree roots to kill a tree. It does not die at once but its slow death is painful to watch.

When trees reach their climax they are ready to go, leaving the sun and air and water to the young comers, but they often cling to life for years until the woodland is a dying forest of ancient trees and sparse, spindly young ones.

When young trees are too thick, they are too thin—crowded together struggling for survival. Thinning trees is no job for an amateur. If you want to do the work yourself, consultation with an arborist is a good learning experience. If you hire an arborist to do the job for you, he may cut the trunks into fireplace log lengths and feed the branches into a chipper that will give you a mountain of wood chips for paths, ground cover, and weed control mulch.

Trees need to go into the winter with plenty of moisture around their roots, no problem where late summer rains spoil many a camping trip, but the conifers' wide branches may leave their root zone bone dry. In the spring, when most trees get

The Brock Shambergs lined a sweeping driveway with conifers, good in summer or winter.

Right: Log pilings, suitable for Alaska, give a regional feeling in this seaside garden in Vancouver, B. C.

their new growth, they need fertilizing, and watering during our normally dry June. (See Chapter 5, Trees and Shrubs.)

LIGHTING, OUTDOOR. The rest of the country thought it was hilarious when a state where it doesn't get dark all summer, went on *double* daylight savings time. But the two-hour leap over the time zones gave the locals more time for fun in the sun.

Garden lighting struck Alaskans, who see no stars from late April into September, as something of a frill. But in the winter when the long darkness descended, and windows and glass doors became black rectangles, reflecting back the scene within, drawing a blank on what lies beyond, they had second thoughts.

You can shut out the blackness with blinds and draperies; or you can light up the darkness and share a curious, friendly scene: snow blowing horizontally across the patio, the shadow of a

shrub against a wall, hoarfrost transforming a twig. Splendid frosted trees, diamonds in the snow. Children skating on backyard rinks, familiar outdoor sculptures suddenly exotic, and big, lazy snowflakes nestling between the needles of a spruce.

Without exterior lighting, there are only the black rectangles. Residential and commercial landscapes that have their tiny white Christmas lights on into the winter months make Alaska's winter a wonderland.

Without entry light, delivery men and guests search for a house number, a driveway, a place to park, a front door. The ubiquitous porch light won't do it. Stairs, walks and pools should be lighted so that a visitor does not stumble blindly into injury. Departing guests should not grope their way to their cars in the dark lest they be divested of their car keys and valuables.

Light provides some residential security—intruders do not relish prowling about in the light. Homeowners feel safer if they can flood their surroundings with light. The mercilessly-revealing yard light, offered at a good rate by power utilities, is flat, harsh, detracting from rather than enhancing the landscape and its amenities. It's great for gas stations though.

Lighting experts like to hide the source of light. They find two floodlights on opposite sides of an area more than twice as good as one. Fixtures should be out of the way, but accessible for changing bulbs. In cities, the best help lies with landscape architects, and with engineering firms, some of which have a staff member who is a lighting specialist. Occasionally a lighting contractor has experience, talent, and an interest in outdoor lighting, but you should ask around because not every electrician has an understanding of this kind of lighting.

If you live beyond the reach of professional help, turn to books about home landscaping—most have a chapter on exterior lighting. An excellent do-it-yourself guide is Ortho Books' *How to Design and Install Outdoor Lighting* (sold in garden centers, book stores, or from Ortho Books, 575 Market Street, San Francisco, CA 941050).

You can experiment with an extension cord and a utility bulb, to see what shadows will do for the night. Twelve volt systems are safer than 110, and cheaper to use. Most electricians can handle their installation.

Squirrel litter from spruce cones makes an effective path cover in a wild garden.

Alaskans keep finding new ways to enjoy the North with landscapes better suited to northern living.

Entry terraces and circle driveways reduce yard maintenance and ease winter access. Outdoor carpeting replaces ice on steps. Tennis courts, backyard skating rinks, and garden ponds take ground out of cultivation on large properties and some innovative homeowners haul in truckloads of Alaska's plentiful, water-worn rocks to create dry stream beds that are virtually maintenance-free.

Alaska is a young country at the top of the world. Alaskans can afford to flaunt tradition and be innovative. We can find ways to collect solar heat and store it in solar mass. We can learn to light up the winter. In a state one-fifth the size of the Lower 48, we can grow what grows best where we live, and re-invent the northern landscape.

CHAPTER 4

LAWNS AND GROUND COVERS

LAWNS, once the minimum standard for residential respectability, are getting closer scrutiny. Middle class neighborhoods' neat lawns and the great greenswards on the estates of the landed gentry are raising serious environmental questions. Lawns' wasteful ways with water and their pollution from nitrogen fertilizers, herbicides and fungicides have called for a second, less approving look at them. That they are equally wasteful of human time and energy is gaining support from their caregivers.

But a lawn is still a handsome frame for a house or a flower border. Grass makes pleasant paths between borders and island beds, and places where foot traffic is required. It relieves the austerity of paved areas, and is hard to beat as a clean play space. Few home owners can forego some grassy areas.

With a fresh look at alternative ground covers for special purposes, lawn areas can be reduced. By careful monitoring of watering and fertilizing practices, their faults are more tolerable .

If the prospect of putting in a lawn does not appeal to you, welcome to a large, vocal majority. It is not a coincidence that lawn rhymes with yawn. If you live in a city, you may not have to put in your own lawn — landscape contractors offer sodding, seeding, and hydroseeding services. If you have a cash flow problem or live in the boonies, here's the deal:

Before **you buy topsoil**, eyeball the soil the Ice Age, or the contractor, left you. Subsoil got a bad name when people called it clay, which it most likely is not. It is simply soil lacking in organic matter. Alaska's soils are young, infertile, recently born of the Ice Age, but very responsive to generous additions of organic matter from peatmoss, animal manures or compost.

Some areas in Alaska have virtually no soil to start with, but like many other such places, they may have abundant coarse sand and peatmoss (the brown, fibrous stuff not be confused with the black peat muck of the muskeg swamps which has no useful place in the garden). Coarse sand and peatmoss make a good soilless growing mix when enriched with a balanced fertilizer (8-32-16 or 16-16-16 or 10-20-10 would be good choices) with lime added, if needed, to bring the acidity of the peatmoss up to a near-neutral on the pH scale. This scale from 0 to 14 is used to indicate acidity or alkalinity on which 7 is neutral with lower numbers indicating acidity and higher numbers alkalinity. Most plants that thrive in Alaska do well in slightly acid soils.

Ask your nearest Cooperative Extension Service to send you a copy of *Establishing a Lawn*. It is by no means racy reading, but there's not much of it and it can save you frustration and expense. We hope you do this in the tawny fall of the year when the September sun is warm on your head and the honkers make big V's in the blue skies over Alaska. Because that's a good day to pick up a modestly priced soil test kit with instructions for taking a valid sample, and you will have made an astute investment. We say fall, because if your soil needs lime, it is best applied then because it takes its own sweet time to work.

Go home and install strips of cedar two-by-fours, or plastic edging around flower beds, shrub borders, and trees for the mower wheel to run on. Unless you get a real charge out of hand edging, a hands and knees shears-type job, resist the temptation to use the free water-worn rocks that came with the place. (See GROUND COVERS, for what to put inside these strips.)

When you shop for grass seed, it should be a mix of Kentucky bluegrasses known to be hardy in Alaska, like 'Park,' 'Merion,' or 'Nugget.' You will no doubt observe that 'Common' bluegrass is considerably cheaper than 'Nugget.' If budgetary limitations make it necessary, sow half 'Common' and half 'Nugget,' and in a couple of years 'Nugget' will have taken over, because it's just a great grass for Alaska.

Grass doesn't grow very well in the shade, but in dappled shade red fescue is better than bluegrass; 'Arctared' and 'Boreal' are good bets. Maybe you should mix bluegrass and red fescue 50-50, depending on the amount of shade. **Grass seed won't germinate if it dries out** and the lot of the hose holder is a tedious one because bluegrass takes 22 days to germinate. A mulch helps preserve moisture, but straw is loaded with weed seeds, and nobody has enough burlap or floating rowcover to blanket a lawn. That leaves clear polyethylene, which has to be removed the minute the grass germinates or the tender seedlings will fry.

While you're at it, ask for the CES fact sheet *Lawn Maintenance*, because you're going to need it when the grass is up and ready to mow. We don't like to deal in dire warnings, but a lawn may be attacked by weeds, disease, winter damage, snow mold, soil compaction, moisture stress, and nutrient deficiency. Choose your weapons with care.

Should you remove lawn clippings or leave them on the lawn? If you mow often enough so that you clip only a third of the blades, they can and should be left on the grass. In a day or so they will have dried up to little nothings. If you can't mow often enough, better rake the take and spread the clippings somewhere in the sun to dry before putting them on the compost pile (where they smell to high heaven if wet). Some mowers are sold as mulching mowers because they pulverize the clippings for you.

Increasingly useful are such power tools as garden vacuums and convertible blower-vacuums. Dealers are listed under 'Lawn Mowers' in the Yellow Pages, but tool rental companies and landscape services may be good for an occasional seasonal need. "Lawn service" is regarded by many home owners as the greatest thing since the discovery of grass.

Power tools that will clean up a paved patio or driveway, and remove grass clippings and autumn leaves from lawns, are great labor savers and are available from rental services in cities. Power weed-eaters are a boon on large properties which may have areas where native grasses on the periphery of cultivated areas scatter unwanted seeds. Small, electric and plug-in types are sold for home gardeners, but commercial services have more powerful ones that make short work of jobs the home models can't cut. An annual assault on wild grasses or mature fireweed can be effective if done before they go to seed.

Spread thinly on the garden as a mulch, grass clippings return some of the nutrients they have been fed, plus organic matter, to the soil, besides retarding weed growth and moisture loss. To dispatch them to the landfill is wanton waste, and increasingly, landfills are refusing to accept bagged lawn waste. Dry leaves that are bagged can be layered with fresh lawn clippings and make quick compost. (By quick we have in mind something like two years). If you limit the stuff to dried grass clippings and birch leaves, turn it frequently and keep it covered with clear plastic, it will do it faster. Even if it isn't finished compost; this organic matter tilled into compacted or exhausted soils works wonders.

Alaska is relatively free of lawn diseases, but there are a few that you may rather not have. Take **snow mold**. It is caused by a cold-tolerant fungus disease complex that thrives on excess moisture. Diseased spots may range from a few inches (usually blamed, in a miscarriage of justice, on the neighbor's dog) to several feet. Snow mold is no killer, so don't panic. If it continues to plague you, a treatment with a fungicide labeled for snow mold is helpful but need not be used if yours is in the first offense class. A filmy coat of snow mold may disperse on the first sunny day.

Fairy Ring sounds sweet, but isn't. It is the dark green circle that appears mysteriously in otherwise healthy lawns. It is succulent growth stimulated by a fungus that feeds on decaying organic matter, like nearby rotting lumber. Treatment is controversial. Some plant pathologists recommend using a broad-sprectrum fungicide.

A recent treatment is liming the entire lawn with dolomite limestone, followed by close mowing and an application of copper sulfate or iron sulfate drench to the ringed areas. Tinkering with soil pH can be tricky. Better check out a soil sample with the nearest Extension agent. Rarely do fairy rings occur in well-tended lawns.

A common fertilizing program is three to four pounds of nitrogen per one thousand square feet of lawn per season, applied in two installments. To decrease fertilizer runoff into the water table, gardeners might apply less fertilizer less frequently and be satisfied with less green, and maybe an occasional fairy ring.

GROUND COVERS are not a lazy gardener's substitute for grass. Ground cover plants must be set out individually, fertilized, watered and groomed like most perennials. Their care, however, is more fun than the mind-numbing tasks of lawn care. The test of their usefulness should never be that they can be walked on or mown; they can't, save for a bit of tennis-shoe traffic on well-placed stepping stones or log rounds.

There are places where grass will not grow well—at the base of trees, on banks too steep to mow, on trampled parking strips, and under roof eaves. There are plants that make better ground covers in such places. They conserve water, act as a living mulch, and they mask dying bulb foliage.

Neither should ground cover plants be considered as last-ditch solutions to problems. They have aesthetic credentials of their own, which grass must concede: contrasting forms, textures and colors, and sometimes flowers.

Grousing about the lack of ground covers for the High North is almost as popular among gardeners as castigating quack grass. Garden centers rarely offer the best ground covers for Alaska, which are native species. If a market existed they would use their off-season greenhouses to propagate them. Among the best for cultivation are:

Aleutian speedwell, *Veronica grandiflora*, grows wild on the Chain and lives it up in good garden soil from Southcentral to Ketchikan. Its small, dense leaves make a splendid ground cover and the little blue-purple flowers are a bonus. It is now propagated by getting a start from somebody, and before long you will be looking for takers, on a U-dig basis.

Arctic willow, *Salix arctica*, makes dense mats and is hardy in Zone l, moving with all the speed of an advancing glacier. **Netted willow**, *Salix reticulata*, is a ground-hugging plant that would make a slow-growing ground cover. Neither is commercially available at this writing. There are several other prostrate native willows that would make serviceable and often handsome woody ground covers, but they have to be collected and propagated by gardeners, and they are slow spreaders.

Bergenia, Bergenia crassifolia, and **B. cordifolia**, often called saxifrage, are bold, evergreen plants that make a dense cover. They have lavender flowers in early summer with leaves that may turn scarlet in fall. They may look tacky after a hard winter of little snow cover. Moose will forage for their succulent leaves and roots. Good for sun or shade, you can grow them from seed or divisions.

Snow-in-summer, *Cerastium tomentosum*, is silver-gray with small white flowers. It comes easily from seed sown indoors six weeks before planting out. It would be effective among rocks or along the top of a retaining wall, but probably not in a wide expanse because it looks ratty in the spring. It is hardy to Zone 2.

Creeping buttercup, *Ranunculus repens*, is a tough, pretty cover that is a rampant invader in milder climates, but responds to guidance here — like being planted between a concrete basement wall and a sidewalk, or on a bank where it can do what it does best — cover the ground.

Creeping phlox, *Phlox subulata*, is a splendid cover for a bank in full sun. Flowers tend toward loud pinks and magentas, but the whites and clear, light blues are delightful. Propagate by division or buy starter plants from a nursery.

Dwarf Dogwood, *Cornus canadensis*, is one of our best native ground covers, but commercial sources are rare. Nursery-grown seedlings are sold at Dinkel's Fairview Nursery in Wasilla. Most

A casual mix of dwarf dogwood, violets, forget-me-nots, starflower, chocolate lilies, and wild geranium is a good choice for sun or shade.

commercial offerings have been collected in the wild. Divisions imported from nurseries at lower latitudes are not reliably hardy in the high north. A handout from a friend, treated well, will spread and provide divisions. If you are lucky enough to have dwarf dogwood growing elsewhere on your property, it can be transplanted. Take the plants in spring, and dig them to a spade's depth. because this may be one that requires a special soil-borne fungus relationship.

Goutweed, *Aegopodium podagraria*, an invasive weed in milder climates, makes a dense, reliably hardy cover in sun or shade where it chokes out undesirable weeds and presents a handsome variegated leaf. It is propagated by division.

Ground Ivy, *Glechoma hederacea*, is a handsome ground cover, especially in shade or filtered sun; it is invasive in milder climates, and it will invade a shady lawn and adjacent plantings in Alaska, but it is one of our best ground covers for shady areas.

Kinnikinnick, *Arctostaphylos uva-ursi.* For such a tough customer, it is surprisingly difficult to transplant, and is not easy to establish. Imported plants are expensive and often not hardy if they were grown at lower latitudes with shorter day-lengths. It should be propagated and sold in Alaska nurseries.

Lamium, *L. maculatum*, is hardy to Zone 3 and useful for small places. It is evergreen and hardy to Zone 4. Nurseries that ship plants require expensive special handling for Alaska. Local nurseries specializing in alpines may offer starter plants at affordable prices. Your best bargain may be over the back fence from a big-hearted neighbor.

Lily-of-the-valley, *Convallaria majalis,* makes a dense groundcover, even in shade. Its brief bloom is lovely and fragrant. Propagate by division or buy "pips."

Nagoonberry, *Rubus arcticus*, is an attractive creeping vine with deep rose flowers. It is aggressive enough to make a satisfactory ground cover and the Plant Materials Center near Palmer is testing promising selections. One named 'Kenai Carpet' has been released for commercial production. It spreads by rhizomes and competes with the surrounding vegetation.

Potentilla species, some of which are native to Alaska should be experimented with. *P. tridentata*, is excellent in our Zone 4 garden and *P. verna* thrives on the east side of the Anchorage municipal greenhouse. Walt Mayr's Nursery at Mile 58 of the Glenn Highway near Sutton offers nursery-grown seedlings of *P. fragiformis*.

Pussy Toes, *Antennaria rosea*, is a flat, rosette-forming, gray-leafed cover that can be contained by mowing once, before the pink flowers on six-inch stems go to seed. Look for it in nurseries that specialize in wildflowers.

Strawberries, especially the Sitka Hybrids, which are often called simply Alaska strawberries, are a pale salmon color. They are so bent on runner production that they make a better ground cover than a berry-producer. Planted on l0-inch centers, they will take over in a single season, producing blossoms in spring, and some berries in summer.

For a dense leafy cover, give strawberries lawn fertilizer; for more and bigger berries, feed them 16-16-16.

The native strawberry, *Fragaria viginiana*, which grows wild over most of Alaska, makes a delightful ground cover, but it is a slow grower and there are no commercial sources.

There is a barren, or fruitless, strawberry that is useful as ground cover to Zone 4. It is *Waldsteinia fragarioides*, listed by Milaeger's Gardens.

Trailing Black Currant, *Ribes laxiflorum*, is a luxuriant native vine that will crawl when there is nothing to climb. It is a beautiful vine.

A mix of plant species makes a charming and practical ground cover. If one species gets wiped out, the whole cover isn't in disarray. Good subjects for this purpose would be snow-in-summer, arabis, forget-me-nots, and a yellow-flowered sedum, all sold in garden centers and all easy to grow from seed. One of our most successful ground covers in partial shade is a mix of oak fern, starflower, false Solomon's seal, Aleutian speedwell, and dwarf Jacob's ladder, all Alaska natives, all easy to grow.

Tundra cover, the thick mat of mosses, lichens, prostrate shrubs, tree seedlings and little wild plants that overlay undisturbed places, often muskeg swamps, is called "overburden" by contractors who bulldoze it off construction sites. Chunks of it can be had for hauling home. Piece it together to make a carpet over ground prepared as for a lawn. Watered until it is established, it will take hold and defy weed competition. If taken from an area where birch and spruce are dominant species, you will get a miniature forest—a

great bargain; if it comes up mostly alder and willow, it's a real swindle.

Wildflower Ground Covers, and **"Meadow Mixes"** work best where soil temperatures permit germination early in the season. For summerlong bloom in Alaska, most flowers need four to six weeks' headstart indoors.

In Alaska, early summer temperatures are cool and favor weed germination. Success with a meadow garden may involve tilling the plot as early as possible and permitting existing weed seeds to germinate. They can then be eliminated by a cover of black plastic or carpeting scrap, a process you may need to repeat a second or third time. As a last resort an application of glyphosate

Forget-me-nots, Myosotis alpestris, *are a lovely sight in early summer. Biennials, their seeds insures good coverage the next year. They come in pink and white as well as the familiar true blue.*

('Roundup'™ or 'Cleanup'™) would eliminate weeds and permit planting in about two weeks.

When the meadow mix is then sown, it will need to be watered and fertilized until it is well established. The first summer the annuals should produce a successful "wild" garden of few, if any, truly wild flowers, with a casual, meadow look. The following year the surviving perennials

A mix formulated by the Alaska Plant Materials Center near Palmer produced this meadow: baby's breath (white, pink, and red), candytuft, cornflower (pink and 'Snowman'), red flax, California poppy, Shirley poppies (single and double), baby snapdragon, and Siberian wallflower (the latter did less well).

should bloom and the annuals that went to seed should reappear. In the meantime, introduced weeds and native weeds that have lain dormant in the soil or been sown by wind or birds will need removing.

Meadow mixes are not maintenance-free plantings but are useful for sunny roadside banks and for real meadows, of which there are many on large residential properties. Commercial mixes may contain perennial species that are not hardy in Alaska or annuals that may not be suitable for our cool temperatures and short growing season. Some mixes include yarrow, a common weed here, or grass or clover which are natural components of a meadow but can take over in cultivation. Some may contain wildflower seeds listed by the Soil Conservation Service as noxious weeds

and are restricted in some states. At best "wild-flower mixes" are inexpensive seeds of cultivars, like bachelor buttons and annual poppies. It pays to read the ingredient labels, although they may list some as "others."

Most companies offer mixes for various climates; select one for the northern Midwest states like Michigan, Minnesota, and North Dakota or one formulated for Alaska.

Be prepared to re-seed in spring, for some plants may not ripen seed in our short summer and will fail to re-up. Many meadow gardeners report that, without infusions of new plants, their "wild" gardens gradually die out as weeds take over.

These Alaskan natives would make good additions to a meadow mix because they tend to self-seed and some are reliable perennials: the wild Portage Glacier pink poppy, *Papaver alboroseum*, ox-eye daisy, violets, chocolate lilies, shooting stars, wild iris, fireweed, wild geranium, pussy toes, chive, monkey flower, alpine lychnis, forget-me-nots, wild roses, johnny-jump-ups, annual poppies, and arabis. All will be more successful if jump-started indoors and set out in a random pattern when the weather warms up.

Coniferous ground covers include junipers, and the dwarf mugho pine. The junipers do well with a cover of rock chips and the pines thrive above a bark cover. To keep the pines low, pinch out their "candles" in early summer. Nurseries offer a good selection of choice varieties of conifers known to be hardy in Alaska. (See SHRUBS, Chapter 5.)

Native grasses make good covers on banks of streams and garden ponds. Several are both ornamental and durable.

Seeds or plant divisions of these grasses are not currently marketed, but could be collected in areas where growing conditions resemble those of your own.

Inert ground covers are sold in garden centers, but rural Alaskans have access to some rich resources that have the advantage of being free. **"Squirrel litter,"** the spruce cone flakes squirrels deposit under spruce trees when they take the cones apart to get at the seeds, works well in paths, under shrubs, and in wild gardens. Flat, **polished pebbles** wash up on some beaches, and

they make attractive rock covers, as does pumice, plentiful along shores out to the Westward. **Crushed shells** from cannery waste can be used where foot traffic is not desired. Water worn rocks keep traffic at bay and look nice if weeds are eliminated periodically.

PATHS. A fairly wide garden needs access for weeding, moving plants, harvesting, and for the daily Grand Tour, whether it be a solitary stroll or a conducted guest walk. If there is no path, a gardener will find a way, but tramping on soil damages its structure, breaks feeder roots, and compacts soil so that it is cold and vulnerable to puddling and thereafter, glaciering. If the garden is too narrow for a path, you may get by with a few well-placed stepping stones or log rounds to reach the farthest plants without compacting the soil.

There is, unhappily, no perfect path-making material. But there are some very good ones:

Grass would be our first choice for garden paths in town settings. Now that spacious lawns are coming into disfavor for their tedious maintenance, water waste, and leaching of fertilizers into the water table, conscientious gardeners are doing the unthinkable: they are carving up large lawns to create beds for flowers, herb gardens or vegetable plots, leaving grassy paths between boxed-in raised or mounded beds. Well-tended grass paths are the most beautiful and comfortable of all for walking; mowing the weeds may be an acceptable substitute in a vegetable garden.

Such paths have to be mowed, so make them in

When the tulips fade, a dense cover of false Solomon's seal, Smilacena stellata, *keeps weeds at bay.*

lawnmower widths. Grass can be expected to invade adjacent beds. Attachments to lightweight tillers make this edging an easy annual task, but if you don't have one of these versatile power tools, hand edging won't kill you. Grass paths may also show traffic wear and are not weed-free. They require water, but only a fraction of that needed for a whole lawn.

If your beds are free-form ones, lay them out with rubber garden hose (plastic hoses are too stiff), marking the outline with a dusting of agricultural lime, then get on the business end of an edging tool.

Shredded bark or **wood chips** are within the budget of the numerous gardeners who have turned to composting and have a chipping attachment for their compost shredder. If a power line runs through your property, maintenance crews will leave you your wood chips if you point to a place their chipper can back up to; the same goes for tree service companies. This would be a first choice for a woodland garden, where grass grows poorly, and artificial materials are a jarring note. If you have to buy wood chips or shredded bark, the cost is daunting if the path is long.

Laying old **carpet strips, black plastic**, or one of the **commercially manufactured mats** is effective, but they require covering with wood chips or fine bark. As the wood degrades, plants will volunteer there.

Log rounds make attractive natural paths. They need to be treated with copper napthanate to prevent early decay, but in time they too will crumble. Big logs (about 16 inches in diameter) work best for solid footing; spruce and birch seem equally well-suited. Four-inch slices are none too thick for paths; steps need 10 to 12 inchers securely buried; a wobbly step is a short step to a plaster cast. Weeds will grow between log rounds and they will have to be hand pulled or treated with an herbicide.

Crab and **clam** shell wastes, **sawdust, pebbles, spruce cone flakes, and beach-harvested pumice** are used in innovative ways by remote gardeners. None is comfortable to walk on and needs to be underlain with matting or black plastic to retard weeds.

Asphalt and concrete are expensive and too permanent for an evolving garden. **Gravel** is attractive but it is not comfortable for walking in dress shoes, and is difficult for handicapped access. Garden centers in the larger towns and building supply companies sell **stepping stones** and **pavers** that are attractive and can be laid by first-time landscapers. Some areas have flat, **water-worn rocks** that make splendid natural stepping stones.

If the space between pavers is small, like an inch, seedlings may volunteer and make neat mounds with their roots forced to go deep for moisture and nutrients, a charming walkway. If the space is large, like several inches, ground cover will be needed to reduce weeding between the pavers, and most plants aggressive enough to qualify as ground covers will invade neighboring areas.

Cracked concrete, often available from landfills and construction sites, makes good stepping stones. If you're buying readymix concrete for sidewalks, driveway, or a patio, you can salvage the leftover mix if you have forms ready. Buckets will make round ones and ham-handed home craftsmen can throw together scrap lumber for square or rectangular ones. If all this seems like too much trouble, pavers sold by building supply companies are easy to lay and nice to look at.

A few generalities about paths are in order. No path should come to a dead-end, nor should it be so narrow that two people cannot walk it together. Straight paths are businesslike ways to get there from here, but a gently curving path lets the viewer discover the garden, rather than having the whole spread laid out before him.

A path should be level so that you aren't puffing at the terminus. If the grade is steep, steps and a bench or a flat rock at seat-height may be needed. Over-hanging plants should be pruned so that the hapless visitor doesn't find that his hat, his glasses—or his hairpiece—is snatched. Plants that encroach upon a path at ground level should be pruned, or transplanted elsewhere.

CHAPTER 5

SHRUBS AND TREES

Shrubs and trees are long term investments. Their selection should be made with the same concern for consequences that you might reserve for, say, getting a tattoo.

Buying a tree when you really need a shrub is the most common of all costly investments. Spruce trees that were nice little inverted ice cream cones when they flanked the sunny front steps grow up to defy mail carrier, deliveryman, and guest. There are south-facing windows around town, big ones, totally shaded all winter by little trees planted too close to the house that grew up to be big ones. Their roots can undermine the foundation and trunks can cave the roof in after a snowstorm.

A row of native spruces along your windward boundary can offer up to a 25% saving in heating cost, say agricultural engineers at the Universities of North and South Dakota, who are intimately acquainted with the winds that sweep across frigid prairies. If you chose a location for your castle in a spot famed for its winter winds, a shelter belt of spruce on three sides will save a whopping 40% of heat loss and trap the winter sun in your kitchen. If you plant a hedge, or build a fence at the **bottom** of a south-facing slope, you trap the cold air .

Buying plants that are not known to be hardy in your Zone can be a budget buster. (It is, however, an avocation of many gardeners.) The U.S. Department of Agriculture and the American Horticultural Society once established hardiness zones for plants, and gardeners found plenty to quibble with them. Recently a new Hardiness Zone map was published that takes into consideration local climatic conditions such as hours of possible sunlight, prevailing wind patterns, precipitation, and elevation.

Local micro-climates are a big deal in Alaska, where 50 feet of elevation makes a difference. In Anchorage, the prevailing winter wind pours down the Chugach Mountains like a waterfall, and low areas off Muldoon Road dip into Zone 2 every few years with anguished moans heard all over town; Downtown, Bootlegger's Cove and Government Hill can be snug in Zone 4 and the South side of the Performing Arts Center smug in Zone 5.

In Fairbanks, the opposite is true. The warm micro-climates are in the high places and downtown temps make the chilling morning newscasts. In Palmer thermometers register warmer temperatures when the Matanuska wind blows than when the air is still, but a place where the snow cover is scoured off by this infamous wind is somebody's little private Antarctica.

Actual hardiness depends on more than temperature comparisons. "It's hardy in North Dakota" doesn't translate to "It should be hardy here." There are a good many places in the South 48 that have lower mean winter temperatures than Southcentral. But they don't have our long late summer days, so not all woody plants get the message that winter is coming. They do not commence in a timely manner the complex process of getting ready for winter.

We dismiss their problem as "winterkill," when the bummer was the summer. Plant dormancy happens in two stages. The first is triggered by declining temperatures that cause the plant to harden; to toughen up for what's ahead. The second stage kicks in on day length, and its exact point varies between species. Some aren't concerned about day length; to others, it is a life and death matter.

Acclimatization takes longer than we once

thought; some woodies need maybe three winters before they're here to stay (the same goes for people).

Moisture stress is a killer. In most of Alaska we have adequate late summer rain, but some years deep watering is needed around conifers to send them into winter with plenty of moisture around their roots. Drying winter winds may call for an anti-dessicant foliage spray to reduce dehydration. A burlap-wrapped cage around a young tree or shrub may make the difference; a clear plastic wrap may be its death sentence. Burlap is not easily come by, but the heat buildup on a sunny day under clear poly can thaw sap that freezes at night and ruptures the capillaries.

A warm Chinook-like wind called a williwaw puts woody plants under stress with its freeze-thaw cycle and the glaciering of puddles around crowns and tree roots. An organic mulch helps keep soil cold until the false breakup is past and spring is really on the way. The sourdoughs had it right: "one williwaw don't make a breakup."

If a shrub or tree that is supposed to be hardy fails to survive, don't give up; next year may be different.

Some Alaska nurseries buy bare root stock in the spring when it can be dug in distant nurseries, sell it at bargain prices and you can pot it up and keep it in your greenhouse until you can dig a hole, preferably before the plant has leafed out. If it has leafed out, treat it like shrubs that have been growing in containers which can be planted as soon as frost no longer lurks in the wings and it has been hardened off. Spring is the preferred planting time for imports; native woodies can be transplanted in the fall if you're on to the 40-degree factor.

Cornell University horticulturists discovered that the last safe planting date is four weeks before soil temperatures fall to the 40-degree point, when root development grinds to a halt. For wanabees—marginally hardy and hard-to-transplant stuff, the date should be earlier. A soil thermometer is not a frivolous expenditure.

Time was when we believed that the planting hole should be amended with good stuff like manure, compost, peatmoss and fertilizer. No more. Nurserymen find that this coddling is not the best way to go. Just dig a hole. Dig it to the depth the plant was growing, but forget the frills about enriching the soil.

Instead make the hole wider, *not deeper*. The roots grow close to the warm surface of the soil, not deep into the cold ground, and they spread out far beyond the mythical "drip line," where the good stuff is needed.

Learning new ways does not come easily to gardeners—after decades of evidence to the contrary some are still planting by the moon. Another pious practice has fallen to scientific proof: the guying of newly planted trees. A young tree standing alone with its top free to move may become a strong tree, better able to withstand the elements, says a University of California researcher. "Many trees do not need and should not have support stakes. Trees having tops that are large in proportion to their roots may be an exception, although many can stand alone with some thinning of branches in the crown." We would add to that caution young woodies planted in areas of notorious fall and winter winds.

The two winters of 1991-92 saw early, heavy, wet snowfalls that took many of Alaska's beautiful white paper birches which have a life expectancy of about 80 years. Some died before their time.

Birches are great self-seeders. They grow too thick for the available moisture and sunlight , and they should be thinned when they are very young, lest the friendly support of their neighbors leaves them bereft of protection. When they are very tall and thin their leafy branches are on their tops and cave in under a heavy snow load, their trunks cracking off at mid-height. When they have reached climax and stand like tribal elders, their fall gives young comers a place in the sun.

Mid-March is a hard time for trees. The sun at Anchorage is 29 degrees above the horizon, almost a third of the way to the top of the sky. A stretch of warm, sunny days thaws sap that on freezing nights ruptures the capillaries. Black-barked and thin-barked trees are vulnerable.

People give trees a hard time. During home construction or remodeling, soil gets scraped off root zones, or heaped on top of them. Four inches' change in soil level can kill a tree, but death comes slowly, puzzling the owner who tries to save trees on a wooded lot he paid a premium price for.

The best guide to transplanting shrubs and trees is a neat fact sheet, *Transplanting Trees Successfully*, free from any CES agent.

PRUNING TREES AND SHRUBS. Harvard's Arnold Arboretum head pruner, Jim Nickerson, had some salty advice for readers of Horticulture Magazine more than a decade ago. Pruning in the spring encourages growth; pruning in the fall inhibits growth. Prune flowering deciduous

Pat Leary, Grounds Supervisor at the University of Alaska Anchorage, corrects moose-pruning in late winter. Photo: Sherrie Kincaid

woodies *after* they flower. Always remove fading blooms from flowering shrubs.

Prune deciduous shrubs every year? How much? Up to one-third every year, says Nickerson. Rejuvenate an old but healthy shrub by cutting it to the ground in the early spring. If it doesn't work, don't grieve. Start over. Don't allow dead, damaged or diseased material to remain on a shrub or tree.

To shorten a branch, clip to just above a bud; clip to an outside bud if new growth is desired, an inside bud for the reverse. Thin a deciduous shrub; don't shear it.

Landscaping for birds. Roger Tory Peterson had it right. "A garden without birds is as sterile as a pond without fish." How do you measure the song of the myrtle warbler, the flash of a pine grosbeak zeroing in on a highbush cranberry, the breathless descent of a flight of waxwings onto a mountain ash heavy with red berries?

To be practical, you might start with the statistics that 80 to 100 percent of the diet of some species for six months of the year is insects; that even the voracious seed feeders supplement their diet with insects to the tune of 40 percent. No one need begrudge them their treats of cutworms, aphids, scale insects, and an occasional pig-out on leaf rollers.

The late Margaret Heller, resident bird authority, said that to attract birds to your garden you have to give them a place on its perimeter to reconnoiter. A lilac bush or a cotoneaster hedge makes for good hiding while the birds assess the lay of the land and stake out bugs and weed seeds. Provide several shrubs or trees with nutritious seeds—like hardy roses, serviceberries, chokecherries, a Mayday tree, a crabapple. Or prop up a wind-fallen branch in the snow near your bird feeder for the birds' lookout post.

The Alaska Department of Fish and Game has a good brochure, *Landscaping for Wildlife in Alaska*, that offers six steps to make Alaska's urban communities alive with beauty, movement, and song, with instructions for making your own property a wildlife sanctuary.

Let the birds clean up the garden weed seeds

in the fall before you offer sunflower seed and peanut butter. After snow has covered the ground, provide sunflower seeds for the chickadees, thistle seeds for the little fellows, suet for hefty eaters.

If traffic is heavy at your sunflower feeder, you may have observed that grass and other plants do not thrive beneath it. Sunflower seeds are allopathic, containing a substance that is toxic to plants, but not to birds. The toxin leaches out into grass and other planted areas. Hulls should probably not be added to the compost pile. You might find a spot for the feeder where there are weeds to which you would like to deliver a low blow.

Smaller seed mixtures attract pine siskins, redpolls, and grosbeaks who do not disdain them but would thank you for some black thistle seeds (we toast ours in the oven for a few minutes to kill any that might take root in our garden). In cold weather a glob of crunchy-type peanut butter and a hunk of suet helps keep body and soul together. A pan of thawed water and a dish of coarse sand to cleanse the palate are much appreciated.

In early summer when mosquitoes are troublesome, there may be great flights of swallows. If you are not landlord to swallows it may be that you cannot provide enough mosquitoes to feed their young, so they move on. Or maybe you put the houses too close together. They don't like to be too neighborly, like closer than 15 feet.

The list that follows is a compilation from the Alaska Horticultural Association, the University of Alaska Anchorage, the Municipality of Anchorage and the aforementioned publications.

EVERGREEN SHRUBS

Evergreen shrubs that are widely adapted to Alaska's austere landscape do not strain the memory. **Arborvitae,** *Thuja species* , make attractive specimen plants in Zone 3 and will make a low hedge in protected locations near a house wall.

Cedars are hardy only in a scrap of land near Ketchikan. The shrubby "cedars" seen around towns in Southcentral, are not cedars. Some are False Cypress, and some are Juniper. They may look like cedars, smell like cedars, and may be called Alaska Red Cedar , but cedars they are not.

There are a couple of dwarf **False Cypresses,** *Chamcyparis* species that are hardy to Zone 4, nice slow-growing conifers that double for cedars. Dwarf Lawson Cypress and Hinoki Cypress are two-footers that do well in Southeastern and Southern Alaska and in protected locations in Southcentral.

The low-growing **Junipers** are useful as ground covers and are described in Chapter 4; the taller kinds are listed as trees in this chapter. **Savin Juniper,** a two-footer, suffers some die-back if snow cover is lacking in Zone 3. **Bird's Nest Spruce,** *Picea abies nidiformis,* is good to Zone 3 and its slow-growing habit makes it desirable for a large alpine garden or shrub border.

The **Dwarf Mugo Pine,** *Pinus Mugho pumilio,* is widely used in Zone 3 for ground cover, but it suffers some foliage burn in windswept locations. Like all the pines, it must be "candled" faithfully to keep it dwarfed. If you want it really dwarf, cut the candles back all the way; if you like some slow growth, cut them back half way.

The taller Mugo Pine, *Pinus mugho mugus,* gets about eight feet tall, but takes its time.

Rhododendrons as outdoor shrubs have challenged Alaska gardeners for many years, and some progress has been made. Some have survived for several years, but those years were in a moderately warming climatic trend. They do better, sometimes stunningly, in Southeastern and on the southern coast.

Much work is being done in breeding rhodies with greater winter hardiness. The 'Lights' series developed at the University of Minnesota is reported to be hardy to -40 degrees. With more than 800 rhododendron species now known, it stretches the credulity if none is adaptable to Alaska's summer day length and winter temperature.

The Rhododendron Species Foundation has 10,000 plants representing 475 species, the largest collection in the U.S. on its 24-acre spread 10 miles northeast of Tacoma, Washington, on the grounds of the Weyerhaeuser Company corporate headquarters. It is open to visitors.

Alaska's native rhododendrons are collectors' treasures, but not easy to acquire. Sitka is lovely in the spring with its display of Kamchatka rhododendron, *Rhododendron camtschaticum,* an undocumented hitchhiker from the Kamchatka Peninsula which has settled there. The **Alpine azalea,** *Loiseleuria procumbens,* is prized by rock gardeners. **Lapland rosebay,** *Rhododendron lapponicum,* grows wild over much of Alaska and is a good low-growing shrub.

The widespread acceptance of sunrooms has opened new opportunities for rhododendrons as indoor-outdoor plants. Nurserymen import container-grown specimens from the Pacific Northwest, where they reach perfection. These are gorgeous plants for patios and decks, relishing our cool, moist summers, then retiring to the sunroom or commercial greenhouse storage for a frost-free winter.

DECIDUOUS, LEAF-LOSING, SHRUBS

These sturdy shrubs don't just stand there. Most make flowers, autumnal fruits, or at least canes that are colorful against the snow.

The **Dwarf Arctic Birch,** *Betula pendula,* is a low-growing birch at home in a wild garden.

Cotoneaster is one of our most stalwart shrubs. Iron hardy, red of leaf in the fall, and accommodating about growing in a container or in a hedge, clipped or left to its natural fountaining form, it is probably our best and most versatile shrub. Its blue berries bring birds in for a feast, and there are red-berried kinds. Sadly, the good, ground-covering kinds like C. *horizontalis* and C. *microphyllus* are not reliably hardy in Zone 3.

Currants offer some interesting possibilities. The **Alpine currant,** *Ribes alpinum,* is a great little shrub for Zone 2 and up. It flares with ruddy autumnal color. We give it high marks as a low-growing shrub that does its stuff in fall when the garden is giving up the fight. Neither do we upstage a food crop that makes an acceptable ornamental: the **Black currant,** *Ribes nigrum* 'Swede's

Black,' is a good one. And we like the native **Trailing Black Currant,** *Ribes laxiflorum,* a fine ground cover. Too bad you can't buy it—register your complaint with your garden center if it has propagation capability it isn't using. The **Yellow Flowering Clove Currant,** *Ribes odoratum,* has been successful in Anchorage Municipality plantings. We have seen a great planting of a single common garden currant, var. 'Red Lake,' which was a handsome shrubby groundcover, and yielded fifty pounds of currants each year. Don't miss these off-beat food crops' ornamental possibilities.

Dogwood means *Cornus florida* to most of us, the winsome tree of the pink or white bracts that enchants with the Redbud in milder climates. Sadly, it is not for us, but the bracts of the ground-hugging Dwarf Dogwood make a splendid ground cover, and **Red Osier Dogwood,** *Cornus stolonifera,* isn't a bad shrub if you don't judge it by *florida's* standard. It grows wild over much of Alaska and accepts cultivation. Its spring prunings will bloom indoors in water. There are red-twigged, yellow-twigged, and variegated forms. Go for the variegated kind, hardy to Zone 3.

Caragana, C. *arborescens,* the Siberian pea, is a familiar shrub in the High North. It is an eight-footer and moose seem to give it a wide berth. Among its other virtues are extraordinary hardiness, pretty yellow sweet pea-like flowers, and the ability to make a hedge with alacrity. If it has a fault, it would be a tendency toward bare ankles, but they can be covered with C. *pygmaea ,* a dwarf form. There is a weeping form, C. *arborescens pendula,* that is grafted onto the taller form. There are several other Caraganas, native to Turkestan, Siberia, and China that are not common in the trade, but may be as commerce with Asia develops.

The **Red Elderberry,** *Sambucus racemosa,* deserves a better press. True, it is prolific in the wild and favors the highways and back roads with its beauty, but it is too rangy for some town gardens. It is a welcome self-seeder on the back side of a fence, in a bare space between trees that will eventually meet, as camouflage for a compost operation or a trash can. It is a survivor in poor soil without water or fertilizer; with care it will grow 12 feet tall and conceal a multitude of sins. Alaska's elderberries are not considered edible. They won't kill you, but an early experiment station bulletin suggests that they "may cause vomiting and headaches."

Euonymous is generally invisible in Alaska, but the University of Alaska Anchorage has *E. alata* on its campus.

Honeysuckle, headily fragrant in rain-washed summer air in milder climates, is hard to forget, and **Tatarian Honeysuckle**, *Lonicera tatarica*, is no substitute for it, but it has credentials of its own. This robust pink Russian native, which also has magenta and white forms, is not fazed by Zone 2 winters. You will probably plant it too close to the house but it doesn't mind being moved around if you are handy with a front end loader.

Lilacs require cold winters to be at their best, and Alaska is pleased to oblige them. If you don't know your way around among the French, Canadian, Persian, and Korean hybrids, you are in good company. The familiar **Common Lilac**, *Syringa vulgaris*, is better than common. It offers good foliage, fragrant blooms, and will sucker like mad to provide you with enough plants to make a hedge or a backdrop for a flower border.

The **Canadian hybrids** sometimes bloom the first year you plant them. They are said to require liming every year, but we have found them responsive to a wide range of soils.

Lilacs grow very slowly and may decline to bloom if black plastic mulch is placed over their roots to prevent suckering and to reduce weeding. They are usually free of insect pests and are said not to be favorite fodder for moose; our observation is that moose will break their branches but not eat them.

In local nurseries look for these kinds that have proved their staying powers, and select different species to prolong the season of your pleasure. **Chinese lilac**, *Syringa chinensis*, and the Korean lilac, *S. meyeri*, top out at a modest three or four feet. The taller Korean Early lilac is *S. oblata dilatata*. 'Miss Kim' is a pretty Korean, somewhat less hardy than the others and needs winter protection. It, too, is small and dainty.

The **Persian** and Canadian lilacs are very hardy, and grow tall. The Canadian *Villosa* is sometimes sold as "Late Lilac." They profit from liming.

Maples. Once maples freeze back, they tend to remain shrub-like, but they do what a maple is

Tatarian honeysuckle's pink form makes a graceful privacy hedge that may grow 12 feet tall and as wide.

Maples are not common hereabouts, but the Louis Strutz' Amur maple, Acer ginnala, flames at the west end of the Denali Park Strip in Anchorage.

supposed to do in the fall—produce leaves in glorious reds and oranges. The **Douglas Maple**, *Acer glabrum*, tops out at four to six feet, can be found in Southeastern coastal forests, where it may make a small tree.

Ninebark, *Physocarpus opulifolius*, is a useful shrub with good foliage, growing to about four feet in Zone 3 but is said to attain real glory in milder temperatures.

Potentilla, the north country's beloved "Tundra Rose," is *Potentilla fruiticosa*, a delightful shrub that occurs widely in the countryside, but has been selected and hybridized and now offers numerous handsome cultivars. The State's Plant Materials Center has introduced *P. fruiticosa* 'Fredericksonii,' which has proved its worth in test sites all over the state. There are other cultivars, not all hardy everywhere, but worthy subjects for

trial. Nurserymen have succeeded in finding the best and the hardiest. They range in color from white, through yellow into orange, and there are numerous named varieties.

Shrub roses are Alaska's consolation prize for the tender hybrids that are difficult to overwinter here, requiring indoor storage or burying.

The **Rugosas** and their hybrids are of very ancient origin, depicted in calligraphic art thousands of years ago. Native to the austere coasts of the Asian Far East, they are very much at home in Alaska. Alaskans call them "Sitka" roses because when the Territory was young, there was an agricultural experiment station in Sitka which distributed *Rugosas* to settlers for trial.

But there are other hardy shrub roses. The **Red Leafed Rose**, *Rosa rubrifolia*, has fine reddish foliage and small pink single flowers. The **Scotch Rose** is a tall one with white or yellow single flowers that bloom on the new wood, so it does not take kindly to pruning. 'Louisa Bugnet' and her

The Rugosas may be single or double, pink, white, or yellow, suckering so freely that a hedge of this handsome-leafed shrub comes soon.

lovely sister 'Therese Bugnet' are pale pink doubles. 'Butterball' ,'Harrison's Yellow' and 'Persian Yellow,' a Rugosa hybrid, are among the scarce yellows.

Many shrub roses tend to produce suckers which can be dug and lined out to make a hedge. If you have in mind a rather more opulent hedge than you can find suckers for, you can grow them from seed.

There are several methods to get them to germinate; this simple one works for us: Select a fully ripe rose hip and remove the seeds. Wash them in a cup of water with a drop of dishwashing detergent in it. Some seeds will float and some will sink. The floaters probably won't germinate, but the sinkers probably will. Dry them on a paper towel and shake them up in a jar of some commercial mix and place them in the refrigerator (not the freezing compartment).

Make a note on your calendar to check them in about three months. If they show tiny, pale "tails," they can be gently removed and potted up in cell packs or small pots and placed in a warm, bright place.

The third year from seed, a Rugosa rose hedge should produce token blooms and begin to look like a hedge.

They will produce small plants the first summer and should be hardened off and planted in a nursery bed where the big plants won't overrun them. The second year they will be big enough by summer's end to be placed in their permanent locations.

Do not be indignant if they are not all replicas of their mother plant. These are very old species and much natural hybridizing has taken place. In our case we chose a light pink single *Rugosa* and got all singles, many of them magenta and one nice white with a pinkish cast.

Silverberry, *Eleagnus commutata*, is plentiful in the wild, transplants easily, and is a nice accent. It is said to grow 10 to 12 feet tall, but usually settles for about four feet.

Soapberry, *Shepherdia canadensis*, is a respectable native shrub that grows over most of the eastern half of the state. It may reach seven feet in height. The University of Alaska Anchorage grows *S. argentia*. The Shepherdias are also called Buffalo Berries. Both male and female plants are needed for fruiting.

Sweetgale, *Myrica gale*, an indigenous plant, grows in a low, dense mound, suggesting that it might be of interest for dried materials because its evergreen leaves are fragrant.

False Spirea, *Sorbaria sorbifolia*, gets mixed reviews from gardeners, ranging from an enthusiastic "I haven't had to paint the garage in years!" to a whining, "I whack it down, but it keeps coming back." This "false spirea" comes to us from Siberia's Ural Mountains, but it is a welcome settler, much like the red-berried elder in its ability to grow big fast, look good, and cover our uglies.

The real **Spireas** include such choice shrubs as the **Bridalwreath**, *Spiraea prunifolia plena*, and the **Dwarf Bridal Wreath**, *S. trilobata.*, although we do recall years when the Bridal Wreaths got wiped out and didn't appear in full bridal finery for a few years. There are other hardy Spireas used by local landscapers, like *Spireae frobelli* and hybrids 'Goldflame,' 'Little Princess,' and 'Van Houtte.' The UAA campus has grown *S. prunifolia* successfully. The native *S. beauverdiana*, **Billiard** spirea, should not be upstaged because in good garden conditions it is a perfectly acceptable specimen shrub, although it doesn't look promising in the wild.

Viburnums are a neglected, small group of fine landscape materials. Our native **highbush cranberry**, *V. edule*, is no slouch, producing nice bushes that are agreeable about making a hedge that turns fiery red in fall, offers enough red berries to keep the pine grosbeaks in business (or make a jelly that is reported to smell like overage tennis shoes if the berries were too ripe). In spring there are white flower clusters.

Nannyberry, *V. lentago*, is hardy to Zone 3 and so is the **Wayfaring Tree**, *V. lantana*, which offers bright fall color and red fruit that turns purple as the season wears on. UAA grows *V. trilobium*, the **American Cranberry Bush**. It is rare in the big part of Alaska.

Willows, are a sore subject with most gardeners. These buggy, sprawling, heavy drinkers often volunteer where they are not welcome. However, the State's Plant Materials Center, near Palmer, is testing some well-mannered *Salix* species that show promise of a warmer welcome in Alaska gardens. See them at the Center's annual open house in late summer.

EVERGREEN TREES

Cedars. Alaska Cedar is no cedar; it looks, feels, and smells like a cedar, but it is **Alaska Cypress**, *Chamcyparis nookatensis*, which grows wild in Southeastern. **Hinoki False Cypress**, *C. obtusa*, and **Sawara False Cypress**, *C. pisifera*, are usually hardy in Zone 4.

Firs are uncommon in the big part of Alaska, but a **Balsam Fir** queens it over my garden, thirty or more feet tall, acquired for 50 cents at one of those card tables the Society of American Foresters set up in shopping malls on Arbor Day to encourage tree-planting. It was a poor thing when I bought it, eight inches tall, single stemmed, in a cardboard tube no bigger around than a quarter.

There is a columnar kind, *Abies balsamea* 'columnaris,' and a dwarf form. Balsams should be hardy to Zone 3. Zone 2 landscapes may have to be content with the **Siberian Fir,** *A. sibirica*, scarce in the market place, but that may change with new trade patterns with Russia.

It is not easy for Alaskans to accept the fact that the only cedars that are hardy in our big state reside in a scrap of land near Ketchikan, but the grim truth is that those conical "cedars" next to house walls in mild micro-climates are either False Cypress or Junipers.

Larch species are not truly evergreens because they lose their needles in the fall after putting on a grand show of copper colored branches that look like dead spruce trees in the winter. We describe them in the section on Shrubs, although some are towering trees.

Pines are not numerous in the big part of Alaska. The **Mugos,** *Pinus mugo,* make small trees if their "candles" are not removed. The **Bristlecone pine,** *P. aristata*, one of the oldest living species on earth, has an interesting gnarled, windswept look that is an asset in the Japanese garden and in rock gardens. The **Swiss Stone pine**, *P. cembra*, is hardy to Zone 3, and the **Shore pine**, *P. contorta*, to Zone 4. The **Lodgepole pine,** *P. contorta latifolia*, is the Rocky Mountain version of the Shore pine and is found in Southern and Southeastern Alaska. Many Alaskans have collected small lodgepoles on their way up the Alaska Highway, and they are found throughout Southcentral, where they are not indigenous.

The **Limber pine,** *P. flexilis,* and the **Scotch pine**, *P. sylvestris*, are marginally trustworthy to Zone 2.

Spruces are a more cheerful story. Our native **White Spruce,** *Picea glauca*, is a grand one, if it does not fall to the spruce bark beetle. The spruces are slow-growers, but their absence from the land would be a tragedy of major proportions. *P. engelmanni,* the **Englemann Spruce** is faster-growing and considered better than **Colorado Blue** or the White Spruces by many landscapers. *Picea glauca* 'conica' is appealing for its neat cone shapes, but it is hardy only to Zone 4. On the Kenai Peninsula the splendid **Sitka Spruce** has hybridized with the native White Spruce; the hybrids are **Lutz Spruce**, *Picea X Lutzii.* Many have been transplanted in the greater Anchorage area and some natural hybridization has occured.

Alaska's native **Black Spruce**, *Picea mariana*, has not endeared itself to landscape professionals nor to casual motorists who find little cheer in its stark, stunted presence in muskeg swamps. Japanese gardeners see great possibilities in it if transplanted early in life to a Japanese-style garden.

Colorado Green Spruce is a tough, slow-growing stalwart, as is **Norway Spruce**, *Picea abies*, and the durable **Black Hills Spruce**, *P. glauca densata*.

Jim and Elva Scott brought several lodgepole pines from approximately the same latitude in northern Canada to their home in Eagle on the Yukon, where they have flourished.
Photo by: David R. Scott

DECIDUOUS, LEAF-LOSING, TREES

Beech. The purple or copper **European Beech** is a Zone 4 plant that rarely shivers through a Southcentral winter.

Birches, *Betula* species, grow wild over most of Alaska. These beautiful trees could be catalog centerfolds if they were not so commonplace in the northern landscape. The **Alaska Paper Birch,** *betula papyrifera*, is hardy to Zone 2. It is a graceful, white-barked that may stand tall and straight or have a tendency to weep. The **Kenai Birch** is a slim black-barked tree, a lovely foil for the white birches. In the Interior the **Yukon birch** has a similar dark bark but is a clump-forming shrub.

The European Weeping Birch, *B. pendula papyrifera*, is hardy to Zone 3, our best alternative to the weeping willow. It is a tree of great grace and few faults, excepting occasional invasions of leaf rollers and the green birch aphid. Its fall branches are an acceptable substitute for grape vines for making wreaths.

All the birches are notorious hosts to the green birch aphid. Bolstering the trees' natural defenses is the first line of defense. They should be protected from injury and receive plenty of water during dry periods. The U.S. Department of Agriculture and the Cooperative Extension Service bulletin, *Birch Aphids* recommends the application of one to two pounds of a complete, high-phosphorus fertilizer per inch of tree diameter by making a circle of eight to ten inches deep in the soil around the tree, starting two feet from the trunk and extending a few feet beyond the drip line.

A hose turned on full blast will dislodge many aphids; it won't get them all but it can make the difference between a nuisance you can live with and one you can't put up with. (See Chapter 7 "Fighting Back.")

Crabapples, *Malus* species, are among Alaska's lovliest flowering trees. Many are hardy to Zone 3 and some to Zone 2. Their blossoms range from creamy whites, to pinks, and deep mauves. Some produce edible fruits that enhance a country ham or a baron of moose.

Among the numerous varieties offered by nurseries are these favored by horticulturists and landscapers: 'Almey,' 'Antonova,' 'Dolgo,' 'Heyer 12,' 'Hopa,' 'Norland,' and the ruddy, red-leafed 'Radiant,' 'Red Splendor,' and 'Royalty.'

Because the apple species are thin-barked, they are susceptible to sun scald and they are not salt tolerant, so their streetside use is questionable. They are attractive to moose. Although the kinds named have high marks for hardiness, they are best when grown on their own rootstock, rather than grafted onto some rootstock like '*Malus domestica*,' a catch-all of seeds marketed as a by-product of cider mills. Hardy rootstocks for grafted crabapples are 'Dolgo,' 'Antonova,' and 'Ranetka.'

Chokecherries of the great *Prunus* tribe, provide some of Alaska's best flowering trees. The **Mayday Tree**, *Prunus padus commutata*, comes on strong in early summer, its creamy blooms like candle flames against the blue skies of June. Less desirable is its country kin, the **Common Chokecherry**, *Prunus virginiana*, which takes room for sprawling and is host to the black aphid, which also relishes delphiniums. Both self-seed.

The **Canada Red Chokecherry**, *Prunus virginiana shubertii*, may be Alaska's best landscape tree, says Nurseryman Sherman Bush of Bush Landscaping. It has a lot going for it—chokecherry blooms in spring, green leaves that redden to burgundy in late summer when the hot pink perennials set it off to dramatic perfection. It is not attractive to insects. The **Amur Chokecherry**, *Prunus maackii*, is desirable for landscape purposes and hardy to Zone 2.

Black or **Rum Cherry** needs discovering. The late Dr. Donald Wyman, Horticulturist emeritus of the Arnold Arboretum of Harvard University and prolific writer on shrubs and trees, calls *Prunus Serotina* a fine ornamental, the most ignored of our native trees. Common from Nova Scotia to the Dakotas, it is hardy to -35 degrees. It produces pendulous racemes of white flowers followed by grape-like clusters of red fruits that ripen to black. They have a rich wine flavor and are used in jellies, pies, wines, liqueurs and cordials. No wonder the birds relish them. Farmer Seed & Nursery offers plants.

Hawthorns are in the almost-but-not-quite class for Southcentral; they do better in Southeastern. The **Black Hawthorn**, *Crataegus douglasii*, occasionally grows wild in Southeastern, but the English '**May Tree**,' *C. oxacantha*, is a better cultivar. Flowers range from rose to red, single and double, and fruits are yellow or red. This is a common street tree in northern Europe where day length is similar to ours, but our Japanese Current is no match for their benign Gulf Stream.

Mountain Ash comes in as a close second. **European Mountain Ash**, *Sorbus aucuparia*, shoots up to 50 feet in a protected location. It has creamy blossom clusters in spring, colorful fall foliage followed by bright red berries that bring the waxwings in for a feast. It is a thin-barked tree, susceptible to sun scald and moose-munching. It self seeds freely. Less well known is *Sorbus decora*, '**Showy Mountain Ash**,' which doesn't get so tall but is equally hardy .

Poplars, *Populus species*,' run from the almighty **Black Cottonwood,** *Populus trichocarpa*, hoary giants on the hillsides that are too massive for any home landscape, down to the **Quaking Aspen**, *P. tremuloides*, which is no substitute for the lovely quaking aspens of the Rocky Mountain country which are *P. tremula.*

The **Balsam Poplar** is a possibility for a yard tree if you can put up with its several faults. The female tree sheds a cottony fluff over whole neighborhoods and telling the girls from the boys when they are transplanting size isn't easy. It is a heavy drinker. To its credit let it be said that it is hardy to Zone 1, is free for digging in the wild where it is very, very common. If more desirable species are hardy in your area, you might pass over the poplars.

The late David Wodlinger was a sort of Johnny Appleseed, importing and distributing many **Lombardy Poplars**, along with other acts of kindness, during his tenure on Kodiak Island. Some of the trees survived and they are possibilities for Zone 4 south.

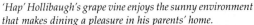

'Hap' Hollibaugh's grape vine enjoys the sunny environment that makes dining a pleasure in his parents' home.

CHAPTER 6

GARDENING INDOORS

When the century was yet young, Alaska was already into indoor gardening. Geraniums bloomed cheerily from cabin windows and "slips" were traded freely between neighbors. True, houseplants were a mixed lot, sometimes potted in coffee cans, but they held the hope of an early breakup and the promise of spring. They were a network between friends and neighbors and the places they came from.

I cherished a beefsteak begonia that had crossed the plains with the Mormon settlers, and leaf cuttings from a homesick neighbor's African violets brought up the Alaska Highway in the dead of winter, taken into roadhouses every night and kept warm on her lap by day.

Houseplants have not always fared well in Alaska's brief winter daylight and desert-level indoor humidity. No longer the province of stay-at-home housewives, indoor plants are everywhere in offices, and atriums of commercial buildings. Increasingly they are becoming collections of related plants that are indoor plantscapes, real indoor gardens.

The interior plantscape industry is largely responsible for showing us what our living spaces and workplaces could be like in the dead of winter. Such companies offer design and installation services, regular maintenance, rotating and replacing plants as necessary. Plant boutiques and florists are educating people to match plants to their growing conditions.

LIGHTING, ARTIFICIAL. If you do much indoor gardening at Alaska's high latitude, artificial lighting is a necessity. At noon on December 2lst, the sun is six degrees above the horizon at Anchorage. The light lasts less than five and a half hours, and many days are overcast. This gives indoor plants a hard time. Most windowsills are too cold, and the places where you want plants, like the stairway landing or the top of the piano, are too far from the source of natural light.

Grounds Supervisor Mary Whybark created this indoor garden in a utility corridor at Anchorage's Providence Hospital, using massive concrete culverts as containers for bulky ornamental cabbage, in scale with the dramatic ventilator system.

The higher the temperature at which plants are grown, the more light must be provided—and the more water and fertilizer. Cuttings taken in the fall and seedlings over-wintered under lights are often woody and lack the compact, succulent growth characteristic of well-grown plants.

The "light-food-water" ratio is fundamental to keeping indoor plants alive. If the light level is as low as a given plant will accept, the soil must be kept on the dry side, and only enough fertilizer given to stave off signs of malnutrition. If there is abundant light and a buoyant atmosphere, more water and nutrients are needed.

Insufficient light produces elongated, spindly stems with pale color and slow growth. Few indoor plants can survive in good health with the low house light levels of the subarctic winter. Fortunately, the choice of artificial lighting has gone beyond the sepulchral lavender glow of the first grow-lights.

Winter plant storage requires a cool place; basement and garage locations require eight hours of artificial light to keep roses, geraniums, and fuchsias in semi-dormancy until seasonal home greenhouses can be opened. It is not economical to start greenhouses before late April or early May, which is too late to sow tomato, cucumber, and many perennial and annual seeds. Artificial light bridges the gap.

Fluorescent lights work well for this purpose. They put out almost three times as much light as incandescent bulbs of the same wattage and last 15 to 20 times longer. You'll need a pulley arrangement to get the tubes down close to seedlings and cuttings—two to four inches is about right, and to raise them as the plants grow. Fluorescents are so cool that plants are rarely burned, even on contact. It's the ballast that gives off the heat, and in a chilly garage you may be glad to have it.

It is not easy to incorporate artificial plant lighting into a home's interior design. Since some general lighting is necessary in the home for several winter months, it can be combined with the need for plant lighting, but this usually requires professional design help.

In the boonies, you're on your own, and you soon discover that books by plant people suggest light setups that are not attractive enough for living areas, and that interior designers' books lack expertise in plant growing. A bank of concealed lights above an African violet, cactus or low-grow-

ing foliage plant collection of similar heights works well.

Recent improvements are the fluorescent tubes that can be used in existing light sockets, and spot lights that can aim at a container plant on the floor. Some have a light output equal to that of a 100-watt incandescent bulb at a fraction of the operating cost. Even as this is being written new bulbs are being developed that conserve energy while putting out more and cooler light.

Inexpensive strip fluorescent tubes can be installed by many home craftsmen. Tiered light carts are good for starting seedlings and for African violet collections. When you get into plants that grow taller, you must either adjust the lights or the plant bases.

Many indoor gardeners do as the plant leasing services do. They display plants that are living on their stored energy, then retire them to growing areas to recuperate—a basement plant room or a garage may be the answer. There, a bank of fluorescent tubes in shop fixtures, or an HID (High Intensity Discharge) lamp is acceptable and the plants can regain their good looks .

Any kind of fluorescent tubes will work above foliage plants, but if you grow blooming plants, a combination of cool white and warm white tubes produce a better plant response—but warm whites are getting scarce in the market place. A better way to go is wide spectrum, plant-growing tubes, which yield a normal, near-day-light quality of light. They cost more, but they last far longer than ordinary tubes.

Lights should be controlled by a timer. If you're simply over-wintering a few geraniums or fuchsias in the corner of a cool basement, eight hours may be all they need. If you have indoor flowering plants, give them 16 to 18 hours; seedlings will need 18 hours, up close to the lights.

In a plant-growing room, all surfaces can be painted white for maximum light reflection, or lined with aluminum foil. Don't neglect dusting the tubes occasionally, and replacing them when the ends darken, which signals a reduction in light that your eye does not detect. When the tubes flicker, they've had it.

For a basement garden you may want to invest in an HID metal halide, mercury or sodium lamp. Plant response exceeds the best fluorescent systems. Longevity is greater and the requirement for power is about one-half. A single HID metal halide lamp will illuminate a sizeable area and require no racks. Sodium lamps are safer and simpler to operate, but they produce a yellow light that is visually disturbing.

Diagnosing indoor plant problems over the telephone or by letter is a lesson in futility, as your friendly Extension Service agent will tell you. Figuring it out by yourself can be baffling. Here are some clues:

The prime enemy of houseplants is salt buildup. Commercial suppliers of indoor plants consider a year the maximum time a pot-grown plant can survive without re-potting in fresh potting mix, says Steve Shropshire of The Green Connection. The first indication of salt damage is wilting of plants that have adequate moisture. Margins or tips of leaves may turn brown and a white powder may form on the soil surface. Clay pots may show white stains.

The cure: knock the plant out of the pot, wash its roots off and cut away any that look dead, then re-pot in a clean pot with fresh potting mix. The commercial soilless mixes are best because garden soil comes loaded with unfriendly pathogens.

Watering practices are the nemesis of most of us, with the anxious gardener an easy victim. If you hover over your plants with a watering can so the soil is constantly wet, stems will get limp and may rot; lower leaves may curl and wilt from lack of oxygen. Too little water and the lower leaves will turn yellow and fall off. Leaf tips will turn brown.

Cold tap water from the earth's icy depths can do wretched things to plants. Water below 50 degrees will reduce leaf size, cause leaf drop, and can eventually kill plants. Tropical plants should never be watered with water below 60 degrees and 80 is better. Even warmer water, as high as 90 degrees, can stimulate growth, Ohio State Uni-

West- and south-facing sunrooms above ground level may serve as solar units, welcome in winter, overheating the house in summer. East-facing structures make pleasant breakfast rooms and escape the heat of summer's late-setting sun.

versity horticulturists have reported.

Bear in mind that body temperature is about 98 degrees, so even 80-degree water will feel cool to your hand. It makes no difference if you water from above or below, but hairy-leaves plants and cacti get unattractive water spots.

Poor drainage takes its toll. The time-honored practice of putting pieces of broken clay pots, pebbles or styrofoam peanuts in the bottom of plant pots does not prevent plants from becoming waterlogged and is now under fire from indoor plant experts. Better to have a fast-draining potting mix and a circle of screen wire in the bottom of the pot than to have a layer of drainage material which may actually inhibit good drainage. If you water the plant thoroughly and the excess runs out the drainage hole, you're in good shape. This is a nuisance, requiring a trip to a laundry sink to let the pot drain.

To avoid frequent watering and the possibility of carpet and floor stains, consider using one of the hydrogels, or soil polymers. They are mixed with the potting medium, and greatly reduce the need for frequent watering. (See Chapter 8, Polymers.)

Houseplant fertilizers come with directions in teaspoons, making it easier to guess how much and how often to feed. However, most are formulated for a gallon of mix, when you had in mind about a pint. You can avoid this frustration by buying a measuring glass marked in milliliters, sold in photographic supply shops. One teaspoon per gallon of water comes out to l.3 milliliters per liter; 1 tablespoon per gallon is 7.8 milliliters per liter.If directions call for l ounce to the gallon, 7.8 milliliters per liter is right on the mark.

If you overdo the fertilizer application, the plant grows lush foliage and few flowers. If you are too parsimonious, the lower leaves lose their good green color and may drop. New leaves are smaller and stems are weak and stunted. Fertilize when the plant is in active growth, tapering off to nothing when the plants are dormant, which coincides with the winter darkness.

When a plant needs to go dormant for a resting period you cannot make it perform by sweet talk, or giving it a double shot of fertilizer and water (and never, never "on the rocks" despite those cute magazine tips about watering with ice cubes to prevent drips).

SUNROOMS, now a common feature in urban homes, add a delightful dimension to Alaska living. They double as dining areas, sitting rooms, offices, hot tub enclosures, entry foyers, (the contemporary version of the arctic entry).

They increase the kinds of ornamental plants you can grow indoors. Their proliferation has produced a market for indoor plants that do more than just stand there. They had better make lemons, or smell wonderful, or produce exotic blooms to cut it with today's sunroom gardeners.

SUNSPACES are extensions onto existing rooms, not separated from them by doors. They are glassed-in on one side and may have glazed end panels. They may have a solid roof and it may have skylights. They are a great facelift for a dark room if it has a wall that can be pushed out.

SOLAR HEATING UNITS are part of the house and can be closed off from the living space. Requirements are exacting for insulation, the mass for solar collection, provision for circulating warmed air, and a control system.

It is true that a sunroom attached to a house entrance fends off cold winter winds and moderates low temperatures, but a solar heating unit's summer temperature can be lethal to plants and uncomfortable for people. If you are considering such a unit, ask the Extension Service to send you its publication, *The Attached Solar Greenhouse.*

Pre-fabricated greenhouse components are another way to go. Their manufacturers usually offer sunrooms as well. Local vendors of greenhouses may be able to recommend a builder who has put up some of their units. If it's the first time around for you and your contractor, a lot of time can be spent studying the manual. Here are several manufacturers (check the Yellow Pages to see if there is a local representative):

Greenhouse manufacturers

❀ Lord & Burnham, Melville, N.Y. 11747

❀ Janco Greenhouses, 9390 David Avenue, Laurel, MD 20707

❀ Everlite Greenhouses, 9305 Gerwig Lane, Guilford Industrial Center, Columbia, MD 21046

❀ Four Seasons Greenhouses, 425 Smith Street, Farmingdale, N.Y.

❀ Solar Additions, 10 Pearl Street, Cambridge, NY 12816

❀ Garden Way SunRoom/Solar Greenhouse, 420 Hudson River Rd., Waterford, NY 10164

❀ Vegetable Factory, Box 2235, New York, NY 10164

❀ Pella, The Rolscreen Co., Pella, Iowa 50219

If you plan to do the work yourself, collect catalogs from the manufacturers and then, for a small charge, obtain the manuals of the ones that interest you. They will give you a good idea of how thorough the manufacturer is in his documentation, and whether the job is within your competence.

Important considerations:

Foundations must go deep enough to prevent frost heaving; a plan for transporting and storing excavated soil must be made. It should not be heaped over the roots of nearby shrubs or trees, nor onto lawns.

Exposure means everything to a sunroom. If it is to be an extension onto the dining room an eastern exposure is delightful; if it is south- or west-facing, it may not be usable on sunny summer days until seven o'clock in the evening and it may generate enough solar heat to make the house too hot in summer.

Ventilation will be required. Most greenhouse fans are too noisy; but vendors of sunrooms have exhaust fans that are suitable. Think twice before you install a fan that can drown out civil conversation and snatch your wig off.

Shading is not difficult with ground-level sunrooms where exterior blinds can be used, but second floor sunrooms pose problems. Companies that sell awnings can install them with interior electrical controls, and drapery dealers have vinyl materials that block sun and heat but permit you to see out.

Solid house walls take on a garden look if covered with commercial lattice or made from lath strips and spray-painted. A lattice makes a good backdrop for a large plant and a support for vining plants.

In winter the expanse of black glass during dark hours is forbidding. With exterior lighting, the sunroom becomes a small jewel and the occupants look out on a magical snowscape, or a garden landscape made mysterious by shadows. If reading the newspaper is part of the breakfast ritual, good lighting must be provided.

You may opt to close the sunroom during the coldest, darkest days of winter. It will still be a buffer against the cold and the wind, and you may be able to pull plants inside and put them under artificial light until the days get longer. From November 15 to February 15 you may prefer the comfort of the fireplace to a sunroom that gets too little sun. If insects on plants have been a problem, a freeze-down gives you a fresh start.

If the sunroom is primarily a plant growing room, access to water, a sink, and a workbench is needed, and perhaps a floor drain. If hanging containers of plants are to be used, a rug is not a practical amenity; ceramic tile is a good way to go and no-wax vinyl an acceptable compromise.

PLANTS TO GROW INDOORS

AFRICAN VIOLET, *Saintpaulia*, deserves to be Alaska's most widely grown flowering houseplant. It tolerates low light levels, but it is a real show-off under grow lights. It enjoys the same warm room temperatures that people do.

The growing medium should be humisy and well-drained, and the plants should be watered with care, avoiding extremes of soggy wetness and drought. Soluble fertilizers with a high middle number keep them blooming most of the year. When the blooms taper off, the plants need to rest, and fertilizing should be discontinued.

Overwatering is the most common cause of problems, and variegated plants need cool conditions to maintain their variegation.

Miniatures are tiny and beguiling. Trailing African violets are gaining in popularity. They produce more flowers and their cascading habit makes them attractive even when out of bloom. The trailers were developed by crossing and back-crossing the trailing *Saintpaulia grotei* with standard varieties. Trailers have been crossed with miniatures to make miniature trailers.

African violets are almost too easy to propagate. You can root a leaf, its stem attached, in a glass of water in about six weeks, pot it up and snip the old leaf off when the young plant is ready to fend for itself. Better, dip the stem end in a rooting hormone powder and set it in a pencil size hole in a pot of soilless mix covered loosely with a plastic bag. There are African Violet Societies in some towns where members exchange cuttings; their plant sales are targets for collectors.

AMARYLLIS, *Hippeastrm*, is a spectacular winter blooming indoor plant. Great flaring lily-like flowers on tall stems push their way up from an out-size bulb and strap-like leaves. Some new hybrids have shorter stems and may yield four or five gorgeous flowers. These plants grow well in a soilless mix at room temperatures, in pots two inches bigger than the bulb, with a half to a third of the bulb above the soil surface.

Amaryllis can be multiplied by detaching offset plants and growing them on until they are blooming size, but few gardeners have Job's patience. The plants tolerate low light levels but do better with supplementary light. Give them a shot of soluble high-middle-number fertilizer after flowering and keep them moist until the leaves die. Store the pots in a cool place until signs of life appear, when you can bring them out into sunlight and keep them well watered.

Authorities (I consulted eight published ones) differ on whether the bulb should be repotted in fresh soil. Most are uneasy about disturbing the bulb's roots, suggesting flushing the top of the soil off under a faucet or hose and replacing with fresh mix.

ASPARAGUS-FERN, *Asparagus sprengeri,* is an accommodating indoor trailer easily grown from seed, but since it outgrows its pot so frequently you may be forced to propagate it from divisions made with a sharp knife. Pot the divisions up in fresh soil; post-operative recovery will be slow.

In sunny locations the plant will bloom and produce red berries inside of which are black seeds which can be planted to produce new plants. Asparagus-fern has a prodigious thirst and will shed its needles if it wants water. Properly

hardened off, it can spend the summer outdoors in a protected location. Don't ask it to live forever in a small pot on the mantle above the fireplace.

AVOCADOS may or may not be an asset to an indoor plant collection. Avocado trees are bred for heavy fruiting, eating quality, disease resistance and harvest time—but not for indoor culture. Since they are freebies, the by-product of produce counter purchases, few indoor gardeners can resist the big seeds, sometimes already sprouting. You might try several and keep any that shape up.

Here's how: plant the seed, big end down, in a container of soilless mix, giving it the same care you would any foliage plant. This works better than impaling it on the traditional three toothpicks in a jar of water.

AZALEAS and **RHODODENDRONS** are very closely related botanically (azaleas have five stamens and rhododendrons have 10 or more). For an Alaska readership they will be treated separately, azaleas being described as indoor plants and rhododendrons as deciduous shrubs (Chapter 5).

Azaleas are splendid florist plants, well suited to cool sunrooms, less so to house temperature and humidity levels. They last a long time if you can give them 45- or 50-degree nights in a cool garage that does not freeze, and days at somewhat less than the 70-odd degrees of the average home. You may even be able to get them to re-up the next year with this kind treatment.

The Japanese use azaleas as bonsai subjects and some are very, very old. During Tokyo's torrid summer, they are refrigerated, trimmed to shapeliness after blooming, repotted in fresh potting mix and they grow more beautiful with the years. You might try it, if you have a second refrigerator.

BEGONIAS are rewarding sunroom plants and some cane types, like the familiar Angel Wing, do well as houseplants. They grow several feet tall, but can be tip pruned to make them stockier. The variety 'Sophie Cecile' has taken her share of prizes. 'Pink Rubra' has smaller flowers but more of them.

The handsome Rex begonias are lovely sunroom plants with marvelously colored and spotted leaves. Many are silvery, but 'Merry Christmas' is a red one. They are so easy to propagate that you can start with a leaf, lay it on a seeding medium, and make little cuts across its main vein, from which infant plants will come. Slip the flat into a plastic bag and keep it out of direct sun. There are too many gorgeous newcomers coming on line to name names, but your florist will have some beauties.

Fibrous-rooted begonias, *B. semperflorens*, are a far cry from the wax begonias that have long been with us as accommodating houseplants. The hybridizers keep producing more magnificent foliage and larger flowers of melting beauty. You might buy a pair of them for indoors, trim them back when they become lanky, root the cuttings, and have enough for patio containers by summer.

Florists' begonias are good bets for the sunroom. They require 60 to 65-degree temperatures at night, high humidity, and good, indirect light. If heat build-up on sunny days is a problem they do not fare as well. There are many species and some gardeners have large specialty collections.

The 'Star' begonia blooms when Alaskans need it most, from February until spring, a colorful foliage plant with star-patterned leaves.

BOSTON FERN, *Nephrolepis species*, is well suited to indoor culture in Alaska if it can be provided its own air space—these ferns detest being handled. They like a moist humusy soil, comfortable room temperature, and a semi-annual dose of a soluble fertilizer in spring and summer.

Bright light, but not direct sun, suits them best, so some sunrooms may be too bright for them in summer. Boston ferns are rambunctious growers and need to be divided when their roots overwhelm the pot. You can multiply your stock by pinning down runners and separating them from the parent plant when their root systems can support the offspring.

BROMELIADS are tropical members of the pineapple family, most of them epiphytes or air plants that make exotic indoor subjects, effective as ac-

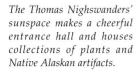

The Thomas Nighswanders' sunspace makes a cheerful entrance hall and houses collections of plants and Native Alaskan artifacts.

cent plants in an all-foliage plantscape or on a sunroom wall. They require minimal care. Most have "urns," little reservoirs that hold and use water as needed. There are hundreds of species, often with spectacular flowers, or more accurately, floral bracts. Leaves have a wide range of color and form.

Although bromeliads grow on tree branches in tropical rain forests they accept pot culture. Soil mixes must be as open as the moss and decaying bark they find in the rain forest. Those that are terrestrial need a mix with more soil and organic matter. Some vendors sell special bromeliad mixes, but you can make your own, starting with one part soil, two parts peatmoss and one part perlite.

Bromeliads are quite sensitive to salt and should not be watered with softened water. Professional growers fertilize every few weeks with one-quarter strength African violet fertilizer or fish emulsion.

The plants are often sold on pieces of driftwood, and they can be grown on bromeliad "trees," usually a dead tree branch with holes bored in its branches in which the bromiliad roots are inserted and secured with raffia or cord, but never wire.

Their common names are descriptive: sword plant, urn plant, painted feather, rainbow plant, painted fingernail. Usually listed in catalogs by their botanical names, look for these spectacular ones, all tongue-twisters: *Aechmea chantinii, A. fasciata, Cryptanthus zonatus, Guzmania sanguinea, Bilbergia amoena, Ananas comosus, Neoregelia carolinae tricolor, Tillandsia ionantha, Niduilarium innocentii,* or *Vriesea splendens.*

BROWALLIA is a great hanging container plant for the summer greenhouse or sunroom. When it has bloomed itself out and gotten lanky it can be cut back and will perform like a perennial, making a comely comeback in the spring; or, it can be treated as an annual since it blooms the first year and is offered in garden centers. The biggest blooms are from *B. speciosa major* in purple or white.

BULBS, FORCING. If ever there was a misnomer, it must be "forcing" bulbs; coaxing is more like it. Most of the big part of Alaska has winter temperatures too low for conventional outdoor bulb forcing, but a modest row of six-inch pots at the back of the bottom shelf of the refrigerator can make spring come early.

Pot up a half dozen tulips or three daffodils or as many narcissus as you can get into a six-inch "azalea" pot of soilless potting mix. Mann Leiser, the multi-skilled founder of Alaska Greenhouses, always told his customers to set tulips so that the flat sides of the bulbs faced outward so the leaves would bend down over the sides of the pots. A couple of generations of Anchorage gardeners have been doing it ever since. Water them well, drain them, and enclose the pots in plastic bags closed with twist ties.

By January or February pale shoots will appear. When they are about three or four inches tall, put the pots in a cool place under fluorescent lights to green-up. When the buds appear, bring them out to enjoy. It would be prudent to take them back to a cool garage at night, so they won't get leggy.

Daffodils have been more difficult to force, but Israeli breeders have introduced some which bloom sooner after planting, without the cooling period which was a problem for many indoor gardeners. Look for names like 'Ziva,' 'Nazareth,' 'Israel,' 'Jerusalem,' and 'Galilee,' which are said to take only three to five weeks to bloom.

Narcissus forcers have often planted their bulbs in pebbles, but growers now suggest that a commercial potting mix (peat-bark-perlite) with a pinch of slow release fertilizer works better. Bottom heat and artificial light help rooting and keep stems from elongating.

The Daffodil Mart (Route 3, Box 794, Gloucester, VA 23061, catalog $1) a respected grower from whose catalog we lifted these tips, also suggests watering with a teaspoon of rubbing alcohol to a quart of water.

CACTI are native Americans, several thousand species of them, oddly at home in Alaska's indoor gardens. They come from the deserts of the Western Hemisphere, but also from high mountains and along sea coasts and other austere environments to which they have marvelously adapted.

They are able, better than most plants, to survive the winter desert conditions in the modern Alaska home, warm and dry by day, but with a cool respite at night. Cacti are succulents, having the ability to store moisture in their tissues longer than vascular plants.

Not all succulents are cacti. **Spurges** are the succulent counterpart of cacti on the African continent, among them the numerous *Euphorbias*, which resemble cacti and are mistaken for them by most world travelers. Cacti and many succulents have similar requirements and are commonly grown together in dish gardens, on window sills, in collections under lights, or in sunrooms.

Among the succulents suited to indoor culture in Alaska are the *stapeliads, hoyas, crassulas, sedums, haworthias, aloes* and numerous others offered by florists, garden centers and mail order cactus nurseries.

The leading cause of failure with these tough plants is overwatering. How often is too often varies with local climate and time of year. From spring into fall, their growing season, water thoroughly when the plants are nearly dry. Soluble fertilizer at half- or quarter-strength can be applied with each or every other watering. Decrease water during the winter, but be alert to signs of shriveling, for some houses are so dry that cacti potted in clay may get too little moisture. If they rot, you are over-watering. Do not fertilize during the winter when the plants need to rest from their growth spurt, or they will not bloom the next spring.

Provide a soil mix that drains readily. Cacti do not thrive in the soilless peat mixtures, so most garden centers offer a special cactus mix. A good combination is one part sandy soil, one part sifted compost, two parts coarse sand or perlite.

A moisture meter is a good investment for gardeners who are unsure about watering. After a few times, users will know when it is time to water but an occasional meter check is a prudent safeguard.

Will cacti bloom for you? Maybe not, if you cannot give them a two or three month winter rest at cooler temperature, as low as 40 or 50 degrees. They need bright artificial light during their growing season, spring into summer, and their growth will tend to elongate without it. Their flowers are worth scheming for, fragile blooms of pure color. Some are less than half an inch in diameter, but those of the Epiphyllum hybrids can be of dinner plate dimensions. Even if they don't bloom, cactus and succulent gardens are so interesting and undemanding that a single plant will soon give rise to a collection—or a mania, since the born collector has little chance of getting them all.

Many of our cultural suggestions were lifted from the brochure of B & B Cactus Farm, 11550 East Speedway, Tucson, AZ 85748. This excellent nursery offers a vast range of plants at low cost. It ships bare root stock to Alaska, or you can take it with you.

Spines come in many colors, designed to reflect intense sunlight, conserve moisture, and discourage animals; they vary in shape and are beautiful in themselves. Dense hair, or wool, or a powdery cover protect some species and offer exotic patterns.

Propagating cacti and succulents is easy and fun. Most seeds germinate fairly quickly, if somewhat unevenly, simply pressed into moist sand. They can be potted up when you get around to it or when they become crowded.

Most mature cacti and succulents produce offsets, infant plants at the base or along the plant's stem, which can be detached with a sharp knife or a razor blade. When a plant gets so tall that it topples, or grows into the light tubes, its top can be lopped to a more appropriate height. Don't throw the "mother" plant out if you want new offsets of the same kind. Such cuttings and offsets should be permitted to heal in the air until a thin skin has formed over the cut. Most plants need re-potting once a year, when their shallow roots have exhausted the soil.

Can you grow succulents outdoors in Alaska?

For sunrooms you would have to look far for something lovelier than "Star of Bethlehem," C. isophylla, which shines in white or lavender.

A cautious yes. Several of the *echevarias*, "hen and chick" plants, do well in rock gardens, and some survive many winters, but it is easy to dig them up and bring them indoors for the winter to serve as pot plants or be stored under lights. Many nurseries market them in cell-packs and you can replenish your supply at modest cost.

A few cacti are tropical and require warm, moist conditions—the familiar Christmas and Easter cacti, for example, and those handsome-ugly epiphytes, the orchid cacti, and the night-blooming cereus. I have been summoned in the middle of a rainy night to witness the blooming of pioneer gardener Mrs. Hans Hanson's night-blooming cereus, and a momentous occasion it was. The huge buds opened slowly, majestically, until great creamy blossoms were wide, releasing a heady, sensuous perfume. It was a suspenseful performance, mysterious and unreal on a rainy night in Alaska.

Out of bloom these gangly plants are not beauties, but the orchid cacti (which are no kin of orchids and come in several colors besides orchid, all gorgeous) produce a phenomenal number of blooms. Conrad Bitter once invited me to see one plant in his collection, with 105 immense, scarlet blossoms. ("You shoulda been here last week when one had 150 blooms!")

Christmas cactus, *Schlumbergera bridgesi*, is an old time favorite houseplant. Thanksgiving cactus, *Schlumbergera truncatus*, is paler pink, has toothed leaves. Flowering in both is governed by day length and temperature. Their awkward stems need pruning once a year to promote compact growth and more bloom.

To get Christmas cactus to bloom for Christmas (when it will clash with red poinsettias but would be splendid with the pink ones), give it short days of eight or nine hours starting in mid-September. Many gardening articles suggest a cardboard box or in a dark closet, and a night temperature of 55 to 60 degrees. The same goes for Thanksgiving cactus, except that you give it the short-day treatment a month earlier, but why bother? They will bloom a little later when they are more welcome. If you keep these plants in a room that receives no artificial light at night and maintains a cool temperature, they will bloom when they get good and ready, which will be sometime in mid-winter.

Easter cactus, *Rhipsalidopsis gaertneri*, blooms as days get longer in the spring, and may bloom for Easter depending on when Easter is.

If you can manage a 50- to 55-degree night temperature, buds will form regardless of day length, and they will rarely form at night temperatures above 70 degrees. After flower buds are well developed they will flower at normal house temperature. After blooming, new growth will occur and during this period more fertilizer and water will be needed for next season's buds.

Florist specimens of these plants are more beautiful than homegrown ones because of cooler temperatures, moist air, and younger plants—unlike the lugubrious specimens home gardeners hang onto for years, but some folks get their jollies from washtub-size antiques. They are so easy to propagate from three- or four-joint cuttings in a coarse potting mix that you should start early looking for good homes for their progeny.

CALCIOLARIA, pouch flower, once a florist's plant, is now within the grasp of home gardeners who like to start seeds in winter for early spring bloom indoors. The 'Anytime' series blooms in four months. Catalogs list it and garden centers stock plants. At the University of Alaska Anchorage, Pat Leary found that they germinated in five to 10 days in daylight at 70 to 75 degrees when seeded the last week in February.

CALLA is a name that can be confusing. The Calla lily is *Zantedeschia*, and it is no lily.

Callas make rather good indoor plants, sometimes producing a bloom or two. The familiar

The Calla makes a good foliage plant and sometimes produces a few blooms indoors.

white one is a robust specimen, but the pink and yellow kinds are interesting rarities, best in sunrooms.

CAMPANULA. The Star of Bethlehem, C. *isophylla*, is offered by some garden centers in cell-packs and it is also a florist's plant. Cut back in fall and stored with minimal light and water, it re-ups in February, but is not worth the bother unless you have no source of fresh plants. My best plants are grown outdoors in pots against a south wall, and moved into the sunroom when they have set buds and nights are growing cool.

CARDINAL CLIMBER, *Ipomea x multifida*, is an annual vine that doesn't make it outdoors in most of Alaska, but is a nice climber for a sunroom trellis.

CARNATION, *Dianthus caryophyllus*, is not a good performer in Alaska gardens but it does well in greenhouses and sunrooms.

CHINESE EVERGREEN, *Aglaonema modestum*, is the lush, dense foliage plant of gray-green leaves that you see in the professionally-tended indoor gardens of modern Alaska buildings.

It is an old-timer, long known for its tolerance of low light levels and house temperatures, but the hybridizers have been tinkering with it and you will find some glamorous hybrids offered in garden centers and florist shops. Some are variegated with white, or brushed with silver. A great, sturdy indoor plant for Alaska. It can be propagated from stem cuttings.

CHRYSANTHEMUMS. Throughout the year potted chrysanthemums are commercially available and make great indoor plants, blooming for six weeks or so. Keeping them over and getting them to bloom again is not easy because of the day length problem.

CITRUS plants are not hardy anywhere in Alaska, but they make elegant and interesting indoor plants, especially for sunrooms. Since most citruses bloom and bear green and ripe fruit simultaneously most of the year, it is an exotic experience to open the sunroom doors to the heady scent of orange blossoms and ripe fruit.

Look for 'Meyer' or 'Ponderosa' lemons, which produce very large fruits on dwarf trees, a 'Rangpur' lime, an 'Otaheite,' 'Calamondin,' or a Mandarin orange.

Sunroom temperatures and light agree with citrus fruits unless they wilt at mid-day in summer when west-facing sunrooms can get too hot. These plants will accept a degree or two of frost. In the event of a power failure, they may lose their leaves, but they usually regenerate after a hard cutting back. They do best if they get supplemental fluorescent light in winter.

You want the bad news? All citrus plants are regarded as delicacies by red spider, mealy bugs and scale. Sprays can be offensive in sunrooms; granular products teased into the soil surface pose a danger to pets and small children; systemic poisons are effective and easy to use, but harvesting fruit from treated plants is risky business for toddlers.

CLIVIA, the Kafir lily, has foliage that resembles its related amaryllis, but the orange lily-like flowers are in dense clusters, unlike the amaryllis' out-facing single blooms. Its long lasting flowers come in early spring and accept the light levels of a bright room or a shady sunroom. It is a rare patio or courtyard in Spain that does not have this plant in lush profusion that rates an *Ole*!

COBAEA, cup and saucer vine, has lavender cup-shaped flowers and is a good bet for a sunroom.

COLEUS is a foliage plant that is most useful in the North as an indoor plant. It is easily grown from seed or tip cuttings and there are as many interesting and colorful forms as there are winter weary plant-swappers. It is widely available in cell-packs. These plants come alive under the sepulchral glow of the old lavender grow-lights.

CROTON, *Codiaeum variegatum*, is a colorful tropical shrub that is well suited to sunroom culture. Some varieties make small pot plants, some handsome shrubs. They are not candidates for outdoor culture in Alaska and they make poor houseplants.

CROWN-OF-THORNS, *Euphorbia splendens*, is a tolerant plant for the house or sunroom. It has long thorns and small red blossoms. Grow it in a container out of harm's way for a splash of welcome winter red. Treat it as a cactus; be stingy with water and generous with light.

CYCLAMEN is a familiar florist gift plant that can be grown from seed by reasonably patient home gardeners. Mine took 15 months from seed to bloom under artificial light in a cool location. Seeds are listed in many catalogs.

They need a place by a cool window or a nightly rescue to a chilly, but not freezing, garage. They make a brief showing as a hospital gift plant because of the uniform 70-degree room temperature and windowsills that are often above heat vents.

CYPERUS, *C. alternifolius*, the umbrella plant, is a durable houseplant, easily grown from seed and offering a pleasant contrast in texture and form to the indoor plantscape. When summer comes, it can go outdoors to flourish at the edge of a pool, happy with its feet in water or mud. If it has a fault, it is its fatal attraction for cats which, inexplicably, relish its sharp-edged foliage and may keep it chewed down to a nubbin.

CYPHOMANDRA, *C. betacea*, is occasionally advertised as the "tree tomato," accompanied by pictures of life-size, tomato-like fruits on a plant that reaches for the ceiling. If the Brooklyn bridge has already been snapped up, you might consider investing in a Cyphomandra. It gets tall. Fast. It may produce fruits that somewhat resemble tomatoes, which are not toxic so far as we know. Its chief claim to fame is its inexorable attraction for aphids and gullible gardeners.

DIEFFENBACHIA, dumb cane, is a stalwart indoor plant. It grows to majestic heights, tolerates indoor temperature and humidity, and somewhat lower light levels than many houseplants, creating a lush, tropical look. It is easily propagated from "logs," cut in two or three-joint sections from the trunk of a cane that got too lanky. Tip cuttings root readily in a pot of moist soilless mix encased in a large plastic bag. Wipe the leaves off frequently because their bold texture holds the dust. This plant is toxic to mucus membranes and paralyzing to throat tissue if nibbled on. Folklore has it that mouthy slaves were forced to chew it for punishment.

Like all indoor plants, it becomes magnificent only with considerate treatment. In a wintry sunroom where it gets all the light there is, it may bloom.

DRACENA is one of our most accommodating indoor plants. *D. marginata* has red leaf margins and grows to be a tall, bare-trunked plant with a contemporary look. (Those bizarre trunks you see in plant shops are produced by laying the plant on its side for a time to get the trunk to grow upward, which is its natural tendency, and turning the pot occasionally.)

D. fragrans, the corn plant, is an impressive leafy indoor plant, a fast-grower that requires little pampering to produce great good looks. Keep the soil evenly moist and give it as much indirect light as you can in the Alaska winter. A fluorescent spotlight trained on such a plant is dramatic. Small plants are sometimes sold in garden centers. Logs cut from a lanky trunk, enclosed in a bag of moist peatmoss, will sprout offsets at the nodes.

FATSHEDERA is a bold plant for Alaska interiors, reasonably tolerant of room temperature, low humidity and low light levels. It has great palmate leaves and will fill a large corner. In good light and humidity, it is impressive.

FIG, *Ficus*. This family of tropical rubber trees, shrubs and vines serves Alaska's indoor gardens well. The Creeping Fig, *F. pumila*, is a small-leafed clinging vine useful in interior plantscapes and in sunrooms. The Benjamin fig, *F. benjamina*, is the lovely weeping tree gracing atriums of office buildings and some spacious homes. It has a reputation for being difficult, arguably, because it does drop its leaves when its environment changes, but in time new leaves appear. It enjoys consistently moist, humusy soil, an occasional tepid shower, and room temperatures that people find comfortable, if it can have somewhat cooler nights.

The rubber tree, *F. elastica*, once associated with dimly lighted funeral parlor decor, is back in fashion's favor. It tolerates a wide range of interior conditions. Its bold leaves and rangy branches require space. The fiddleleaf fig, *F. lyrata*, is similar, a welcome addition to the interior garden.

GARDENIA, *G. jasminoides*, is a deliciously fragrant small shrub for the sunroom in Alaska and it can, with some effort, be a satisfactory houseplant. It accepts room temperatures by day, but at night needs a cool 60 degrees to set buds. Sunrooms can manage this, besides offering the sunlight the plant needs, but in the house you may find the only place cool enough at night is in front of sliding glass doors. Windowsills above heating convectors are too warm.

Gardenias like higher humidity than most homes can offer in winter, so they are plagued by red spider and mealy bugs, which look for dry environments. They need an acid soil with a pH around 5, an occasional watering with an iron chelate solution sold in garden centers under various trade names, like GreenGuard, and in drug stores as iron sulfate. A half ounce in a gallon of water, applied once a month, should do the trick. Use a balanced soluble fertilizer every two weeks while the plants are blooming, but ease off when they show signs of wanting a rest.

Bud drop is perhaps the most frustrating problem for growers of gardenias, which can be caused by a maddening variety of things, like over- or under- watering, dry air, too many dark days, or indoor air pollution. Allowing only one bud per shoot to develop, seems to help. Moderate watering (with tepid water), not allowing the soil to dry out completely, is a wise precaution.

In spite of their outbursts of temperament, it would be hard to forego the pleasures of a gardenia when you run across a small one, in bud, at an affordable price. You don't have much to lose if it isn't with you long; a plant of majestic size loaded with buds will need good care and a space to its rather finiky liking, or it will languish.

GERBERA, a florist plant until the introduction of 'Happipot,' is now a fixture in Alaska sunrooms and in patio containers. Gerberas can be grown from seed sown in March and plants are sold by garden centers. They are usually mixtures of spidery, double, or tufted daisies of red, orange, yellow, pink or cream.

If you keep your sunroom going all winter, a mature plant may produce multiple blooms, but you'll need supplemental light.

GERMAN IVY, *Senecio mikanioides,* is a familiar houseplant that prefers higher humidity than most homes have. When well-grown, it is a good addition to an interior plantscape or to a sunroom. It should be kept evenly moist in good light. Laundromats grow excellent German ivies which live it up in those big windows with humidity from the washers and dryers.

GLORIOSA LILY, *Gloriosa superba,* is an exotic vining tropical plant with red and yellow lily-like flowers that makes a good sunroom choice. Start it from purchased tubers. It rests in winter.

GLOXINIA, *Sinningia speciosa,* is closely related to the African violet, and makes an elegant houseplant if you have room for it under artificial light. These gorgeous plants take up a fair amount of space with their big leaves and flaring trumpet flowers.

Easy to grow from seed listed in most catalogs, they will bloom in about six months. When they need a rest, the leaves fade and drop off and the plants look like losers. Left to their own devices, they will send up new growth when they get good and ready in two to four months.

Gloxinias are sensitive about over-watering, especially if water gets into the crown.

GRAPE-IVY, *Cissus incisa,* accepts moderately low light levels but is a star performer in good light. It will make a luxuriant hanging basket plant if you pinch it. Let it dry between waterings, and prune it to induce branching. It is a star performer in laundromats.

HERBS make poor houseplants. They do not even do very well in sunrooms without supplementary lighting when the fall days get shorter—and cooler temperatures than sunroom occupants enjoy. Those that accept declining daylight and coolish room temperatures are sage, lemon balm, thyme and rosemary.

Digging up an outdoor-grown herb and potting it up for indoor culture works very poorly. Better to start a new batch in mid-summer and gradually acclimate the young plants to indoor growing conditions.

HOYA, waxplant, is tolerant of neglect; it will twine itself up a curtain rod or trail from a hanging container. In a south window or a sunroom, its blossoms, reminiscent of flowers on little girls' hats of long ago, are almost too fragrant. There is a variegated form that is not quite so vigorous.

HYDRANGEAS are tempting florist plants for sunrooms, but tend to be short lived houseplants.

IMPATIENS (pronounced impatience) is a captivating plant that does not deserve its odious common names, "Busy Lizzie" and "Blooming Idiot." It is an indoor-outdoor plant that needs cutting back occasionally to keep it compact. Garden centers sell these plants in spring in numerous colors, all luscious, singles and doubles, bicolors, with plain or variegated foliage, in heights ranging from five to 12 inches. The doubles are especially appealing, like tiny rosebuds. The New Guinea hybrids have variegated, pointed leaves. Grow at least one in a pot for indoor culture. Or, take cuttings of your outside favorites and pot them up for houseplants.

JADEPLANT, *Crassula argentea,* is the obliging houseplant that has dark green, pulpy leaves and is tolerant of poor light and indifferent care. It comes into its own if it can have good sunshine, daytime temperatures in the 70's and cooler nights. Under optimum lighting it may produce pink flowers and, in time, will develop a thick trunk and take on bonsai airs. You can buy an inexpensive starter plant, or beg an easily rooted tip cutting from a friend.

MONSTERA, *Monstera deliciosa*, is a vining tropical plant with huge leaves, deeply cut. When young it is often mistaken for the cutleaf philodendron. It is an indoor plant in the north that requires good light and even moisture, and is very easy—and impressive.

NIGHT-BLOOMING CEREUS, *Hylocereus undatus* (see CACTUS).

ORCHIDS, once considered too difficult for Alaska's indoor gardeners, have made such limitations obsolete due in part to newer hybrids, and the advent of sunrooms. There are many orchids that can be treated as indoor plants, and they are sold in Alaska nurseries, and in plant and florist shops at affordable prices.

Orchids are usually classified by temperature requirement. The warm-natured ones require a night minimum of 65 degrees. Intermediates (60-65 degrees) accept the comfort requirements of most homes. Sunrooms can satisfy the cool-loving orchids' preference for 60 degrees or less at night.

A cool-vapor humidifier and a circulating fan plus a fluorescent light fixture with a couple of grow light tubes and a pair of cool whites makes an acceptable orchid growing space.

Orchids often bloom only once a year, but it is possible to have one or more in bloom every month of the year, and some blooms last for weeks. Their producers' computers have them in flawless bloom for Easter, Mothers' Day, Christmas, and June weddings.

Out of bloom, orchids don't look like much, so a shelf in the basement or in a utility room, can maintain good growing conditions, with the plants brought out into living areas to do their stuff.

Most orchids are epiphytic: they grow by attaching themselves by their roots to a tree. When grown in pots they must dry out between waterings. Terrestrial orchids, like the *Cymbidiums* and the *Paphiopedilums*, grow in soil which needs to be kept evenly moist, but not wet.

If you start small, with three- or four-inch pots of orchids, you will probably have to water twice a week, less often as they are potted up into more commodious containers. They require free drainage — osmunda fiber and fir bark chunks are popular potting media so they will need fairly frequent feeding, perhaps a dilute soluble fertilizer every third or fourth watering. Occasionally the pots need to be held under a faucet to leach accumulated fertilizer salts.

Among the most accommodating orchids for interior gardens are the *Phalaenopsis*, moth orchids, lovely flat-faced white, pink, or lavender blooms on graceful, arching stems. Another beginner's orchid is the *Paphiopedilum* species, which were once classified as *Cypripediums* or Lady's Slipper orchids.

The *Cattleyas* are what people think of when they think orchids. They are, happily, easy for amateurs to grow. These are the great "orchid" colored ones, the corsage blossoms. They appreciate warm room temperatures and slightly cooler nights. Since orchids can be hybridized between genera, there is a fantastic number of cattleya hybrids from which to choose, in more colors than we can come up with mouth-watering words for.

The *Oncidiums, Brassias,* and *Epidendrums* relish intermediate temperatures and moderate light levels. The *Vandas*, known to Alaskans who return from Hawaii wearing leis, also make good indoor garden plants. The *Ascocenda* hybrids are not so tall, a miniature *Vanda* better for indoor gardens.

When you're in Washington D.C. be sure to see the Smithsonian's Office of Horticulture Orchid Collection, one of the finest in the world, a brief walk from the Mall.

PHILODENDRON'S numerous species (about 200) accept low light levels, house temperatures, and casual care. In hanging containers the leaves will be small, but these naturally vining plants will put on an impressive show against a trellis. They make sumptuous plants in a greenhouse or sunroom and respond to good care by being gorgeous.

Some kinds have leaves shaped like calla-lilies,' or heart-shaped like *pothos,'* or are deeply cut like *Monstera deliosa*. Some branch from their base and are slow growers but may reach an eight-foot ceiling in a few years. The Saddleleaf philodendron is one of the best.

All philodendrons look dreary with neglect, their leaves drooping and dull. In good indirect light, when treated to an occasional shower or sponge bath, and nourished with one of the houseplant fertilizers, they are aristocratic indoor foliage plants.

PIGGYBACK PLANT, *Tolmiea menziesii,* is native in Southeastern, and is a common houseplant everywhere. It is an interesting one, forming plantlets in the base of its heart-shaped leaves. Any houseplant potting mix and a steady source of moisture will please it. When it is not pleased, it simply collapses in a heap.

POINSETTIA, *Euphorbia pulcherrima,* is a splendid indoor plant for Alaska. It is widely available, grown in Alaska at Christmas time in colors that include not only the traditional red, but creamy white, shades of pink, rose, yellow and bicolors.

Alaska growers who first experimented with elaborate shading and lighting programs to induce bloom by December, discovered that Alaska's natural day length at the critical season was ideal if the plants could be protected from artificial light at night, and that new hybrids were less sensitive to day length. They now produce thousands of poinsettias for retail sale and wholesale to local supermarkets and garden centers.

Poinsettias initiate flower buds when days are 10 hours long and nights are 14 hours, which occurs in September in Anchorage. Under home conditions, to induce a poinsettia to bloom for the holidays, begin no later than early October to place the plant in the dark every evening at five

o'clock. A closet, an unlighted room, or a cardboard box will do, or cover the plant with a black plastic bag.

Return it to bright light no earlier than seven the next morning. Once the color shows, around Thanksgiving, you can discontinue the treatment. If you fail to give it this light-dark regimen, a poinsettia will bloom around March to say Happy Easter.

Producers are trying to make poinsettias more than just a holiday plant, manipulating flowering time and offering colors suitable for other seasons. More than 65 varieties are now sold, ranging from lemon yellows through the hot pinks to a wide choice of reds. The modern hybrids last much longer than older kinds. Plant breeders are breeding for more compact foliage, and double flowers.

When you buy, look for compact stems, large flower bracts, with little or no pollen showing. Be sure the plants are well-wrapped and go into a warm car—even brief exposure to low temperatures can spoil them. Sixty- to 70-degree daytime temperatures and night temperatures of 55 to 60 degrees prolong flower life.

If bracts begin to drop, the plant is getting more water, heat, or fertilizer than it should have for the light it receives. Avoid extreme temperature changes. Water the soil completely when the surface dries. Water should drain out the bottom. A soluble houseplant fertilizer once a month will prolong bloom.

When the colorful bracts fade, the leaves often remain and make the poinsettia an acceptable foliage plant. If the leaves drop, it is an indication that the plant is ready for a rest, and it can be turned on its side and not watered until new sprouts appear at the leaf nodes. Brought into the light of day, it will regain its foliage

STREPTOCARPUS plants appear in the nurseries when you need them most, in early spring when the February sun is finding the windows. These are African violet kin and need the same conditions as their prolific cousins. Give them a moist African violet soil, whatever humidity you can muster, and cooler nights .

UMBRELLA PLANT, *Cyperus alternatifolius,* resembles a clump of palm trees about a foot tall. It is easy to grow from seed, makes a good foliage plant indoors but can go outdoors for the summer. It requires lots of moisture and would like nothing better than to have its feet in the mud beside some little pool or stream.

WAX PLANT, *Hoya carnosa,* is a durable houseplant and a useful hanging basket or vining subject in the interior plantscape. In good sunlight it will bloom; the flowers look like artificial nosegays and are almost too fragrant.

YAM. As an indoor vine or hanging basket subject, yams are not a bad choice if you can find one at the supermarket that is sprouting—most have been treated with a chemical to prevent sprouting. Suspend the bottom half in a jar of water, or plant the bottom half in a pot of potting mix and place it in a bright window or under lights. Pinch ungainly stems to make it branch.

INDOOR PLANT PROPAGATION

When Alaska was young and a drop-in visit from a friend from up the creek was a an event, an African violet leaf was a nice hostess present, or a slip of a "Swiss cheese" *philodendron* that had traversed the Inside Passage.

Rooting these treasures in a jar of water sometimes worked, and still does, but it works better if the stem is inserted in a pencil-size hole in a sterile potting mix and covered loosely with a plastic bag. Dipping the cut stem end in a fungicide wards off the dreaded "black leg" and the use of a rooting hormone speeds things up and produces stockier plants.

Airlayering came within the competence of home gardeners when "baggies" hit the market. A lanky, ceiling-tall dieffenbachia, among others with bare legs, can be shrunk to a manageable 12-inches. Fill a square of polyethylene with moist peatmoss. With a sharp knife or razor blade cut part way through the stem where you want roots to form. Dust the cut with a rooting hormone powder and slip a toothpick in the cut to keep it open. Wrap the peatmoss-filled plastic around the cut and fasten it securely at both ends so that it is airtight.

Watch for white roots to appear and when they have filled the plastic, cut the rooted top off and pot up in fresh potting mix. The parsimonious will save the old stump, which will produce more offsets at the joints. Dieffenbachia is not called Dumb Cane for nothing. It contains a paralyzing juice. Best not to grow it while the kiddos are putting new experiences in their mouths.

Cuttings have been used for propagating plants in Alaska since the Russians came. Before the modern garden centers were here sourdough gardeners were passing out "slips" to friends, who were grateful for the handouts, even if they produced pitiful plants, because the only rooting method they knew was rooting in water. We know more about it now.

We know that rooting a "slip" in water works well with only a few plants, and that they are apt to be leggy and lacking in vigor because plants rooted in water usually lose their lower leaves and produce gangly stems. We are onto the hazards of unsterilized garden soil as a rooting medium, which can do us dirt, and that we get a high success rate with the commercial soil-less mixes. Homemade mixes are good too, so long as they are fairly gritty and contain no unsterilized soil. Geraniums and other succulent plants can be rooted in mason's sand. (Perlite alone is a bit more difficult to anchor the cuttings in; a mixture of perlite and builder's sand works better).

Plastic bags and clear plastic wrap have replaced panes of glass for cover, frequently prescribed in older horticultural literature.

The fungus diseases, like "black leg," that once took a heavy toll of homegrown cuttings, have succumbed to fungicides and rooting hormones that promote rapid and vigorous root systems, reducing the time in which cuttings are exposed to pathogens.

A dozen fuchsia tip cuttings taken in March will most likely net even the novice gardener a dozen little fuchsia plants two or three weeks later. A single wax begonia plant purchased in a four-inch pot may yield enough for a window box by planting time.

A lanky geranium can be chopped up for cuttings, the severe pruning making the mother plant more compact and floriferous. Don't slit your wrists if you lose a higher percentage of geranium cuttings than you do with other kinds of plants; even commercial nurseries have problems with geraniums.

DIVISION is a means of propagating plants that is within the competence of the ordinary gardener. For decades divisions of plants have been passed over the back fence between neighbors. After several years some perennials' spirits lag, the stems become spindly and the center of the crown may die—an indication that division is in order to give it a new lease on life. This happens with trollius, columbines, the native iris, delphiniums, shasta daisies, rhubarb, oriental poppies, the native iris, veronica, comfrey, and Russian ("flame") lilies, among others that get carried away.

Lift such a clump, dispose of any dead parts, and divide the remainder into segments. Prune off a third of the top growth and set the segment you're keeping in soil augmented with peatmoss and fertilizer. Water it in with a slow-running hose to settle the soil (instead of tramping it in with your feet) and protect it from sun and wind if necessary.

Division will work with shrubs, especially those clump-formers that send up many suckers. Don't try it with plants that grow from a single stem.

OFFSETS. There is a kind of delight when you discover that a favorite plant is having an offspring. Many indoor plants produce offsets, or "pups," miniature duplicates of themselves, with which you can increase your stock and have little plants to give to deserving friends or contribute to a plant sale.

Most cacti and other succulent plants are generous with these little plants. You simply wait until they are of handling ease and cut them off with a clean, sharp knife. Let them lie on a clean surface until a callus has formed and pot them up in small pots of a fast-draining mix.

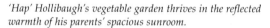

'Hap' Hollibaugh's vegetable garden thrives in the reflected warmth of his parents' spacious sunroom.

CHAPTER 7

FIGHTING BACK

It's enough to make a gardener throw in the trowel. Weeds, insects and plant diseases. Moose in the cabbage, rabbits in the hybrid lupines, birds freeloading in the strawberry patch. In the bad old days the word was "Quick, Henry — the Flit!" Integrated Pest Management and the garden supply industry have newer ploys to help you fight back.

Integrated Pest Management courses and research programs are now offered by virtually every major university in North America and IPM is being vigorously promoted in Alaska by the Cooperative Extension Service, which deploys technicians in both farm communities and urban areas, and has the urgent endorsement of all responsible garden publications, including this book.

IPM has brought more prudent, effective and cheaper ways of controlling the garden spoilers. Commercial growers who employ their own pest scouts must balance their labor cost against the high cost of pesticide use, and they report a modest profit from the pest scouts.

New products are coming on line and gardeners should make their acquaintance. Full service garden centers and garden supply catalogs are pushing the new technology.

American Horticultural Society President Mark Cathey's 'New Garden Ethic' is having an impact on gardeners who are learning when to accept tolerable pest levels and to make pesticides a last, rather than a first, line of defense.

The first line of defense is in plant selection, choosing plants with built-in resistance, and plants suited to the environment in which they will have to grow. Trying to coax survival from plants not native to high latitudes, and subjecting them to insects and diseases to which they have no resistance, is a loser's game and adds to problems we already have.

Many seed catalogs indicate disease-resistant varieties and extensive research is being done on plant species that have a natural repellent factor for certain insects. The cucumber 'Sweet Success' is a sweet example, the bitterness factor having been bred out of the fruit but left in the foliage, where the insects do the damage.

Chemicals toxic to insects but not to mammals have been discovered in many plants. A plant maintained in vigorous good health, uncrowded, receiving enough nutrients and water, and not stressed by unsuitable environment can keep the spoilers at bay; plants stressed by poor cultural methods are vulnerable to attack. The gardener who puts high nitrogen fertilizer on everything in sight is inviting insects that relish succulent new growth, not to mention pollution of the water table. Crowding plants, in the wistful hope that they will crowd out the weeds, deprives them of beneficial air circulation and light on all sides. Rotating crops prevents the build-up of soil-borne pests. Except in areas prone to winter winds, fall tillage exposes many weed seeds and insect eggs to the harsh winter—and hungry birds.

Planting large blocks of one plant family concentrates vapors that attract their enemies. Ask any grower of an acre of roses, or a field of cabbage. A mulch of aluminum foil repels aphids from rose bushes and the planting of sage, mint, and mustard among the cole crops discourages insects attracted to them. Aphids are not fond of garlic's fragrance.

WEEDS

Weeds have been with us since the Ice Age and are adapted to the temperature and daylength of the High North better than any of the introduced cultivated plants, which is why desirable plants don't "crowd out the weeds." To add insult to this injury, most weed seeds require light to germinate, and Alaska has more than enough daylight to boost the germination rate.

Instead of pulling one weed at a time, the use of the Cape Cod weeder and similar hand tools make short work of small weeds.

Here is by no means the end of a long list of noxious weeds that plague the gardener. Some are prevalent in one area, not in another.

Keeping them from going to seed is the first control. Sometimes a plant becomes a weed because it is so aggressive in the conditions you have to offer that it tends to crowd out other desirable species. In my garden, I have had to eliminate such "weeds" as *Aquilegia brevistyla*, *Arnica montana*, our native wild geranium, "butter and eggs," and a wild *Erigeron* I collected in Finland which became invasive. Watch introductions that come "over the back fence" for aggressive tendencies and impose sanctions before you have to resort to chemical warfare.

Wayne Vandry, the Alaska State Horticulture Specialist, writes that "Weed prevention can be accomplished by reducing existing seed populations, increasing plant competitiveness, and preventing the introduction of new seed. The key to long term control of annual weeds is preventing seed production. Dealing with perennial weeds such as quack grass and horsetail is more difficult because you have above-ground reproduction through seeds and below ground vegetative reproduction to contend with. Destroying the top without the bottom doesn't work. Destroying the root system or both the top and bottom does work."

Truer words were never said.

CHICKWEED is easily the most aggravating. It is in the soil everywhere. It germinates before seeds of cultivated plants do. It goes to seed while your back is turned. It reproduces not only by seeds but by rooting at the nodes, so if you leave a scrap of it on the ground, it becomes a rooted cutting. Instead of pulling one at a time, the use of the Cape Cod weeder and similar hand tools make short work of chickweed and other small weeds.

If you attack chickweed with a hoe or a cultivator, be deft about it; plant roots spread out close to the warm, moist surface. If you rely on pulling chickweed, take along a container; any left in the garden will root and become new plants. In some areas where chickweed has been allowed to go to seed you may have to leave such ground fallow for a year, covering it with black plastic, carpet scraps, or roofing paper.

If you opt for the herbicide route, glyphosate, marketed as Roundup™ or Kleen-up,™ is effective and degrades so quickly that plants can be set out in two weeks. Bear in mind that glyphosate is a grass killer; you may need to do some fancy footwork if you must cross a lawn in your spray-boots.

DANDELIONS are a tap-rooted weed, ill suited to attack by hoe or hand weeder. There are tools that permit you to stand while pressing down with your foot on a clamp that gets the whole root if your aim is right on target, and there are hand tools that go deep to get the root. Picking dandelion blossoms before they go to seed is an exercise in futility because the plant will redouble its efforts to produce seed. Allowing the plants to go to seed spreads the airborne seed over whole neighborhoods.

The common dandelion came into the country with European settlers, but it found plenty of related species that came the way Alaska's early settlers did — over the Bering Sea land bridge to spread throughout the hemisphere. Alaska has numerous species, probably twice as many as the Lower 48 states.

In the countryside dandelions are an important source of nectar for bees, provide nutritious vitamins and minerals as food for people, and make a wine that has a long history in Europe.

The French dip the blossoms in batter and deep fry them. It is their incursion in lawns that arouses the wrath of urban dwellers.

The most effective control is, unhappily, one fraught with danger. 2,4-D, the ingredient in many commercial herbicides in common use is a systemic weed killer that does not kill on the spot, but works as it spreads throughout the plant's system. It is specific to broadleaf plants and does not kill grass.

Tomatoes are incredibly sensitive to minute amounts of 2,4-D that gets into greenhouses from winddrift and on the clothing and hands of gardeners and guests. Some products are designed to be sprayed on lawns with a garden hose; others incorporate it into weed-and-feed formulae that damage or kill neighboring broadleaf shrubs and herbaceous plants. It is bad news for family pets if it gets into their water dishes or if they get it on their coats from a freshly sprayed lawn.

Probably the safest application method is to use a coarse spray nozzle inserted in a 46-ounce juice can that has both ends cut out. Moving the can from weed to weed is tedious business but much safer than spraying the whole lawn. The applicator should consign his clothing to the washing machine and take a shower. The equipment used should be reserved for that chemical alone and the container stored as far from the greenhouse as possible and out of the reach of children and pets. Scary? You bet.

FIREWEED, *Epilobium angustifolium,* is either a weed or a wildflower, depending on your point of view. As a wildflower it has a lot to offer: rosy spikes that can make a wild garden out of a weed patch in summer, and a splash of fiery foliage in autumn. Its young shoots are salad green fodder and fireweed honey is tasty.

If it grows where you'd rather not have it, it can be a troublesome weed, germinating by the millions. Moose enjoy it for munchies at the

The native fireweed is a welcome fiery introduction to fall, but it can be a troublesome weed.

Alaska Zoo, and it draws them to suburban gardens.

In a dwarf dogwood ground cover we pulled fireweed to reduce competition for the desired dogwood. The next summer, native annual grasses sprouted where the soil had been disturbed. That year we hand-cut the grasses and remaining fireweed close to the ground, depriving them of their ability to photosynthesize, and our weed problem was virtually solved. A single weed-cutting each summer keeps this 20- by 40-foot expanse of dwarf dogwood weed free.

NATIVE GRASSES are not difficult to control in lawns because they do not respond well to management. They are a problem in cultivated areas, and a fair number of agronomists believe that grass is the climax crop which would take over if ground is left to its own devices.

Using a hand cultivator works, but it has to be repeated frequently. To prevent seed-set is the goal, best done when the grasses are small, even with a hand cultivator. If it has set seed, it's worth a pass with the pruning shears to prevent mature seed from spreading on the wind.

QUACKGRASS, *Agropyron repens*, is probably Alaska's most vicious perennial weed, a European import. It is spread by seed and by creeping under-ground roots, which can sprout new plants at every node. In good garden soil it can travel fast and can take over a large area in a single season. It is exceedingly difficult to eradicate. The stems are dark green, one to four feet tall, the lower part being hairy. The seeds are smaller than the familiar Red Top wild grass and somewhat resemble oat seeds, but are smaller.

Tilling can worsen the problem by chopping up untold numbers of viable cuttings and spreading them throughout the entire plot. Pulling quack grass may also be among the worst methods of control, for it leaves behind fragments of rootstock that make new plants. Cutting it at ground level is better, depriving it of its ability to make chlorophyll, but this is one of the most mindless tasks known to man.

There is no easy method of control. It can be smothered by black plastic or roofing paper, which may take a year, and underground roots may find their way outside the smothering blanket. Glyphosate, the herbicide marketed as 'Round-up'™ and 'Kleen-up'™ is an effective control.

Glyphosate is not a volatile compound so it does not vaporize to damage adjacent plants, but care must be taken to protect desirable plants nearby from its spray. It degrades rapidly enough that you can plant in a matter of days after application (read the directions carefully for maximum effectiveness and minimum danger—your foe is an implacable one). The first sign of a kill may be in about 10 days, depending on how warm the

weather is. When yellowing stems turn brown, look for any remaining green ones and spray again.

If your garden is free of quack grass, be alert to its incursion. It is not too difficult to eradicate

The late Dr. Christine Heller photographed this water hemlock on Cottonwood Creek near Wasilla

if the area is small, but it is virtually impossible to rid a whole garden of this invasive weed once it takes hold. When it has made thick sods that almost no tool will penetrate, the last resort is to lift the surface sods and take them to the city landfill for burial. Apply glyphosate to the soil and surrounding area, repeating if necessary, before replanting.

If quackgrass is present in the neighborhood, it will almost certainly appear from windblown seeds. Cutting seed heads is probably helpful but it is tedious and if you miss one stem, it has the potential to germinate many new plants. This is a truly vicious weed requiring more aggressive measures than good gardeners like to use. It is not as dangerous in lawns where weekly mowing keeps it in abeyance, but in areas you opt to leave out of cultivation, it is a menace—and cultivating is no solution.

WATER HEMLOCK, *Cicuta spp.*, is common in Alaska in wet places. It is deadly poisonous, the more treacherous for its close resemblance to the non-poisonous water parsnip, *Sium suave.* It is not uncommon around lakeside cabins at the water's edge.

WILD MUSTARD is a problem because it is host to insects more troublesome than the weed itself. Pull it or hoe it before it goes to seed.

INSECTS

Alaska has fewer kinds of garden insects than the other states, but their numbers are growing due to importation, and carelessness.

Insecticides become less effective as their targets build up immunity. There are mounting concerns about their safety.

The Cooperative Extension Service employs technicians in the summer months who dispense information by telephone and often make house calls.

Commercial growers who employ their own pest scouts balance their labor cost against the cost of pesticides, and they report a modest profit on the pest scouts. To avoid individual plant inspection they use "sticky traps" to see what insects are present by monitoring a sampling of plants instead of a whole field or greenhouse bay. If the infestation can be held at a tolerable level by less lethal measures they can avoid overkill and the killing off of beneficial predators. This monitoring trick can be used by home gardeners.

Sticky traps are usually yellow plastic ribbons coated with a powerful glue. It has long been known that many insects are attracted to the color yellow and will zero in on a sticky yellow strip, and stay stuck there. (So much for the old wives' tale about marigolds fending off insects.) Some insects are more attracted to other colors. Red sticky traps work better with insects attracted to

poinsettias. Blue strips lure thrips and gnats.

Some full service garden centers and national garden supply catalogs sell sticky traps. (If one gets stuck to greenhouse glass, acetone — as in nail polish remover — will take it off, but if your hair gets stuck, better settle for a scissors.) Other traps are cards with holes for hanging, or you can attach them to stakes for use outdoors. Home concoctions work too — heavy motor oil or honey smeared on colored cards or boards will trap insects. One commercial source is the catalog of Barrington Industries, P.O. Box 133, Barrington, IL 60010.

Insecticides should be specific to the pest and the least harmful to beneficial insects, people and animals. Home gardeners are learning to tolerate low levels of insect populations and disease, something that commercial growers cannot do if their products are to be marketable.

Keeping plants in vigorous good health so they can fight off insect attack calls for careful attention to meeting their needs for water and nutrients, and eliminating weeds, which often are host to damaging insects.

Rotating susceptible crops helps keep insect buildup at tolerable levels, and separating crops of the same plant family prevents a concentration of the vapors that attract the insects. A strong stream of water from a hose washes off many harmful insects, and a shower under the kitchen faucet or bathroom shower will work on houseplants if you do it before the insects have established a major beachhead. You may have to repeat the operation every few days to catch new generations.

Floating row covers over susceptible vegetable crops prevent insects from laying eggs as well as promoting growth and providing protection from inclement weather. In our home garden, long targeted by root maggots, a floating row cover stretched over arches of PVC pipe and anchored to the raised beds with staples so that egg-laying flies could not get in, worked perfectly. When we were too sparing with the staples, the flies got in and had a field day.

With good coverage, susceptible radishes,

turnips, and green onions reached harvest size with no sign of maggot damage. Row covers attached to one-by-two boards worked well, and the edges of floating row cover sealed with soil or rocks did less well. The row covers were installed when the seeds were sown and remained on until the vegetables were harvested.

Early gardeners cut flat round discs from roofing paper and placed them around the stems of the cabbage family starter plants, or used small tin cans at planting time to create collars. A ring of wood ashes offered some protection from slugs, but had to be repeated after rains or watering.

Removing over-age radishes and other susceptible vegetables from the garden so that larvae won't move out of roots into the soil and overwinter as pupae is important. These methods are useful techniques; they come from the writings of Wayne Vandre, the State horticultural consultant.

Looking for Mister Goodbug is a rewarding search. Many natural predators and parasites exist. Exterminating them with broad spectrum insecticides is counter-productive. Beneficial insects and the benign bacterium, *Bacillus thurengensis* (BT for short), are marketed by several companies. You may find them in garden centers or they can be special ordered for you. Remote gardeners will find that some seed catalogs list them and offices of the CES maintain a list of vendors' addresses.

Birds have a voracious appetite for insects. They will gladly work over your garden in exchange for shrubs and trees to reconnoiter from and sneak fruit, and water for a bath and a drink. Until you have watched a bird enjoying a shower in your sprinkler and preening itself on your garden fence, you have missed one of the keen pleasures of gardening.

Shrews are not popular with home gardeners because they tend to seek shelter from the cold indoors, but they have hearty appetites for insects. The **orb-weaving spiders** that make such beautiful webs, are adept at catching flying insects, and they don't let go.

Removing infested plants from the garden

and consigning them to a tightly covered trash can is far better than composting them; compost piles do not always get hot enough in all parts of Alaska to kill insect eggs. Putting infested plants on a weed pile is a very bad idea.

There are numerous insecticides on garden center shelves and listed in seed catalogs. When you must resort to chemical warfare choose a weapon that is specific to the problem insect rather than a shotgun product that kills insects you don't have or exterminates beneficial ones you don't even know you have.

Aim for minimal toxicity. Soap drenches have long been used to do battle with insects. Some plants are easily damaged by soap and some insects are immune to it. Two tablespoons of dishwashing liquid to a gallon of water will control soft-bodied insects, but if not rinsed off may damage some plants. Insecticidal soaps sold in garden centers and listed in seed catalogs are one of the safest insecticides, but label directions should be followed carefully if the treatment is to be both safe and effective. Hard water minerals may bind with the ingredients, so soft water or distilled water is a better way to go.

Safer's markets a botanical insecticide derived from the neem tree, seeds of which have been used for centuries in Asia to keep insects out of stored grains. USDA Agricultural Research Service entomologists report that mixing one cup of a vegetable cooking oil with one tablespoon of liquid dishwashing (not dish<u>washer</u>) detergent makes a stock solution. For spraying, mix one to two teaspoons of the stock solution to a cup of water. This gives good control for spider mites and is nearly as effective on aphids and the dread whitefly.

Spraying should be done every ten days. The lowest rate is advised for cauliflower, red cabbage and squash plants, which are sensitive to leaf burn. Spraying the undersides of leaves is important because that's where insects hang out and lay their eggs. Since some plants are damaged by even this innocuous spray, maybe you should try it on a trial plant first.

Rotenone and pyrethrum are botanicals—derived sprays that have low toxicity to people and pets; they kill a broad range of insects. However, rotenone is toxic to honeybees and fish; pyrethrum is safe for them but degrades under sunlight.

Dormant oil sprays made from fish, or petroleum fractions control many troublesome insects, including aphids on trees.

Read the label each time you use a pesticide and never decant it into an unlabeled container. Make sure that it is for the plant you want to use it on and that your timing is right on the button. Many are not acceptable for edible plants, and those that are have strict intervals to observe before harvesting. Keep a written record of application dates or have a calendar for that purpose.

Foliar systemics are absorbed by the plant tissues and kill insects as they feed. Soil systemics take longer to act but are effective longer. Avoid using systemic insecticides on trees and shrubs that have berries or seeds on which birds feed.

Contact insecticides kill on contact and are widely sold. They also kill beneficial insects that eat or parasitize aphids. Observe label warnings about eye, skin, or lung contact with great care.

(See GREENHOUSE MANAGEMENT, for control of greenhouse and indoor plant insects.)

ANTS are more nuisance than menace in Alaska gardens. The carpenter ant is more than a nuisance because it moves into houses, excavating inside walls and insulation for nest building material, where it can do considerable damage. What to do?

First, find the nest. You may be able to trace ants to it and nail them on the spot, but that may not be easy. Look for places where there is excessive moisture, or rotting wood. Old wood piles and decaying stumps harbor carpenter ants which also use Styrofoam or expanded insulation materials for nest building, bad news if you find traces of these materials in your house.

Diazanon mixed with bread crumbs or jelly works by being tracked into nests where other ants feed on it and die. Malathion sprinkled along an ant trail is helpful, but sprays are safer than granules or dusts, which can be dangerous to pets and birds. Baits come in cans with ant-size holes. Study insecticide labels to be sure the product is effective against not just any ant, but *carpenter* ants. The CES has a helpful free bulletin, Carpenter Ants.

APHIDS are also more nuisance than killers, but they do spread diseases. They may damage a plant so badly that it cannot easily be restored to beauty; control measures may be more damaging than the insects. There are several kinds of aphids and their life cycles differ, so you need to know which of the little suckers you're dealing with. Some lay eggs and can reproduce without mating, a neat trick.

Female aphids can produce live females that start giving birth in 10 days or less. Their reproductive capability is so impressive that you may be inundated before you know that you have them. Do not delude yourself into thinking that you can get rid of aphids; they can out-produce your most deadly ploy, but you may be able to contain their numbers to tolerable levels. The good news is that most aphids are plant specific, confining their feeding to one species, like the black aphid to which the chokecherry tree is host. The bad news is that the minority that frequents gardens has eclectic tastes and will feed on anything from arugula to zucchini.

Besides sucking the vital juices from a plant, the varmints excrete a substance called honeydew, which is disgusting when the green birch aphid drips it onto stairs and railings, cars and sidewalks, and attracts ants in battalion force. Honeydew is not easily removed, requiring hot soapy water and elbow grease.

The Extension Service has a good bulletin, Birch Aphids. Birch aphids may beleaguer a town tree, but rarely kill one, but the honeydew nuisance may get so troublesome that you will want bulletin #A-O-063.

If you catch them before the population explodes, a hard blast from a hose may control aphids, but you have to repeat the cold shower frequently to keep up with their reproduction. A spray of liquid soap solution (two tablespoons to a gallon of water) works on plants that you can reach with your sprayer, but there's more bad news—you have to reach the undersides of the leaves because that's where these suckers hang out, and the soap must be rinsed off a few minutes after application. This is a daunting task when the birch trees in question are 60 feet tall. Safer's soap, sold in garden centers and advertised in garden magazines, is effective but it too must be applied according to label directions to avoid plant damage.

It is true that ladybug beetles, syrphid flies and lacewings are big aphid-eaters. They eat something like 100 aphids a day apiece and snack on thrips, mites, scale, mealy bugs, leafhopper nymphs and caterpillar eggs. They keep birch forests under control, but town birches are subject to more stresses, and so are the little beneficial predators. It is easy to kill them off when you go after the aphids.

Ladybugs are flighty, too, and may leave your beleaguered columbines for a romp in the wild raspberries. This is because they are programmed, like the salmon, to return to the place of their birth—and the ones you buy were probably collected in the forests of central California where they are plentiful and easily harvested.

To make beneficial insects your ally takes more guile than spraying poisons. First, you have to ID the enemy, then deploy his natural predators, and keep the supply and demand in balance — not as easy as saying "Quick, Henry, the Flit," but very satisfying for those who delight in seeing Mister Goodbug do his stuff.

Southeastern Alaska is often plagued with the spruce needle aphid which feeds on older needles of the Sitka spruce. Needles turn yellow, then brown, and fall, and infested trees have thin crowns. A strong blast from the hose will decimate their numbers and a soap spray will help control them, but must be repeated several times. Ask an IPM technician or an arborist for help.

CUTWORMS are low on the list of gardeners' favorite things. They are the gray or brown caterpillar stage of the little moths that lay eggs on newly set-out or germinated plants. Some have learned to climb and feed on buds and leaves. Others go underground and cut stems at ground level. These work nights and sleep days, just under the surface of the soil. By scratching the soil around a freshly toppled plant you can usually find the culprit and execute him.

Eliminating weeds before planting the garden helps because the moths are attracted to them at egg-laying time, mid-June into August in Alaska. Making collars of roofing paper or small tin cans with both ends cut out may deter the caterpillars if the barriers are at least one inch below and above ground, but these methods come with no guarantee. Using floating row covers will keep out the egg-layers effectively, if they are moth-tight, and so will screen wire stretched over arches of wire. Since muskmelons, outdoor cucumbers, and squash depend on insect pollination, the covers have to be removed when the plants begin to bloom. Chemical controls are Dylox™ and Sevin.™

One species of cutworm overwinters as caterpillars, another as eggs which hatch into caterpillars. Both feed on plants in their caterpillar stage. So, control weeds early in the season, protect plants with collars or row covers, and when all else fails, resort to chemical controls.

FUNGUS GNATS are more nuisance than menace, although in huge numbers they can damage indoor plants. They are tiny black flies hovering about plants. Fungus gnats feast on rotting organic matter, so their presence may indicate that your indoor plants need re-potting in fresh potting mix. They also show a preference for plants that are kept too wet.

ROOT MAGGOTS are the spoilers in the cabbage patch, attacking all the crucifers—broccoli, cauliflower, kale, turnips, rutabagas, radishes—even ornamental cabbage or kale in flower beds. Only kohlrabi is safe; it bears its fruit above ground.

ONION MAGGOTS tunnel into onions. Waiting to plant onions until mid-June or later out-foxes

IPM Technician Beth Schultz points out root maggot eggs on a susceptible cabbage family plant.

them. Both kinds of flies, which resemble ordinary house flies, lay visible eggs on the soil or leaves. They can be rubbed off onions by hand, a task that is nobody's idea of fun (use a tissue) but it works better than most measures.

Fall tillage reduces maggot numbers but may be an erosion problem in windy areas. A relentless search-and-destroy mission is needed to keep these pests from overwintering. Leaving a maggot-ridden plant on the garden is an invitation to an invasion next year. Crop rotation is a necessity. As a chemical control, diazanon is probably the best, repeated every seven to 10 days until no more eggs are found. Lorsban™ and Dursban™

are probably better killers but can only be applied 30 days before harvesting, no good if you're succession-planting radishes.

This wisdom is confirmed in the CES bulletin *Root Maggots in Alaska Home Garden* free at the nearest CES office.

SLUGS. There are several native American slugs and 20 or more foreign species have come in despite the USDA's quarantine. Both male and female reproductive organs are in a slug, reports an excellent CES fact sheet imaginatively titled *SLUGS*.

Slugs lay eggs under dead leaves, in the soil and other protected places, like under planks and rhubarb leaves. They do not crawl, but secrete a slime in which they slide to their targets. Some species feed on the ground, others higher on plants, and some eat roots. Many eat 30 or 40 times their weight each day (which never shows on their hips) and they are not picky eaters, relishing a rare alpine with the same enthusiasm as a rutabaga. Several kinds may live in a garden at the same time, each having its own population peak.

Nobody likes **slugs** and gardeners have been known to quit gardening rather than fight a no-win war. Slugs are more numerous in some gardens than others, particularly those that are watered in the evening (a poor cultural practice for other reasons). Slugs lay their eggs in late summer, and if there is a long, mild fall, they may lay more than one batch. Some overwinter as eggs, hatching when spring comes, and their kids have big appetites, devouring whole rows of plants. Some assault tactics work better than others.

There are several slug poisons, which may be hazards to birds and household pets. They can be placed in containers with slug-size holes, but you still have the unappetizing task of picking up dead slugs so the birds won't get a poisoned one. Sprinkling salt on slugs kills them, but is toxic to the soil. Picking slugs and dumping them in a container of salt is environmentally sound and aesthetically disgusting. A spray bottle filled with equal parts of household ammonia and water is useful and satisfying, but it's not very good for plants.

Ducks and geese are big slug-eaters and they eat weeds too. They also eat vegetable crops and flowers and newspaper carriers, and their vocal powers and manure production are impressive, so some towns have ordinances banning them.

Slug baits are not poisonous, and not so deadly effective either. You still have to collect the victims, because they will crawl away after pigging out. Beer is a popular bait and slugs do drown in their debauchery. Dr. Whitney S. Cranshaw of Colorado State University, tested 12 brands of beer and a nonalcoholic malt beverage. The beers, reported in the horticultural press, varied in effectiveness, but the slugs' favorite was the nonalcoholic beer.

Homemade solutions using active lager yeast (sold in home brewing supply stores) and baking yeast were tested, and brews made from lager yeast worked best. To make your own bait, mix one tablespoon sugar and 1/8 teaspoon yeast with each cup of water. Pour the liquid into a shallow pan and set it in the garden with the rim flush with the ground surface. Excess solution can be refrigerated for months. In the garden it should be changed frequently.

Some slug enemies say home brew works better than commercial beer and the dregs in the bottom of the bottle are even more effective. Slugs must be harvested each morning lest only the little ones drown and the big slugs stagger off to return in your absence. Nice way to start the day, right?

Half grapefruit rinds, banana peels, cabbage or rhubarb leaves have their supporters.

It is widely believed that slugs will not cross a rough surface like ashes, cat litter, crushed eggshells, or crushed glass. Not so, unless there is a back-tilted barrier behind the rough stuff that they cannot climb, report slug commandos. One that works better than most involves cutting window screen and forming a lip at the top so slugs can't climb over it. Place the screens flat on the ground around plants in need of protection. By removing several lines of wire at the edges, a sharp border is produced, for which a slug will never forgive you. When under attack you need to use more than one weapon. This is one war in which you can't get an unconditional surrender. But you can be hateful.

SPRUCE BARK BEETLES have killed many acres of trees in the Anchorage and Kenai Peninsula areas, a painful sight. The beetles attack older trees, rarely young ones unless they are under stress. For what comfort there is in it, it may be nature's way of renewing a forest, letting aged trees succumb to make way for new vigorous young species.

The new beetle generation comes on from mid-May into June. If you have a neighbor with an infested tree, your trees are at risk. There is now an EPA-approved pesticide that can be safely used on endangered trees. If you elect to spray, be sure that the chemical used is specifically for spruce bark beetles. It is a job best done by a professional pest control contractor. There is no chemical treatment after the beetles have bored into the bark. If you have an infested tree your only recourse is to cut it down, debark it, and dispose of the bark. The wood is safe to use for construction, landscaping, or firewood.

In the home landscape, newly-felled trees and windfalls with the bark left on are prime targets, as are the stumps of infected, recently cut trees. There are de-barking tools, the mechanical ones being dauntingly expensive and the manually operated ones too enervating for many home gardeners. Arborists, listed in the Yellow Pages, have power tools.

The Extension Service has a useful fact sheet on spruce bark beetles that you should have if you are in a danger zone.

The best defense is to keep landscape spruces well-watered and fertilized, giving their foliage a stiff spray with the hose to dislodge other insects that may be stressing the tree. A good soaking of the ground under and around the tree is needed

because little rain reaches the ground under conifers. For a spruce, it's a prolonged drought from
late summer through a long winter. Trees that
have been injured or water stressed are at high
risk.

WASPS, HORNETS, and YELLOW JACKETS
occasionally take up residence where they are
least welcome, in a deck or patio area. They build
nests under the eaves or in the ground, are not
always observed until the nests reach maximum
resident capacity of a few hundred to many thousands. They are more aggressive than the lazy
bumble bees and busy honey bees. Their sting is
more painful and, unlike that of other bees, can
be repeated. Some people have a serious allergy
to their sting and may need emergency room care.

To their credit, these pests consume many
damaging insects. Resort to chemical warfare as
a last resort if they become troublesome. An IBM
technician advises baiting for them. A fish head
in a bowl of water will attract hundreds of these
insects who drown in this good stuff.

When you are truly beleaguered, you may
have to go on the chemical war path. If the nest is
out of reach, a trained handler may be needed to
get the nest into a heavy plastic bag, a job fraught
with some danger to the amateur commando.
Garden centers and hardware stores have spray
cans of insecticide specific to these insects. They
are used more safely at night when the enemy has
responded to call to quarters and is less hostile
after a long day of combat. Directions on the can
should be followed precisely and the prudent will
wear protective clothing, and be prepared to
sprint for cover.

Wasps, hornets and yellow jackets seem to
be cyclical, building several nests one year and
none again soon. When three of them stung IPM
Technician Beth Schulz-Blitz in our garden, she
gamely treated the stings with an ice cube and a
shrug, "They're just getting even."

Once in a while somebody sounds an alarm
about the Africanized honey bee, the cross between our sweet-tempered honeybees and the
accidentally-released African bees, by far more
hostile to people. Research indicates that somewhere in the United States there will be a geo-
graphic or climatic boundary to their northward
migration. True, the African bees survive in the
Andes at 10,000 feet, and at elevations in southern Africa where snow cover may last a week or
more. Their incursion into Alaska is a remote possibility.

WHITEFLY is one of the most dreaded insects of
the greenhouse or indoor plant gardener. You
know you have it when the touch of your hand
brings a swarm of minute white flies from a plant.
Prevention is light years better than cure. Quarantine any plant to be introduced into greenhouse,
home or sunroom for several days and watch it
closely for white fly and other pests before introducing it to clean plants.

If you find it, consider dumping the plant into
a plastic bag and sealing it for disposal. If the infestation is caught early, yellow sticky traps work
well.

The tiny parasitic wasp *Encarsia formosa* lays
its eggs in immature white flies, killing them. Full
service garden centers have sources for special orders and the CES maintains a mail order list.

The synthetic pyrethroid, resmethrin is a de-
gradable, low toxicity chemical that kills all stages
of whitefly except eggs. A newer one is sumithrin;
both are sold in garden centers and listed in garden supply catalogs.

WOOLY APHIDS harass spruce trees but rarely
kill them. Spring fertilization and watering usually enable a tree to withstand an attack. With
minor infestations where the tree does not appear
to be damaged, frequent hosing-down will usually control this pest. If it gets out of hand, a two
percent soap spray may do the trick. As a last resort, a systemic insecticide may be called for.

PLANT DISEASES

Diagnosing plant diseases is complicated and can
be a frustrating effort. We list some of the most
common, easily recognized ones. Your first line
of defense may be a call to the IPM technician in

the CES office nearest you. He/she has special training in diagnosing plant disorders and suggesting treatment. If your problem requires more research, CES personnel have access to State and Federal agency specialists. Even plant pathologists can't always diagnose diseases over the telephone or by letter. If you are remote from technical help, your best bet may be quarantining suspicious plants .

A full service garden center near you may have a copy of the Ortho Problem Solver book prominently displayed on a stand. Take a notebook; don't expect the salesperson or the owner of a garden center to be a plant pathologist. If you take a diseased plant specimen with you, take it out with you when you leave, and don't touch their plants.

As with all the ailments to which plants are subject, prevention is infinitely simpler than cure. Here are some preventive measures gardeners can take.

Wash your hands frequently. Do not touch seedlings unnecessarily. Give plants enough space so that one sick one won't infect the whole crop. Never put diseased plants on the compost pile. Control weeds on which disease-carrying insects congregate, especially in the home greenhouse. Provide good drainage so that excess moisture does not gather around plant stems. Provide for ventilation and air circulation.

Be wary of using any chemical that you may have left from a previous purchase. Any chemical three years old is outdated and its use only builds up resistance in the very pathogens you are trying to control. If it is no longer stocked by vendors it may have been recalled for recently discovered problems. Always read the labels before using any pesticide because they say what the product can be used for and warn of dangers to plants, soil, ground water, and people. But the print is exceeding fine.

BLOSSOM END ROT on outdoor-grown squash and greenhouse-grown tomatoes is a common complaint. It first appears as a sunken spot on the blossom end and turns black. It is caused by a lack of calcium in the nutrient mix, aggravated by fluctuation in soil moisture, and excessive salts in the growing mix. To avoid this disheartening plague, try to keep moisture on an even keel, avoid the use of manure, and go for the more costly soluble fertilizers like calcium nitrate. Be sure that the soil is well drained, and when you water, do so generously to leach out salts.

The **DAMPING OFF DISEASES** are no longer the home gardener's nightmare that they once were. The name, "damping off," of this complex of bacterial diseases that causes seedlings to keel over, or fail to germinate, implies that over-watering is the cause, which is not strictly true. The real cause is disease pathogens. The conditions that favor germination—heat and moisture—create favorable conditions for disease among seedlings, so get your germinated seedlings out into good light and coolish temperatures as soon as they germinate. And wash your hands before handling seedlings.

Use one of the soilless mixes that is sold by garden centers or mix your own. Here is a recipe: to four parts each of sphagnum peat moss, horticultural grade vermiculite and perlite, add two tablespoons of ground limestone and two tablespoons of a balanced fertilizer. Moisten with water the night before you need to use it.

If you plant sterilized seeds in a sterile planting mix, you may not need to wash pots if they have held only soilless mixes. If you begin to have a problem with damping-off, start sterilizing your containers again. You can soak used pots in a tub of one part laundry bleach to nine parts water for 10 minutes and let them air-dry before using. Wash your hands with soap and water and take pains to see that anything that touches seeds or a seeding medium has not come in contact with soil.

FUNGUS DISEASES are often the cause of **leaf spots**, and **stem or root rots**, some plants being more susceptible than others (roses are notoriously prone to leaf spots and geranium cuttings to the ominous "black leg"). Maneb and zineb are two wide-spectrum fungicides which control a number of such diseases. Fore is one which is useful for controlling **lawn diseases** like snow mold.

POWDERY MILDEW is common during rainy or cloudy weather and Phaltan or Domain are used to control it.

ANIMAL INCURSION

The number of moose visitors varies from year to year, influenced by snow, availability of browse, the proximity of protected areas like parks. They quickly become habituated to certain areas and to foods that are not ordinarily part of their natural diet. Although they are browsers they have learned that farmers' hay or straw stacks offer acceptable fodder. They will kneel to get at vegetables in town gardens, and have acquired a taste for the bark of apple and mountain ash trees. They like fireweed, and although I am gracious about sharing a meadow of it with them, I am irate when they get into my little hoard of white fireweed. They are said not to like lilac branches, but they will break them down to see if they just might be tasty. They keep the currant bushes and the Rugosa rose hedges pruned somewhat more severely than necessary.

Although one of the great things about living in Alaska is seeing these magnificent animals close up, it is disheartening to lose a season's veg-etable garden to a single night visit or to see expensive trees and shrubs ruined. Many methods have been tried, from mothballs to firecrackers. Most of these will work at least once or until the animals become habituated and pay no attention to them. The first few times I banged a cookie sheet on a deck railing, a family of moose took off in panic; now they pause in their browsing to look up and acknowledge that it's only the lady with the cookie sheet.

Onion bags of coarse red netting tied over young apple tree branches help but some damage still occurs. Young trees and shrubs can be protected by wooden frames and wire cages left in place over the winter. When the cages are covered with snow the moose may get entangled and can drag one for long distances.

Irish Spring soap and mesh bags of mothballs seem to be deterrents. Fabric softener sheets tied to susceptible plants have worked for a Maine gardener reporting in Organic Gardening Magazine. A commercial spray called DeerAway™ has been useful in other states where deer have become an urban nuisance.

Motion detectors that turn on flood lights, an intermittent sprinkler or a barking dog or howling wolf recorded message have been somewhat effective. A portable radio tuned to a 24-hour station works in places where it does not provoke neighbors to target practice.

Animal incursion usually means **MOOSE.**

An eight-foot chain link fence is effective, but expensive, and no great asset to the landscape.

RABBITS, or more accurately, hares, are cyclical and some years they plague gardeners. They are not fussy eaters, but show some preference for legumes, like Russell hybrid lupines and garden peas. If you are fortunate enough to have a resident bald eagle, they will be scarce the following summer.

You might try a Have-a-Heart™ trap, sold in farm supply stores and some garden centers. You bait the trap with the animal's favorite food, inspect the trap the following morning, and re-locate the animal to a more suitable habitat. A frequent catch: the neighbor's cat.

The next best defense is caging of ornamen-tals and a fence around the vegetable garden.

BEARS have always been troublesome in remote areas but are periodically a problem in towns or near campgrounds where they have acquired a taste for garbage. Compost piles have the potential to attract bears if melon and citrus rinds are there. If you have a surprise encounter with a bear at the compost pile, back off.

Janice Shamberg's petunias thrived in a little hot spot beside her greenhouse.

This raised bed on an earthquake crack overlooking Turnagain Arm of Cook Inlet gets sun-warmed water from a hose-filled barrel.

Right: Homer gardener Toras Fisk put a pump in his garden pond to get sun-warmed water to his crops.

CHAPTER 8
FROM GREENHORN TO GREEN THUMB

GETTING STARTED

If you're a newcomer, ask a gardener in your neighborhood when it is safe to set out plants and sow seeds directly in the ground. If there is an office of the Cooperative Extension Service in your area an agent will answer questions, or refer you to a Master Gardener. The Master Gardeners are seasoned gardeners who have taken special training from an Extension horticulturist. Their services are free. If you plan to grow vegetables, ask to have a copy of *Vegetables and Fruits for Alaska, Recommended Variety List* sent to you. There are versions for Southcentral, Southeast and Interior Alaska. If you visit the office pick up a copy of *Sixteen Easy Steps to Gardening in Alaska* and *A Key to Flower Gardening in Alaska*, for which there is a small charge.

While you're at it, pick up a soil testing kit, the best investment around. When the results come back you will know how much of what kind of fertilizer your soil needs and its status regarding organic matter. Fall is a good time to take the sample and till in organic matter like peatmoss, animal manures, or compost and add lime if the test indicates need. Spring is the best time to apply fertilizer.

HIT THE NURSERIES. Most town gardeners start their gardens with plants purchased from commercial greenhouses, full service garden centers or other local entrepreneurs; some order from specialty nurseries rare or choice plants that are not sold locally. If you have a home greenhouse, sunroom, or a fluorescent light setup in the basement or garage, you can buy better plants earlier and grow them yourself. As their roots begin to show through the drainage holes, pot them up into individual containers so they don't become pot bound or leggy. You may be able to buy around April 15th, but the heating cost often outweighs the advantage over buying about May first.

Look for plants that are small and stocky—they get leggy fast as nursery benches get jammed. If roots have filled the cell packs or small pots, the time is right to pot them up into slightly larger containers to avoid any growth set-back. Weekly feeding with a dilute soluble fertilizer will keep them growing until a week or ten days before planting out time when they can go outdoors under floating row cover or into cold frames for hardening off.

If there are several garden centers or commercial greenhouses in your area, visit all of them. They know what they're doing and will offer the most popular kinds of flowers, vegetables, trees and shrubs which do best in your area, but their specialties differ.

Act as though you know your way around. Pick up pots and cell packs to see that roots aren't trailing out the drainage holes and that the plants are stocky with a good dark green color. (Greeenhorn gardeners sometimes snap up the one cell pack of a kind that is in bloom which the grower planted early to show what the flower would look like). Or they'll grab the biggest one, although a younger plant would overtake it and be a better buy. Buy individual pots of flowering plants in groups of at least three so you'll have a nice clump or drift—odd numbers work better than evens, and a mass of a single color makes a more emphatic statement than one of mixed colors.

Denali Seed Company offers seeds of many recommended vegetable varieties. Thompson & Morgan have many English varieties that do well in similar Alaska climates. Seeds Blum specializes in northern and high altitude needs. These and other seed companies will have seed racks in many garden centers. Commercial greenhouses and garden centers try to stock varieties with good local potential.

The best seeds cost more; it is not good judgment to base purchases on the cheapest plants or seed packets.

STARTING FROM SCRATCH. If you live in the boonies, or if you like choosing your seeds from a wide range of catalogs, consider sending for several. Consult the Addenda at the end of the book for suggestions of catalogs that list varieties well suited to the High North. They make exciting reading after you've put the holiday decorations away.

Each year the seed catalogs describe new varieties that are not yet on the Recommended Variety list, but which may be good bets for Alaska. If it's a kind of vegetable known to do well here and is labeled "All-America Selection," it's worth a try. If the "days to maturity" are shorter than existing kinds, give it a whirl. If a new variety of a vegetable that is marginally successful here shaves a few days off the days to maturity, go for it.

"Days to maturity" can mislead Alaska gardeners, for we may have enough days, but not enough "degree days," to ripen some varieties and some crops. But we also have more hours of summer sunlight than in the lower latitudes, giving Fairbanks, for example, a longer growing season than Chicago.

Get off to a fast start. With a growing season of only 108 days, give or take a few, depending on what part of town you live in and whether the neighbor's spruce trees are between you and *el sol*, many vegetables and flowers need a headstart indoors to get to the finish line before first frost. Some need eight to 10 weeks, others do best with only three weeks, and some need only a few days' time for pre-sprouting. Check it out in the listings in appropriate chapters.

Even with a garden diary that goes back several years, it's not easy to guess right on sowing times. Until you have learned about your own growing conditions, you may find yourself starting more than one batch of seeds, pitching the first if it gets too big, or the last because it was started too late—but there are so many seeds in a packet that you can afford to hedge your bets. Keep a garden diary of when you planted, the variety name and your evaluation.

Disregard the time table on seed packets and the magazine articles aimed at gardeners in the Lower 48, and be wary of any calendar for Alaska planting that suggests specific dates. They may be too early for your part of town, or not take into account the difference between dwarfs and tall-growing types, and whether you're starting at room temperature or in a cool garage under fluorescent tubes.

The good earth can do you dirt. Start with a sterile sowing medium. Garden soil comes equipped with fungal and bacterial diseases. The "damping off" complex of fungus diseases that causes seedlings to keel over and die is soil-borne.

The soilless potting mixes drain well and are not contaminated by disease organisms or herbicide residues. If you use a lot of potting mix or live in the Bush, here is a recipe for one of the Cornell mixes, which commercial nurseries use and sell under several trade names.

4 gal. #2 grade vermiculite

4 gal, shredded peatmoss

8 Tbsp. ground dolomitic limestone

1/2 cup balanced fertilizer like 10-20-10

You can sterilize moistened soil in the oven for 30 minutes at 180 degrees. Don't start the count-down until a meat thermometer in the middle of it registers 180, and more is not better. A turkey-size "brown-in" bag is a good container. Microwave ovens with a temperature probe can be used to sterilize two quarts or more of soil at a time. Set the controls at 180 degrees and the time for 30 minutes.

Sterilize plastic pots in a tub of one part chlorine laundry bleach to nine parts water for 10 minutes, or use paper cups with holes punched in the bottom. Styrofoam cups recycled from the trash can under the office coffee maker work as well, but new ones add to our existing problem with solid waste.

If you're using a seed-sowing mix, start the night before by pouring some warm water in the plastic sack it came in so that it will be pleasantly moist by morning. This is not necessary with vermiculite, which sucks up water thirstily.

Sow thinly so that you can prick the seedlings out without damaging their hair-like roots. Coarse seeds are easy to space; if they're fine as dust, add a pinch of coarse sand, give the packet a shake, and sprinkle the contents sparsely on the medium, and press for firm contact. Susan Miller, Grower at the Anchorage Municipal greenhouse, has a neat trick that works for fine seeds like petunias; she moistens the tip of a pencil, picks up the tiny seed and deposits it on the surface of the medium. She built up speed and accuracy with practice. Some fine seeds are pelleted by the seedsman, worth the extra cost for beginners.

Barely cover big seeds. The seed packet may suggest soaking or nicking them with a file to help them germinate. Rubbing hard seeds lightly over a food grater helps some to wake up, as does rolling them in a damp towel and keeping them overnight in a warm place, like the top of the refrigerator.

If you're sowing seeds of something that rebels at being transplanted—like beans, pumpkins, squash or cucumbers—sow their seeds directly into individual pots. Peat pots do not degrade at low soil temperatures and should be used with caution, removing any portion above the soil line, which acts as a wick to dry out the soil. Plastic pots work better, but you should tap the contents out of the pot, never gouging them out.

Enclose pots or flats in a plastic bag or cover them with plastic wrap. Seeds germinate over a wide range of temperatures but there is a known optimum for each. Most germinate at 65 to 75 degrees, but there are enough exceptions to exasperate you.

Some vegetables—celery, lettuce, and potatoes—germinate best in light. There are small table-top greenhouses with fluorescent lights and heating cables for starting seeds, and there are commercial heating cables and mats, but make-shifts work pretty well.

A cardboard box cut to fit over a heating convector or transom, a shelf built over the hot water pipe under the sink, the top of the refrigerator or hot water heater are warm spots. As soon as seeds have sprouted they need to get into bright light and cooler temperature, around 60 degrees.

Pre-sprouting is a useful ploy for peas, beans, and potatoes. A plastic bag of moist peatmoss works for peas and beans, and a paper sack in a warm, light place produces potato sprouts quickly.

Pre-sprouting very small seeds is best done with the fluid-gel method, a technique developed at Michigan State University. It is based on the fact that seedlings will grow in soil cooler than seeds will germinate in. The seeds are sprouted at the optimum temperature for their germination on a paper plate covered with moist paper toweling and checked twice a day until sprouts emerge.

To prepare the gel: mix three or four level teaspoons of corn starch in a cup of water. Bring it to a boil, stirring. Continue stirring while cooling the pan over cold water. Put a sandwich size plastic bag in a cup, one corner down, and pour in about half a cup of cooled gel. Drop the germinated seeds in and stir so the seeds are uniformly suspended. Close and fasten the bag with a twist tie. (In case of bad planting weather, the bag can be refrigerated for a few days).

To plant the seeds, cut off one corner of the bag and squeeze the gel into the furrow, as you would toothpaste. With a steady hand, the seeds will come out at uniform intervals. Cover the gel with a quarter inch of soil and water immediately. This technique makes thinning virtually unnecessary.

Most seed packets contain more seeds than you need; you can save leftovers, but germination may decline with age. Some kinds are viable for years, and some only when freshly harvested. You can test viability rate by sowing l0 seeds and counting the number that comes up for a guide to how many to plant for the number you need.

Store seeds in a cool, dry place. A tablespoon of dry skim milk powder folded in a facial tissue will keep them dry in a jar in the refrigerator, or you may hoard the little vials of silica gel that come with prescription drugs.

Pricking out is a delicate task best done with something like a meat skewer. When the seedling has one or two sets of true leaves, hold it by its leaves, not its stem, and gently insert its roots into a hole in the potting mix that is deep and wide enough for the fragile roots. Two-inch pots or cell-packs are big enough for the first go-round, and you can pot up as their roots ask for it. Keep your thumbs out of the pots; a better way to firm the soil is to tap the pot on the table. Best root development takes place in a mix that is well-aerated and "sharp" from the addition of coarse sand or perlite.

Finding a cool, bright place for your nursery isn't easy. Sunny windowsills get baked by heating convectors beneath, and at night the glass gets too cold. If you don't have a greenhouse kept around 60 degrees at night, scout the basement, garage or laundry room for a place to hang a fluorescent light fixture with three or four tubes, which need not be special plant-growing lights. Give seedlings 18 hours of light a day and check often to see that they don't grow into the tubes, which should hang four to six inches above them.

Hardening-off before planting is giving plants a little exposure to ultra violet rays today, more tomorrow. After about 10 days they can stay out all day and all night. If you have only a few, set them out in a shady place and bring them indoors in the evening.

Packing a lot of trays in and out gets old. A plastic shelter or a cold frame is better.

FRAMES. Cold frames and hot beds are as good as a pay streak in Alaska gardens. A cold frame sits on, or in, the ground and has a cover of glass or rigid plastic. If you put a heating cable under it, it becomes a hot bed. Frames are useful for germinating seeds, raising seedlings, rooting cuttings, and wintering over tender plants. A frame can be a box on the south side of a building, framed by logs or scrap lumber, with storm windows or rigid plastic to cover it. It may have an excavated foundation, masonry walls, a buried heating cable and maybe a vent that is thermostatically-controlled.

Backing up to the side of a building is a good way to go. A frame's size can range from an arm's reach in width to the length of a building, but it should be divided so its covers can be lifted individually. (It would be lovely if they were hinged and if there was a hook to hold the lids open or closed.) A frame can be as high as a rabbit's eye to protect a row of hybrid lilies, or tall enough to be a "corn house." It can be low enough to shelter a batch of alpine seedlings so small only an alpine gardener can see them, or tall enough so that an arthritic gardener need not bend or kneel.

The prudent builder will use one-inch lumber and treat his cedar boards with copper napthanate, not "penta" or creosote. He will make the back six inches or so higher than the front, so that the frame slopes to catch the sun and to allow run-off of rain and melting snow.

He will spread six inches of mason's sand in it, into which he will sink small pots of seeds. When the first warm day sends his neighbors to their icy greenhouses to jab a tentative trowel into the frozen soil, he will be setting out infant plants of spinach, lettuce, and leek to be harvested long before his vegetable garden looks alive.

The lid, when closed, is a passive solar collector. When daytime temperatures get into the 50's the lid can be raised a bit, then lowered before the afternoon chills.

After the garden is planted and the cold frame is forlorn, is a good time to sow seeds of slow-germinating alpines and perennials, which can remain snug in their protected nursery until the following spring. In areas with severe winters you might throw a carpet scrap over the frame to hold in the earth's warmth; if your frame is a hot bed, heated electrically, use the carpet scrap to keep the escaping heat from melting the insulating snow cover.

Lacking a cold frame, a good substitute is setting the plants on a table, or on the ground if you must, covered with floating row cover stretched over arches of heavy gauge wire or PVC pipe. The plants will be protected from wind and too much sun and a few degrees of chill, and be no worse when the fickle spring weather has settled down.

Planting-out day will vary from mid-May to mid-June, depending on where you live. It's a killer on the thigh muscles, but very, very easy on the spirit. As soon as the snow is gone (you can speed things up by spreading wood ashes or coffee grounds) pick up a handful of the good earth and if it crumbles in your hand, it is ready for planting seeds of hardy plants like peas, potatoes, and the cabbage family. Wait until daytime temperatures are in the 60's to set out plants.

Susan Miller of the Anchorage Municipality, uses a transplant solution containing rooting hormones when plants are set out and finds that it also gives an advantage to container plants. She sprays plants with an anti-dessicant before setting them in the ground, to help them retain moisture and resist sun damage. If you guessed wrong and frost is predicted be prepared to cover them with clear plastic, floating row cover, or newspapers.

Writers captivated by Alaska's mystique tend to rhapsodize over its million acres of rich, fertile land that has never known a man's plow. It is true that there are vast areas of potential agricultural land, but the rich, fertile part is more literary license than scientific fact. **Alaska's soils are young and lean, only recently born out of the Ice Age.** They are enormously responsive to fertilization, but they lack organic matter—the good stuff that comes from centuries of decaying vegetable matter. By digging under the layers of decomposing leaves in old birch forests you can find the brown fibrous peatmoss that aerates soil and makes it moisture retentive, but well-drained.

In urban areas much of the overburden, as contractors and road builders call it, is gone, bulldozed off to get at the subsoil for footings. Early construction was on the high ground; later on drained peat bogs—and **peat and peatmoss are not the same.** Peatmoss is derived from sphagnum mosses and is spongy, brown, fibrous stuff. You can buy it in bales at garden centers and often by the pickup load from excavating companies and topsoil vendors. It should be visually inspected to be sure that it is not the black, car-

bonaceous material found in swamps, which is not useful in potting mixes. It is sometimes used as an amendment in heavy clay soils, which are rarely found in Alaska. (Gardeners who complain of clay-like soil usually have subsoil lacking in organic matter.)

Animal manures (but not that from dogs and cats) is another good source of humus. If it comes from animals that have been on pasture it should be composted to destroy weed seeds. Purchased steer manure is an expensive substitute for organic matter and a balanced fertilizer. Poultry and rabbit manure should be used cautiously. Both are good organic sources of nitrogen and if used too liberally may burn, or produce plants with abundant leaves and too little fruit. Fresh manures also come equipped with damaging salts, but so do commercial fertilizers.

In seaside communities kelp is a source of humus where little else may be available. A green manure crop of oats and peas, or barley, can be turned under to provide humus. Organic gardeners will want two free publications of the Cooperative Extension Service, *Organic Fertilizers* and *Animal Manure as Fertilizer*, both free.

Mulches of dry leaves, dried grass clippings, bark, leaf mold, squirrel litter from spruce cones, and pea vines all help supply humus.

COMPOST has great merit as a source of humus in our young, lean soils. Composting is a better way to dispose of garden and kitchen wastes than consigning them to our fast-filling sanitary land fills.

FROM BAGS TO RICHES

Bagged yard waste comprises as much as 50 percent of municipal solid waste in the summer and fall. Many cities have municipal composting programs (Seattle Tilth being one of the best) and many ban all yard wastes from landfills. An economical and efficient alternative is making compost.

Newer lawnmowers chop dry leaves where they fell, which can be used as winter mulch held in place in wire cages above tender perennials, eliminating the need for cage storage and deterring some moose incursion.

If you clip only an inch or so of grass at each mowing, you can leave lawn clippings on the grass and provide your lawn with a top dressing that has some residual fertilizer in it.

Contrary to common belief, this practice does not cause thatching; thatching is caused by dead roots and other dried plant parts. Thick covers of wet grass clippings are not a good mulch, but fresh clippings can be applied in a thin layer that will dry quickly and more can be added at

A compost pile need not be an elaborate structure. David Harrington simply layers lawn and garden clippings and kitchen wastes onto a pile covered with clear plastic.

the next mowing. Layered with lawn clippings, dry leaves decompose more rapidly than older methods of simply dumping kitchen and garden wastes on a heap to decompose in time.

Where temperatures are very low, decomposition occurs with all the alacrity of a receding glacier. Without a compost chopper or grinder, large chunks may not decompose. If they contain edible garbage like melon rinds and vegetable trimmings, they can be attractive to bears.

If the pile is too wet, which it may well be in areas of heavy rainfall, anaerobic bacteria work it, and it reeks to high heaven. If it is too dry, decomposition is glacially slow. With moderate rainfall you may not need to wet the pile. Many English gardeners do not add additional water, believing that it cools the pile and slows decomposition. Neither do they turn their piles with a garden fork, for the same reason.

It may take two years to get finished compost; then it will have to be sieved to produce the crumbly stuff that would send little shivers of pleasure up a hoe handle, but loam was not built in a day.

If you have a shredder but don't have a compost bin, and don't want one, the choppings can be spread on the garden in the fall and tilled in. This adds needed organic matter to our young, lean soils and re-cycles modest amounts of residual commercial fertilizers. For small gardens, electric shredders will chop wastes up to an inch and a quarter in diameter. Garden supply catalogs list a less expensive "leaf eater" that can handle leaves and grass clippings. Gasoline- and electric-powered machines will grind or chip wet or dry branches up to three inches. Hand-operated grinders are woman-killers.

A compost bin about 12 feet long and four feet wide, with two dividers, will make three four by four-foot bins. Keep the slats loose for good ventilation. Don't put a floor under it, so soil bacteria can work and good drainage can be maintained.

Or, make bins of snow fencing, wire fencing or chicken wire. Form the wire into a circle about four feet in diameter and fasten the ends together with protruding ends. You will need four or five stakes pounded into the ground with the wire reaching to the top of the bin. Set the bin on the ground where beneficial soil organisms will speed decomposition.

Many compost heaps are simply heaps with the weekly take of wilted lawn clippings added to bagged autumn leaves. Cover such a heap with clear plastic for faster decomposition and less stuff blowing around.

For the bottom layer of a more ambitious heap, chop coarse stuff like hedge clippings or broccoli stalks. Layer the finer stuff—grass clippings, leaves, spent flowers, adding a cup of commercial fertilizer or a shovelful of manure. Include kitchen wastes if they do not contain meat or fats. Coffee grounds are good but tend to mold unless you scatter them thinly. Sawdust takes considerable nitrogen to decompose and modest amounts of nitrogen, often from animal manures, are helpful.

It doesn't take much—cow, chicken, rabbit and other grain-fed animals' manure packs a heavy payload of nitrogen—too much if used too liberally, resulting in lush leafy growth at the expense of flowering and fruiting crops.

Here is a sampling of stuff for the compost heap and the percentages of the analyses (bear in mind that the first number represents nitrogen, the middle number phosphorus, the last number potash) and analyses will vary from one sample to another):

cannery waste 3-1-2
dried cow manure 2.5-5-l.5

fresh cow manure .5-.3-.5
coffee grounds 2-.5-.5
poultry manure 3.5-3-l.5
dried poultry manure 4-3-3
seaweed 3-1-5
tea leaves 4.5-.5-0
wood ashes 0-1.5-7
garden wastes 2-1-1
horse manure 4-.2-.4
dried rabbit manure 2.4-.6-.05

You don't have to wait for finished compost—once the stuff has broken down into unrecognizeable material it can be spread on the vegetable garden in the spring.

Finished, screened compost is valuable for working into the soil, filling holes left when plants are moved, adding to potting mixes, top dressing lawns, and mixing into planting holes. It is also a useful mulch to be placed over the root zone of recently planted trees and shrubs in early fall to hold in the summer's heat before the soil has cooled off. Wait until the ground is frozen to do this with bulbs and perennials lest they think it's spring and send up tender new growth.

Compost activators are sold in garden centers and listed in catalogs. Many compost-makers say that the best activator is old compost, or soil that is rich in organic matter. Others think

Dick Green and Sue Adams -Green of Natural Garden Supply (4711 Kupreanof, Anchorage) fill their deep raised beds with a compost rich with rabbit manure and earthworm castings to produce impressive plants.

earthworms are the best activators.

The Cooperative Extension Service issues free bulletins, *The Compost Heap in Alaska* and *Composting in Coastal Alaska*. Be wary of books with names like *Make Compost in One Month!* Or advertised products that promise compost in two weeks. It takes longer in Alaska. Don't get skewered.

POLYMERS, hydrogels, are compounds that absorb water when mixed with soil, reducing the need for frequent watering of hanging baskets, window boxes, indoor plants, seed trays, and germinating lawns. Many garden centers carry these products under a variety of trade names: Broadleaf P4, Supersorb, Viterra Planta-Gel, and Water Grabber. The product looks like rock salt.

The polymers work best if moistened before mixing with soil, and if incorporated in the root zone of the plants rather than the surface. They absorb warm water more readily than cold.

It should come as no surprise that reading the directions pays off in success rate. The effectiveness of polymers varies with soil type and with plant varieties. You may need to experiment before deciding whether polymers are helpful in your garden. Former results were mixed, but they were a boon to sun- and wind-dried container plants and in the soilless mixes used for plugs. Landscapers find it useful to make a polymer slurry to dip the roots of bare root shrubs and trees in before planting.

Full service garden centers stock these products but if you are far from a source here are several:

❀ Broadleaf P4—Broadleaf Industries, Inc., 3802 Main St., Suite 3, Chula Vista, CA 91911; 1-800-628-7374.

❀ HydroSource. Western Polyacrylamide, Inc., P.O. Box 790, Castle Rock, CO 80104.

❀ Soil Moist. JRM Chemical, Inc., 13600 Broadway Ave., Cleveland, OH 44125; 1-800-962-4010.

HYDROPONICS, a system of growing plants in nutrient solutions, rather than soil, proved itself on coral atolls in the South Pacific during World War II where our troops got fresh vegetables, grown without soil. Its possibilities have held a certain fascination for home gardeners ever since.

Here is a way of growing plants that requires no soil, no addition of organic matter, carries no soil-borne diseases or insects and requires no weeding.

Like soil culture, hydroponic culture, has its own problems. It is not immune to diseases and insects. A mistake can show fast consequences without the buffering action of soil. Without a submersible pump on a timer, the nutrient solution must be flushed through the growing medium by hand two or three times a day. Although plants grown hydroponically grow faster than their soil-grown opposite numbers, total yields may be no greater. There is no difference in plant composition between the two systems.

Most hydroponic greenhouses utilize an aggregate medium like pea gravel, or rockwool, and flush it with nutrient solution, which can be replenished as it is evaporated and used by the plants. Aeration is necessary. If you are talking about a quart-size pottery piece with a miniature rose bush in it, you can aerate by blowing through a straw a couple of times a day. If it is a big container, an aquarium bubbler would be better. In a greenhouse operation, you would need to automate the system with a submersible pump on a timer.

Gardeners who use a soilless mix in which to grow seedlings are using a form of hydroponic culture, ideal for seedlings and small plants. If you'd like to try further hydroponic growing, combine one part perlite to two or three parts coarse vermiculite and water it with a one-quarter strength soluble fertilizer.

Hydroponic production is successful in many commercial operations, but in small home greenhouse situations, the gardener should study the ramifications carefully before making a sizable investment.

LIME is calcium carbonate. The best sources for gardens are, in descending order, dolomitic limestone, ground limestone, and (a last-ditch resort) hydrated lime. Wood ashes are a good substitute but require twice as much as ground limestone.

When soil pH is too high or too low, some essential nutrients are not available to plants, and desirable soil bacteria and fungi do not flourish. Punctilious gardeners may be overdoing liming of lawns, vegetable and flower gardens. Alaska soils are moderately acid, an environment in which most grasses, vegetables and flowers grow well. In general, soils in rainy country are inclined to be acid and some require liming to bring the pH up to a tolerable 5.5. It is rarely necessary to bring an entire garden up to 7.0.

Never apply lime without a soil test, preferably done in the fall so that it has time to become effective. The Cooperative Extension Service supplies a soil testing kit for a small fee. The lime should be tilled in, and not applied at the same time as fertilizer or manure. Lime and sifted wood ashes are the consistency of flour so this is a hand job for a windless day.

Hydrated, or slaked, lime is a quick acting, but highly caustic, form of lime to be used only in emergencies and with protective covering of eyes and hands.

WOOD ASHES are a good source of calcium and potash. Wood ashes should not be used on potato ground, where a high pH is conducive to potato scab disease. To be effective, ashes should be stockpiled under cover, safe from leaching by rainfall. If you burn bones in your wood stove or fireplace, so much the better, but burning magazine-type paper should be avoided because of its cadmium content.

WARMING THINGS UP

Cool soil and air temperatures limit the growth of many plants. Alaskans use this limitation to their advantage. They grow flowers and vegetables well that don't do well in hot climates. They use plants for ground cover that are weeds in milder climates. They can do their weeding in the heat of the day and not suffer heat stroke.

But mostly Alaska gardeners are preoccupied with warming things up, and they're mighty ingenious about it.

FINDING MISTER GOODSPOT

Finding the elusive Mr. Goodspot is right up there with coming across a paystreak. Why should it be that there is only one south side of the house? With only one southern exposure to a customer, gardeners erect solid board fences along their northern lot line to create another sunny side. Choosing a gentle south slope for a vegetable garden is like striking the mother lode. But there are ways of raising soil and air temperatures around plants that are successful in the lay of the land dealt you. (See ROW COVERS, RAISED BEDS, and PLASTIC MULCH.)

GETTING OFF TO A FAST START

You will need a starter solution to get your plants get off the dime. There are commercial products sold in garden centers that contain useful plant hormones, but you can make your own booster shot with a half-strength mixture of a soluble fertilizer that has a high middle number, which stands for phosphorus, needed for root development. Or soak a half cup of 8-32-16 granular fertilizer in a three-gallon bucket of water and let it steep overnight.

PLANTING OUT

First you dig a hole. Then you tap the plant out of its container with a sharp rap from your trowel or on a fence rail or a stone. Set its roots gently in the hole and pour in a half cup or more, depending on the size of the root ball, of starter solution, and back fill with crumbled soil. Protect the infant plants with a row cover from too much sun, or wind, or hail or whatever it is that usually happens on Memorial Day weekend.

Then, stand back! All this is beastly hard on knee joints and cuticle, but you will survive. And you are off and running toward your first garden in Alaska.

NOTES THAT GARDENERS WRITE TO THEMSELVES

ADDENDA

COOPERATIVE EXTENSION SERVICE DISTRICT OFFICES

Anchorage District Office
2221 E. Northern Lights, #118.
Anchorage, AK 99508-4143
279-5582

Bethel District Office
Box 556 Bethel Native Corp. Bldg
Bethel, AK 99559
543-2503

Delta Junction District Office
P.O Box 349, Jarvis Bldg.
Delta Junction, AK 99737
895-4215

Fairbanks-Tanana District Office,
1514 Cushman Bldg.,
Fairbanks, AK 99701-6285
452-1530

Fairbanks-Tanana Chiefs Conference Office
122 First Avenue
Fairbanks, AK 92701
452-8251

Juneau District Office
9112 Mendenhall Mall Road
Juneau, AK 99801-7112
789-2666

Kodiak District Office
202 Center Street, Suite 206
Kodiak, AK 99615
524-3011

McGrath District Office
P.O. Box 269
McGrath, AK 99627
524-3011

Nome-NW District Office
Box 400, NW Community College
Nome, AK 99762
443-2320

Palmer Mat-SU District Office
809 S. Chugach St.,
Palmer, AK 99645
745-3360

Sitka District Office
1297 Seward Avenue
Sitka, AK 99835
747-6065

Soldotna-Kenai District
34820 College Dr., Suite 2
Soldotna, AK 99669
262-5824

CATALOGS

These catalogs have been selected from among those with which we have had personal dealings, because they contain many varieties of plants that are adapted to the High North but there are many more that you may find useful. Several add a surcharge for Alaska orders, some so high that you should study the order form before you lose your heart to a packet of seeds whose shipping and handling charges may be more than the price of the seeds. Surcharges are justified when live plants are shipped to Alaska when we are experiencing freezing temperatures, but a packet of seeds that can come for the price of a first class stamp is another matter. Some companies pass their shipping costs along to their customers by using UPS rather than owning a truck and hiring a driver to stand in line at the post office.

SEEDS BLUM
Idaho City Stage
Boise, ID 83706
Vegetables, flowers, herbs, rare varieties

W. ATLEE BURPEE & CO.
Warminster, PA 18974
1-800-888-1447
Vegetables, flowers, herbs

B&B CACTUS FARM
11550 East Speedway
Tucson, AZ 85748
(602)721-4687
Cacti and Succulent plants

CANYON CREEK NURSERY
3527 Dry Creek Road
Oroville, CA 95965
(916)533-2166
Perennials

THE COOK'S GARDEN
P.O. Box 535
Londonderry, VT 05148
(802)824-3400
Gourmet vegetables, herbs, recipes, supplies

THE FLOWER AND HERB EXCHANGE
3076 North Winn Road
Decorah, IA 52101
($5 annual dues)

FOX HOLLOW HERB & HEIRLOOM SEED CO.
P.O. Box 148
McGrann, PA. 16236

HARRIS SEEDS
60 Saginaw Drive
P.O. Box 22960
Rochester, NY 14692-2960
Vegetable and flower seeds, supplies

HIGH ALTITUDE GARDENS
(Siberian Edition)
P.O.Box 4619
Ketchum, ID 83340

JACKSON & PERKINS
P.O. Box 1028
Medford, OR 97501
1-800-292-4769
Roses, perennials, shrubs

JOHNNY'S SELECTED SEEDS
Foss Hill Road
Albion, Maine 04910-9731
(207)-437-4301
Vegetables, flowers, supplies

KALMIA FARM
P.O. Box 3881
Charlottesville, VA 22903
Onions, other rare Alliums

MILAEGER'S GARDENS
4838 Douglas Avenue
Racine, WI 53402-2498
(414)639-2371
Perennials.

NICHOLS GARDEN NURSERY
1190 North Pacific Highway
Albany, OR 97321-4598
Vegetables, herbs, flowers, books, supplies, rare items

PARK SEED Co.
Cokesbury road
Greenwood, SC 29647-0001
(803)223-7333
Flowers, vegetables, herbs, supplies

SHEPHERD'S
30 Irene Street
Torrington, Connecticut 06790
(203)482-3638
Vegetables, herbs, flowers

STOKES SEEDS INC.
Box 548
Buffalo, N.Y. 14240
Vegetables, flowers, herbs, supplies

TERRITORIAL SEED COMPANY
20 Palmer Avenue
Cottage Grove, OR 97424
(503)942-9547
Vegetables, flowers, supplies

THOMPSON & MORGAN
P.O.Box 1308
Jackson, NJ
(908)363-2225
Fax (908)363-9356S

TOMATO GROWERS SUPPLY CO.
P.O.Box 2237
Fort Myers, Florida, 33902
(813)768-1119

GARDEN SUPPLIES

CHARLEY'S GREENHOUSE SUPPLY
1569 Memorial Highway
Mount Vernon, WA 9827
1-800-322-4707

GARDENERS EDEN
Mail Order Department
P.O.Box 7307
San Francisco, CA 94120-7307
1-800-822-9600

GARDENER'S SUPPLY COMPANY
128 Intervale Rd.,
Burlington, VT 0540
802-660-3500
Fax 802-660-3501

WALT NICKE CO.
36 McLeod Lane, P.O. Box 433
Topsfield, MA 01983
(800) 822-4114

WINTERTHUR—Museum, Garden, Library, Gifts
Winterthur, Delaware 19735
1-800-767-0500

SEED EXCHANGES

THE ALPINE GARDEN SOCIETY
Lye End Link, St. John's,
Woking, Surrey, England.

THE AMERICAN ROCK GARDEN SOCIETY
15 Fairmead Road,
Darien, Connecticut 06820

THE SCOTTISH ROCK GARDEN CLUB
21 Merchiston Park,
Edinburgh EH10 4PW, Scotland

THE JAPAN ROCK GARDEN SOCIETY.
2-8 Tatsuno-machi
Himeji 670 , Japan

FLOWER & HERB EXCHANGE
3076 North Winn Road
Decorah, IA 52101

HARDINESS ZONES. Plant hardiness zone maps were developed by the U.S. Department of Agriculture in cooperation with the American Horticultural Society, based on average annual low temperatures. These hardiness zones were revised in 1990. Zones 1 to 7 describe Alaska pretty well.

Gardeners familiar with the old hardiness Zone map will see at once that the main difference is that the zones are in increments of five degrees rather than the old ten-degree dividers. Closer study of the new Zone map reveals that other factors have been taken into consideration. Alaskans have long known that low winter temperature was not the only factor that determined winter hardiness. "It's hardy in North Dakota" doesn't make it hardy in the Matanuska Valley, although winter temperatures in North Dakota may go lower and winds resemble those in Palmer.

Not only are there many locations in the northern tier of the contiguous states that have lower winter minimum temperatures, but they have longer, warmer summers. Cool summer soil and air temperatures in Alaska often call the shots: zinnias aren't keen on 70-degree days.

Summer day length is the nemesis of hardy chrysanthemums which do not set buds until days are short and they don't get short enough soon enough to see flowers before freeze-up. Many woody plants don't get the message that winter is coming, so they don't go dormant to sleep safely through the cold winter. Poinsettias, left to their own devices, may bloom in time for Easter, lousing up the springtime color scheme.

Some plants are not hardy where winter winds scour the insulating snow cover off, but are star performers 40 miles away where snow comes early and lingers late.

Mail order nurseries tend to be too lenient about the hardiness limits of perennials, shrubs and trees and hopeful gardeners order plants they do not find in local nurseries. Nurseries in distant states follow the Zone requirements and often will not ship plants intended for sunroom culture until their Zone maps indicate that freezing temperatures are past, unaware that you had in mind to grow them indoors until planting-out time.

They also fear that spring shipments will freeze in mailboxes before somebody comes home from work, so they use more expensive alternative shippers and levy a surcharge on top of their shipping and handling fee for the non-contiguous states. Before you get your heart set on a mail order plant, check the order form's fine print to see what the surcharge is before you dial the 800 number.

Chain stores that get into the garden supply business in April receive their shipments based on Zone numbers, and frequently offer plants that are not suitable for us. Alaska nurserymen who are in the business year round have more at stake and are not apt to offer plants that are not suitable for Alaska conditions.

INDEX